COLONIAL BLACK AND
INDIGENOUS CULTURAL LEADERS

COLONIAL BLACK AND INDIGENOUS CULTURAL LEADERS

John Fitzhugh Millar

RESOURCE *Publications* · Eugene, Oregon

COLONIAL BLACK AND INDIGENOUS CULTURAL LEADERS

Resource Publications
An Imprint of Wipf and Stock Publishers
199 W. 8th Ave., Suite 3
Eugene, OR 97401

www.wipfandstock.com

PAPERBACK ISBN: 979-8-3852-5066-0
HARDCOVER ISBN: 979-8-3852-5067-7
EBOOK ISBN: 979-8-3852-5068-4

VERSION NUMBER 10/29/25

Contents

Preface | *vii*

1   Introduction | 1

2   Music Composers | 24

3   Architects, Sculptors, Master-Builders, Painters, Potters, and Silversmiths | 49

4   Writers, Poets, Business People, Actors, and Clergy | 58

5   Military Heroes and Political Leaders | 128

Addenda to Colonial Black & Indigenous Cultural Leaders | 193

Index | 197

Preface

COLONIAL WILLIAMSBURG IS THE world's largest outdoor historical museum, founded in 1926 (with a tip of the hat to the 150th anniversary of American Independence in that year). Until recently, it consisted of 88 original buildings plus several dozen reproduction buildings based mostly on solid evidence. Visitors can enjoy authentic gardens, farm animals (yes, animals were very different back then from what you find on a farm today), authentic furnishings, and well-trained people wearing appropriate clothing of the period. Visitors meet craftsmen demonstrating numerous crafts, in which they have served as apprentices and then journeymen, before finally becoming masters: Apothecary, Basket Maker, Blacksmith, Bookbinder, Brickmaker, Clothing makers for men and for women, Cooper, Furniture maker, Gunsmith, Leatherworker, Musical Instrument maker, Printer, Shoemaker, Silversmith, Tinsmith, Weaver, Wheelwright, and Wigmaker. Some employees are specially trained to impersonate people from 250 years ago, such as George & Martha Washington, Thomas Jefferson, and the Marquis de Lafayette, but also people you have never heard of, such as Black or Indigenous men and women, explaining how they saw themselves fitting into society. Musicians present large and small concerts of period music, played in the same way that instruments were played back then (generally quite different from the way modern instruments are taught). Sometimes, the Fife & Drum Corps in their colorful uniforms march along the street, and sometimes you can watch a cannon or a musket being fired. You can go out to dinner in one of the Historic Taverns and eat more or less authentic food, and maybe sing along with authentic historical folk songs. At the western end of Duke of Gloucester Street, you can visit William & Mary, the second oldest college in North America with the oldest college building in North America, dating from 1693 (six years before the City of Williamsburg itself was established). William & Mary, presently state-owned, is nor-mally rated as fifth or sixth best public college in the country. In the year 1776, officials at William & Mary founded a club for its top students known as Phi Beta Kappa, a club that has now reached to colleges all over the world.

Willliam & Mary's charter required it also to educate Indigenous young men, and it was decided that they needed a separate building. The Brafferton Endowment left behind by the great English physicist Robert Boyle, was asked by William & Mary to pay for that separate building in 1723, known as Brafferton Hall. Brafferton Hall is now used by the university administration, and an almost identical building built in 1732 across the courtyard in front of the original college building is the resi-dence of the president. Indigenous students today are an integral part of the student body.

Very recently, the Bray School building of 1760 was discovered, making an 89th original building for Colonial Williamsburg. In the 1720s, English priest, the Reverend Dr. Thomas Bray, who never man-aged to travel to America, started raising money to educate Black boys and girls in America, both enslaved and free. He died before he could ac-complish his plan, but a group of his friends, including Benjamin Frank-lin, brought the plan forward. By 1760, they had built 22 Bray Schools from Nova Scotia to the Bahamas, most of which were deemed to be a success. However, only fifteen years later, the American Revolution broke out, and the British refused to allow any money to cross the Atlantic, even for such a worthy cause. Without the money from Britain, the schools all had to close, although some Bray trustees expressed the hope that local residents in America would continue to pay for these schools which were clearly in their own interest. As it happened, most of the buildings were destroyed, and the land sold for development.

Two Bray School buildings survive today. The one at 47 Division Street, Newport, Rhode Island (sometimes known as Mrs. Brett's School) became a residence, the Peter Bours House, now beautifully restored, and the recently discovered Williamsburg Bray School, once known as the Dudley Digges House (and sometimes called Mrs. Wager's School), has been carefully restored for interpretation as a school for Black chil-dren at the corner of Francis and Nassau Streets. The Williamsburg Bray School had to change buildings part-way through its career because the first building (originally located on North Boundary Street before being moved to the William & Mary campus) was too small for the work it was being asked to do, and the second building (which has not been standing since before photography existed) stood on the same exact site to which the first Bray School building has now been moved for restoration. Most Bray School buildings were simple wooden structures, but the school in New York City was built of brick, and designed by colonial America's greatest architect, Peter Harrison. The New York building was replaced in modern times by a skyscraper.

I used to live in Newport, only one block from its Bray School, and now I live in Williamsburg about five blocks from its Bray School. I was so impressed at the work being done for the Williamsburg project that I decided to write a book about all the colonial-period Blacks and Indigenous who made a real difference in their fields: music composers, architects, painters, silversmiths, writers, poets, actors, clergy, political leaders, and military leaders. The total number came to eighty. Unfortunately, none of them is known to have studied at any of the Bray Schools, although Newport Gardner – a genuine polymath – is believed to have taught briefly at the Newport Bray School. He went on to found and operate his own school after the Revolution, and that lovely building is still standing (on School Street, of course). Gardner is included in this book. The Williamsburg Bray School had a total of about 400 students go through it during the fifteen years of its existence, and an impressive number of modern residents of Williamsburg think that they can trace their ancestry back to one or more of those students.

The Williamsburg Bray School was placed in a supervisory but non-financial relationship with William & Mary; the Bray trustees in London many times expressed the hope that local residents would see it as in their own interests to pay some of the increasing costs of operating the Bray Schools, but the schools attracted very little local financial support. The Bray School at Fredericksburg, Virginia (about 90 miles distant) was probably too far away for William & Mary to have shared such a relationship. The Bray School in Charleston, South Carolina may have had a similar supervisory but non-financial relationship with the College of Charleston after that college had been founded in 1770. Similarly, the Bray School at Philadelphia may have had such a relationship with the college that we now call Penn, and it is possible that Moravian College in Bethlehem had a similar relationship with the closest Bray School. King's College in New York certainly had such a relationship with the New York City Bray School. What we now call Brown University was not founded until 1764 as The College at Rhode Island (although its first

major building in Providence was not available for use until 1770), but
it is possible that it was asked at some point to supervise activities at the
Newport Bray School, despite the distance of almost forty miles between
Newport and Providence; more likely, Trinity Church in Newport provided all the supervision needed there.

I have noticed that an increasing number of visitors complain that
Colonial Williamsburg is 'too woke,' which I hope is a passing fad. Colonial Williamsburg's presentations are grounded in extensive research by
real experts. I know that many politically motivated people are fond of
discounting anything that an expert says, but you can be sure that these
experts have not spent a lifetime of study inventing false history for their
own amusement. The history presented here is as accurate as it is possible
to be, but you can also be sure that if and when more accurate documentation can be discovered, the presentations will be up-dated accordingly.

When I had recently graduated from college, I noticed that the
200th anniversary of US independence was just around the corner. I lived
in Newport, from which the impetus for founding the Continental Navy
sprang in 1775. I raised the money and did the necessary research to
build full-sized, operational copies of two ships of the War of Independence. The larger ship was the 24-gun frigate *Rose*, which had been sent
by the British government in order to stop Rhode Island merchants from
legally participating in the rum trade, and it was to get rid of that ship
that the American Navy was founded on 13 October 1775. Many years
later, she starred with Russell Crowe in 'Master & Commander: The Far
Side of the World,' and she's now on permanent display (under her movie
name of *Surprise*) at the Maritime Museum of San Diego.

Quite a few of the Black people covered in this book served in the
Royal Navy, so I was able to write my experience of sailing *Rose* into their
stories. In particular, for years I and several other people sang frequent
concerts of period sea songs and chanteys, and then for sixteen years at
Colonial Williamsburg I sang the same music in the historic taverns at
dinner-time, telling patrons that if they did not sing along, they would
not receive any dessert. That experience reflects the experience of the
peg-leg Black sailor William Waters, as shown in this book.

I also raised the money and did the research necessary to build a
full-size operational copy of the 12-gun sloop *Providence*, which was
the first vessel authorized by Congress for the Continental Navy on 13
October 1775. That sloop, along with the other ships of the Continental
Navy, is believed to have had a crew in which ten to twenty percent of the

enlisted men were free Black sailors, mostly from Rhode Island. Unfortunately, we know very little about those sailors, except that tiny Rhode Island supplied many of them. The rebuilt sloop is now on permanent display on the waterfront of Alexandria, Virginia, just across the Potomac River from Washington DC, and she sometimes takes people on short cruises around the harbor.

My experience with the *Rose* also offers another connection with the book, in a way. My late friend, Dr. Alex McBurney (urologist) in Newport, asked my opinion about a painting that he had received from a Black patient. The painting showed a Black sailor wearing parts of the dress uniform of a captain in the Royal Navy. I recognized the ship at anchor in the background as the 20-gun Rhode Island privateer frigate *General Washington* from 1779. I concluded that the painting was genuine, and that the frigate had captured a British merchant ship bound for New York City. Among the cargo was this uniform that a Royal Navy captain based in New York had ordered from his tailor in London. The Black sailor had used his share of the prize money to pay an artist to paint his portrait wearing that uniform, so this was obviously the first painting of a Black sailor from the Revolution. McBurney generously permitted images of the painting to be published in many books and magazine articles, but after a while he sent the painting to Boston to be professionally cleaned.

The Boston experts carefully inspected the painting, and then informed McBurney that while the painting was in fact genuine, the sailor had originally been a Caucasian. However, in the 1950s someone had scraped off the white head and hand, and replaced them with a Black head and hand. Would McBurney prefer that the white person be repainted, or would he prefer to keep the sailor Black? He opted for keeping the sailor Black, but he felt obliged to notify all those books and magazines that had published the painting that it was partly fake. This Black sailor, being bogus, of course has no entry in this book, but it shows that I had a sort-of connection a long time ago with a Black sailor of the period.

1

Introduction

THIS IS A LOOK at eighty Black and Indigenous people, born before 1790 (the date when all thirteen original states had ratified the US Constitution), who established themselves as leaders in their fields—in fields of endeavor framed by white people, of course. Some were classical music composers, some painters, architects, potters, silversmiths, poets, writers, accountants, actors, clergy, political leaders, and military leaders. It hardly needs to be said that there were countless Black and Indigenous people who established themselves in leadership positions within their own Black and Indigenous societies, but they did not generally register in the parts of the world run by white people. Maybe someone else can write essays or books about them.

Slavery or involuntary servitude has been a feature of human existence since before written records existed. References to it can be found in the Bible and early Greek literature (such as *The Iliad*), as well as oriental literature. In many cases, slavery was imposed on people who happened to be on the losing side in local battles or in huge national conflicts. Often, but by no means always, the enslaver and the enslaved were of different races.

In early modern times, more than 200 Black people lived in Tudor England, and another 150 in England in the first half of the seventeenth century, and a few hundred more in parts of the rest of Europe. Some of these were actually enslaved, but others were highly respected members of society, such as the accomplished poet and playwright Afonso Alvares in Portugal.

Spain (or its constituent parts) was the first area in Europe where Blacks were found in noticeable numbers (including Juan Latino, the Latinist scholar and writer), mostly because North African Muslims owned much of Spain until they were pushed back by Christians, and many of those North Africans were Black. Some of those Blacks were made prisoners and then slaves by the Christians, so when the Christians began to flood across the Atlantic it must have seemed natural to some of them to bring enslaved Blacks with them to America. The first Blacks arrived in Hispaniola in 1502, and were followed by thousands more in Cuba, the South American mainland, Central America, and Mexico.

The Phoenicians from Lebanon and other parts of the Mediterranean regularly sailed up the Mississippi and Illinois Rivers 1700 BCE to 650 BCE in order to bring back copper from Lake Michigan for making Bronze Age weapons, sculptures, and tools; some of their crewmembers included Hebrews and Egyptians, and they were among the first world navigators. Knowing nothing of what the Phoenicians had already done, the Portuguese were among the first world navigators closer to our own time. They explored the west coast of Africa in the 1400s and established colonies such as Angola there, and Mozambique on the east coast. Afonso, one of the Black kings of Congo, sent one of his sons, Henry, to study in 1508 with the Society of St. John the Evangelist in Lisbon. Henry was later consecrated as the first sub-Saharan Roman Catholic bishop, and possibly the first Black bishop since the Apostle Thomas consecrated some for his church in the area of Chennai/Madras, India in the first century AD. No other Black bishops were consecrated in sub-Saharan Africa for about 300 years after Henry. This was reported by Miranda Kaufmann in her book *Black Tudors*, Oneworld Publications, 2017.

During the fifteenth and sixteenth centuries, a series of popes established various regulations about how Christian Europeans should treat enslaved people. Although Henry VIII and English church leaders broke the Church of England away from control by Rome in 1534, the papal policies about slavery survived mostly unchanged in England, largely because those policies were soundly based on rules laid down in the Old Testament.

In England and most other European countries in the sixteenth century, if a resident were to be arrested for committing any of various petty crimes, such as stealing a chicken, the criminal might often be sentenced to death. However, many judges might commute such sentences to seven years of servitude. Why seven years? The Hebrew Bible (Exodus 21: 2–6; Deuteronomy 15: 12–18; Jeremiah 34: 14) states that servitude should not last for more than seven years. At the end of the seven-year sentence, the person who had bought the criminal was obliged to release him and provide him with some land, a house, utensils of his trade, and a small amount of cash, so it was not entirely a one-way street. In England (and in English colonies), this was part of the Common Law.

It turns out that West Africans, many of them living in Muslim communities, where Muslim leaders assiduously read the Old Testament as much as the Christians did (even if Muslims today generally do not), had an almost identical system of dealing with their petty criminals. Servitude "brokers" in the Old World often arranged for both Black and white seven-year slaves to be sent to the New World to serve their sentences. This was NOT "indentured servitude," which was similar, but somewhat voluntary: if a man thought that he was shortly going to have to commit a crime in order to stay alive, or if he were bankrupt, he could sell himself to a court-supervised broker for seven years. During that time, of course he would be fed, clothed, housed, and have rudimentary healthcare, and that was indentured servitude. Indentured servants worked alongside slaves, and were generally not distinguished from them.

Until 1696, nearly all African people in servitude brought to English America were transported by ships of the Royal African Company, which held a monopoly from its founding in 1660 until then. The Royal African Company had one of its principal offices in Southwark on the south bank of the Thames opposite the City of London. The company's seal was an African elephant with a howdah (a sort-of castle) on its back, so that section of Southwark is still called today Elephant & Castle (with a tube-stop and a prominent pub with that name), and the steps down to the river, so you could board a pedestrian ferry to the north bank, were called Elephant's Stairs, and the steps are still there (obviously not intended for real elephants to use). Historian Eleanor Herman has reported in her book *Sex with Kings* (HarperCollins, 2001) that when George I departed Hannover, Germany to accept the British throne in 1715, he brought with him two German mistresses. One of them was short and fat, Sophia Charlotte Kielmansegge, and local wags nicknamed her as a result Elephant & Castle. The King adored her sparkling personality, and enjoyed her educated conversation, and the fact that she loved sex.

The Royal African Company was initially expected to bring gold and ivory back to England from West Africa, but gradually the directors found that it was more profitable to transport seven-year African slaves to sell in the Americas. Obviously, after African slave merchants began selling prisoners of war as permanent slaves in 1663, the Royal African Company saw its profits from selling slaves skyrocket, until the company lost its monopoly just over thirty years later. The first ship independent of the Royal African Company to bring slaves for sale in Rhode Island was Captain Thomas Windsor's *Seaflower*, bringing fourteen seven-year slaves on 30 May 1696 (Windsor's ship contained a further thirty slaves to be sold elsewhere). It is asserted that the Massachusetts ship *Elizabeth* may have brought one or more slaves to Rhode Island in 1681 "off the books." From 1696 to 1775, Rhode Island ships are said to have brought 59,067 slaves to British America, but only a handful of them were actually brought to Rhode Island (in 1770, the highest number of slaves living in Rhode Island was 3761; most of these were working on plantations in King's County, later Washington County, popularly known as South County). Rhode Island ships were generally so small that they could not carry more than a few dozen slaves at a time, so the well-known engravings of the interiors of slave ships carrying hundreds of people crammed closely together bound for tropical America have little to do with British North America.

The first seven-year slaves imported to Virginia had been captured from a Spanish slave ship by a Dutch privateer ship in 1619 (the same year in which Virginia acquired the New World's first elected legislature, and the year after Virginia established its first institution of higher learning, the short-lived Prince Henry's College, slightly down the James River from where Richmond stands today, but on the other side), and we know that one of the slaves was called Angelo (or, more likely, Angela). Many modern commentators baldly state that slavery began in English-speaking America in 1619, which is not the case. What began in 1619 was simply the arrival of petty crooks serving a relatively brief sentence, normally seven years or less. Both English and African seven-year slaves and English indentured servants (indentured servitude, although superficially similar, was actually rather different from seven-year servitude) who were brought to Virginia were typically granted land on the Eastern Shore of the Chesapeake Bay when they were set free. Because that land was rather sandy and non-productive, the wealthy and influential Virginia tobacco planters had less interest in the Eastern Shore than in mainland Tidewater Virginia. Today, thanks to centuries of cultivation and fertilization, it is among the most fertile land in Virginia. In 1640, it was reported that seven-year Virginia Black slave John Punch was a slave for life, which almost certainly means simply that he had in the meantime been convicted of a further minor crime.

Seven-year slave Mathias de Sousa, a Roman Catholic from the Portuguese colony of Angola, spent the first three years of his seven-year servitude working in Barbados, but when the Catholic colonists who were headed to found the new colony of Maryland met him in 1634 (it may seem strange today, but the best way to sail from England to Maryland with the clumsily-rigged ships of the 1630s was to travel via Barbados), they bought his remaining four years to be worked in Maryland. After he gained his freedom, he ran for, got elected to, and served in the Maryland Legislature in March 1641. He was the only Black ever elected to a North American legislature in the colonial period, which was even more important for him than it sounds: the English were the only colonizers of the day who supported elected legislatures for their colonies at all. The story of Sousa was once told by an exhibit at Jamestown Settlement Museum near Williamsburg.

Fast forward to somewhere between 1661 and 1663: when English slave importers of the Royal African Company arrived in their usual West African port, they were told, "Sorry, we're fresh out of crooks. You've got them all." In order to discourage the slavers from sailing elsewhere in search of seven-year convict-slaves, the local authorities sold them an unlimited supply of prisoners of war. Prisoners of war in Africa were not limited to seven years of servitude, but could be kept enslaved forever under African laws or customs, and many of the hundreds of African tribes seemed to be frequently or even permanently at war with each other. This situation produced so many slaves that they did not know what to do with them. The various North American colonies quickly changed their slavery laws in order to reflect the new reality on the ground. Therefore, slavery in North America really began in 1663, not 1619, an important difference from what is usually related.

Tiny Rhode Island, however, alone of all the colonies, never made that change, and slavery there was always supposed to be for seven years under Common Law. In the case of young slaves, on the other hand, the seven-year clock did not start running until their 21st birthday (even supposing that most of them could know or prove their date of birth). Rhode Island slaves who had served their seven years were required to petition a justice of the peace before they could obtain their freedom. The Rhode Island justices of the peace were not inclined to release slaves until they could prove (through the offer of a relatively high-paying job) that they would not become a financial burden on the community. That is how Rhode Island, alone among the US states, was able to supply an entire regiment (the Rhode Island First Continental Regiment) whose enlisted men were entirely composed of free Blacks (and a handful of Narragansett Native Americans; the officers, of course, were still white). Freed Blacks could surely not be a burden on the community if they were off fighting and being paid. From the beginning, Rhode Island was the first and only place in America to accept the testimony of free Blacks and Native Americans in court – a great many criminals in other colonies (including murderers) went free because the only testimony against them came from Blacks or Native Americans.

Many other Rhode Island former slaves ensured their freedom by enlisting in the Continental Navy or the Rhode Island Navy or aboard privateer ships or simply merchant ships. It is estimated that as many as ten or twenty percent of the enlisted men in the Continental Navy were Blacks, most of them from Rhode Island. According to W. Jeffrey Bolster's book *Black Jacks* (Harvard University Press, 1997), more than a few former slaves who crewed on merchant ships became officers and even ship-owners and captains. One Black man, Mark Startin or Starlins, was promoted to captain of the Virginia State Navy armed schooner *Patriot* for many successful years in the Revolution (replacing her previous captain Richard Barron), but when the war was over, he was not hailed as a hero, but instead he was reinstated as a slave where he had served before the war! Since the schooner is likely to have mounted only four carriage guns, Startin's commissioned rank would have been lieutenant, but that is higher than any other Black made it in an American naval force. The Virginia Legislature, several years after the end of the war, awarded freedom to some Blacks who had served with distinction in the Virginia Navy, but Mark's failure to appear on that list suggests that he had already died. Incidentally, at the moment, documentation is lacking, but it is asserted that some merchant ships and even privateers in eighteenth-century Rhode Island were commanded by capable women, who had stepped into the shoes of their late husbands with no fanfare. So far, no names or dates have been discovered.

Patriot leader John Laurens of South Carolina proposed that 3000 slaves there be freed so that they could form a Continental regiment from

South Carolina. Although Laurens received the approval of Congress for his proposal, yet it was resolutely and successfully opposed by South Carolina's bigoted leaders.

COLLEGES AND SCHOOLS

Education of Indigenous people, and later of Blacks, was of interest in colonial America. English America's first college, Prince Henry's College, was founded in 1618 and located on the south bank of the James River at modern Dutch Gap (a few miles down-river from modern Richmond on the opposite bank). Its student body was intended to include Native Americans from the 34 tribes of the Powhatan Confederacy (properly pronounced PO-atan). However, before that could happen, Obechecanough, the new paramount chief of the Powhatan federation of tribes, replacing his late brother Wahunsonacock, organized an uprising in 1622 intended to drive the English out of Virginia. He succeeded in killing about one third of all the English in the colony. In the meantime, the Virginia government had inaugurated the first elected legislature in the world outside Europe in 1619 (and Bermuda followed suit one year later; Bermuda's elegant still-standing 1620 Statehouse is the oldest purpose-built legislative building in the world!) closed Prince Henry's College in 1622 until such time as the colony should have the resources necessary to re-open it. It never was re-opened, and in the early twentieth century the Lone Star Cement Company from outside Virginia obliterated the remains of the college buildings in order to extract gravel, before archaeologists could have a chance to record their appearance.

The colony of Massachusetts had been founded in the 1620s, and a few years later in 1636 Harvard College was established at Cambridge on the Charles River. Harvard was intended to educate Native Americans as well as whites. As a practical matter, when Englishmen first started exploring and trading in New England in the sixteenth century, they brought diseases with them (including measles and smallpox) that killed the majority of Native Americans, so very few Native Americans were enrolled at Harvard in the seventeenth century, and the majority of those absconded when they found Latin and Greek too difficult or too irrelevant.

In 1693, a new college was founded in Virginia, William & Mary. It was so named because some English and Scottish pirates from the 14-gun ship *Batchelors Delight*, made fabulously wealthy from pillaging ships and settlements along the west coast of South America, agreed to surrender a large portion of their treasure when on trial in London. The treasure was handed over to Queen Mary, and she donated it to the Virginians who had asked for money to found a college. Two alternative designs for the main building were drawn by Elizabeth Wilbraham (1632–1705), the world's first woman architect. Her more elaborate design around an octagonal courtyard included three classical domes (there were no domes at all at colleges in Oxford and Cambridge at this early date), but the local builders felt that they would be unable to build domes. Since a woman could not then be seen to be an accomplished architect, the building built from her second design became known as the Wren Building, after her student Christopher Wren. The Royal Charter specified that the college should educate Native Americans. Some chiefs complained that they saw no reason to send their tribe's young men to learn worthless subjects in a college while no English boys were sent to learn useful things like tracking and hunting that were taught by Native Americans. Some Native American youths tied their sheets together in order to escape out their windows from the college, and melt away into the forests, but others remained and seem to have benefitted. In 1723, the College of William & Mary received major assistance from the Brafferton Endowment in England that had been established by the famous physicist Robert Boyle (1627–1691). They used it to build a special building, Brafferton Hall, designed by former Governor Sir Francis Nicholson (who had learned architecture from Elizabeth Wilbraham), to educate Native Americans. The building still stands, now used as administration offices, mirroring an almost twin building to the north across the courtyard, the 1732 President's House. Brafferton Hall was somewhat of a success, in that the college did educate a number of Native Americans, and a significant number of their parents were sufficiently impressed as to send their young men there.

Brafferton Hall was intended for fairly local Native Americans, such as members of the Pamunkey, Mattaponi, Chickahominy, Monacan, Nottoway, Cherokee and Shawnee tribes. Most of the tribes closest to the coast spoke Algonkian, but those further away from the coast spoke other languages, which made matters more difficult for teachers at the college. Some of the success stories of Brafferton Hall include those of Robert "the Scholar" Marsh (a Pamunkey lad with excellent penmanship, who served as a notary) and Charles Murphy (a Cherokee who served as Patrick Henry's translator during the War of Independence). Marsh enlisted in the American army, was captured at Charleston, and then fought the British at Yorktown in 1781. Some researchers believe that Native American students from as far away as Canada enrolled to study at Brafferton Hall.

In 1701, Congregationalists similar to those who had founded Harvard started a new college in Connecticut named Yale, named after a benefactor who had made a lot of money in India. Like Harvard, Yale was expected to educate Native Americans, and like Harvard, Yale had little success in doing so. After a false start, Yale made its permanent home at New Haven.

Christopher Codrington was an extremely wealthy plantation owner in Barbados. He left in his 1711 will a huge fortune to build Codrington College near Bathsheba, Barbados, intended to provide a theological education for Anglican clergy in the Caribbean. It was designed by Sir Francis Nicholson in 1713, but it was not completed until 1745. Codrington also intended it to be helpful to educate young Black men, although that did not necessarily happen very often. He gave another tranche of his fortune to his alma mater at Oxford, All Souls College, to build a fabulous library, originally designed by Elizabeth Wilbraham (constructed mostly to her designs by Nicholas Hawksmoor), but because Codrington had been a prominent slave-holder, Oxford University has recently removed the Codrington name from the library.

The next account about educating Native Americans was a near miss. Irish clergyman and philosopher, the Very Reverend Dr. George Berkeley, the Dean of Derry (he was the man who asked: If a tree falls in the forest and there was nobody there to hear it, did it make a noise?), talked George I into promising money to found St. Paul's College in Bermuda to educate Native Americans in 1727. Some observers asked why build a college in Bermuda to educate Indians when there were no Indians living in Bermuda, to which the answer was that any imported students who decided to drop out would find there were no tribes to which they could melt away. Berkeley (pronounced Barkly) took members of his proposed faculty with him to Newport, Rhode Island in order to wait for the king's money, which never came, partly because the King had died. Eventually, Berkeley returned to Ireland, where they made him a bishop, and Bermuda never received a college. Meanwhile, many of the faculty members (notably Carl Theodore Pachelbel the music composer and John Smibert the painter) settled down in America and raised the whole tone of intellectual life there.

George II soon showed why he had not sent Dean Berkeley the money that had been promised by George I. It was because he preferred to finance retired General James Oglethorpe, who wanted to establish the new colony of Georgia (named, of course, after George II). Oglethorpe was apparently a breath of fresh air. He wanted the new colony to ban permanent slavery (seven-year slavery, of course, was acceptable), but also to give a leg up to the poor of London. The first colonists arrived in 1733. Among them were German-speaking Moravians, originally from what is now the Czech Republic who had become the world's first Protestants almost a century before Martin Luther. Two Anglican or Episcopal priests accompanied them, John Wesley (who later founded the Methodist Church) and George Whitefield (a major figure in the Great Awakening), who claimed that the Moravians were a great influence on them. Architect Peter Harrison was asked to design Whitefield College for Savannah in 1738, where it was thought that both Native Americans and Blacks could be educated, but the project for the college was finally ended with nothing constructed in 1776, by which time no money had been raised to construct it.

Worse still, almost ten years after the settlers had arrived, it was decided that running Georgia without slavery was not going to work, so permanent slavery was suddenly encouraged. At that, all the Moravians departed for Pennsylvania, where they founded the town of Bethlehem on Christmas Eve, 1741. The following year, they founded Moravian College (now Moravian University) in Bethlehem, which promised to educate whites, Blacks, and Native Americans. Although most Moravians generally spoke German, this was also the first college in the English-speaking world to admit women. At least one of the original college buildings still stands. Moravians do not toot their own horns, so many readers are unlikely to have encountered that piece of history.

Architect Peter Harrison received a special invitation to visit Quebec City in the early 1740s (often off-limits to British subjects), and while there, he was invited to design an enlargement to the Jesuit College. The college was destroyed during the British capture of Quebec in 1758, but it is believed that a handful of its students had been Native Americans, who were presumably being trained to become Roman Catholic clergy, but apparently none of them ever made it to ordination.

The next American colleges were from the 1740s and 1750s. King's College, New York City was founded in 1754 by the Reverend Dr. Samuel Johnson (same name as the man who wrote the famous Dictionary), who had been a great friend of Bishop George Berkeley. He made sure that his Episcopalian college, named after King George II, attempted to educate Lenape Native Americans, but apparently without great success. After the Revolution, the college was renamed Columbia University, and moved to a different location in the same city. Peter Harrison designed the first major building, which has long since been destroyed. Nearby in New Jersey, Presbyterians founded what they called The College of New Jersey in 1746, but it floundered in various locations until it moved to Princeton in 1756. It was eventually renamed Princeton University, and its original major buildings (still standing but greatly altered) were designed by Peter Harrison. In the 1770s, the Reverend Dr. Ezra Stiles of Newport, Rhode Island sent two former Black slaves, John Quamino (*sic* Kwame) and Bristol Yama to be educated at Princeton by President the Reverend John Witherspoon, so that they could be trained and sent as missionaries back to Ghana, Africa. Witherspoon insisted on educating them himself, segregated from all the rest of the students, but with the coming of the War of Independence, the whole scheme fell apart. Both students lived the rest of their lives in the United States.

In 1749, Benjamin Franklin founded an Academy School in Philadelphia. By 1755, the school had been enlarged and elevated to the status of a college, eventually renamed the University of Pennsylvania. Some people hoped that it would be available to educate at least some Blacks and Native Americans, but with the coming of the American Revolution such advanced ideas had to be at least temporarily dropped. Peter Harrison designed the first major buildings for the campus, now destroyed. Harrison's design for the college chapel was used for Saint Thomas' Church in 1792, the first Episcopal Church built for Black Americans.

In 1764, elected Governor Stephen Hopkins of Rhode Island, knowing that his tiny colony had a surprisingly large income derived from the rum trade (the British saw the rum trade as illegal, but technically it was within the conditions of Rhode Island's exceptionally liberal royal charter of 1663), together with like-minded people, founded what he called the College at Rhode Island, later renamed Brown University because the four Brown brothers of Providence and their descendants had endowed the institution. Peter Harrison designed the first major buildings (still standing) on the hill at Providence. There being a substantial population of free Blacks and of Narragansett Indians in colonial Rhode Island, it would be right to expect some of them to have been students there, but no record has survived of them, if indeed there ever were any.

In 1766, officials of the Dutch Reformed Church in New York and New Jersey established Queen's College (named after Queen Charlotte, wife of George III) in New Brunswick, New Jersey, and the principal building was designed by Peter Harrison. One might expect the college to have educated Lenape Native Americans, but the college's finances were in terrible shape, so that never happened. In the early nineteenth century, Colonel Henry Rutgers made a substantial financial contribution, so that the college was renamed Rutgers University. In the 1950s, the state of New Jersey contributed a large infusion of cash, and the university then became a state institution. The Dutch Reformed Church also used Harrison's alternative design for Queen's College as Erasmus Hall School (a public high school) in Brooklyn, New York, and that school building is still in use today.

Dartmouth College, named after British government official in charge of the colonies, William Legge, the Earl of Dartmouth, was founded in 1769 by Congregationalist minister the Reverend Eleazar Wheelock, who claimed that it was to educate Native Americans. He even asked the brilliant Native American the Reverend Samson Occom, whom he had trained, to go to England and raise the money to build the college. Occom raised all the money that anyone had expected, but Wheelock dishonestly changed the purpose of the college so that it did not offer education to any Native Americans. Occom was crushed. Peter Harrison designed several buildings for the campus, only one of which was built at Hanover, New Hampshire, the rest being built in Canada after the American Revolution in the Province of New Brunswick.

The College of Charleston was founded in South Carolina 1770. Peter Harrison designed several buildings for the campus, one of which survives today. South Carolina residents had little or no interest in educating Blacks or Native Americans at their college. In North Carolina, it was a very different story. Presbyterians who settled in the mountainous interior at the town of Charlotte (named after George III's Queen) asked Governor William Tryon for permission to build Queen's College there, and he quickly complied in 1771. Remember that, unknown to the people in rural North Carolina, there was already a Queen's College in New Jersey. However, officials in London over-ruled the governor's permission because they did not like Presbyterians, who they thought (accurately, as it turned out) might be quick to declare independence. Tryon told the college promoters what had happened, but suggested that they could re-name the college the Queen's Museum and get around the prohibition.

They did so, but the Revolution arrived just as the building (designed by John Hawks) was completed, so they renamed it Liberty Hall. The building did not survive long, probably due to serious fighting in the area. A new, unrelated college, now renamed Queen's University, was built in the nineteenth century. It is likely that the builders of the original college intended to encourage Native Americans, such as the Cherokee, Choctaw, Chickamauga, and Creek, to enroll in the college, but the disruptions of the Revolution probably prevented that. Regardless of that, many of the Cherokee and their affiliated tribes became committed Christians, thanks to the efforts of the Moravians in Salem, and at least some of them built sophisticated English-style houses, some with Flemish-bond brickwork, and some three stories tall. They even took enthusiastically to English Country Dancing, which is still taught in some of the elementary schools of Oklahoma, the place to which 60,000 Cherokees were disgracefully forced to move by President Jackson and his allies in the 1830s in what was named The Trail of Tears. Hampden-Sydney College was founded by Presbyterians near Farmville, Virginia, just south of Richmond, in 1775, and they are said to have used the same plans by John Hawks as the North Carolina Queen's College for their first main building.

The Reverend Dr. Thomas Bray in England (1656–1730) worked hard for the Anglican Church (in the USA, that is usually called the Episcopal Church today). He founded the Society for the Promotion of Christian Knowledge (SPCK) in 1699 and the Society for the Propagation of the Gospel (SPG) in 1701. The former worked exclusively in Britain, and the latter operated in the colonies. One day, Bray, who had been wondering how to educate Black children in America, received a large sum of money from the will of Abel Tassin Sieur d'Allone, who had been a high official of King William's government, asking Bray to use the money for educating Black children in America. Some of Bray's friends formed a group known as the Associates of Thomas Bray, and in the 1750s they tried to establish schools at Savannah and Charleston, but the schools failed in the face of hostility from bigoted white leaders. The Associates asked Benjamin Franklin what he thought, and he suggested that schools be established in Boston, Newport, New York, Philadelphia, and Williamsburg and perhaps elsewhere. The schools were established in those cities and several others, and many proved to be a success in 1760. Additional schools succeeded in Annapolis, Maryland and Fredericksburg, Virginia, whereas those in Chester MD, Yorktown VA, Norfolk VA, Edenton NC and Bath NC were all less successful. Schools in Nova Scotia thrived in

Digby (near Annapolis Royal), Halifax, Hammonds Plains (near Halifax), and Birchtown (near Shelburne), as did one at New Providence, Nassau in the Bahamas. Most of the children ranged from six to thirteen years old. They were taught to read and possibly to write, and in some cases to do arithmetic. Girls were also taught sewing and knitting. Some of the students were enslaved, and others were free. The Bray endowment paid for a school-mistress to be in charge of each school, and in some cases to purchase or rent or construct a suitable building. The Bray program covered as many as 22 schools ranging from Nova Scotia to the Bahamas. With the outbreak of the Revolution, the British shut down the whole program because they would not permit any money to be sent to the colonies for any purpose, regardless of how noble it was. The only school to resume after the war was the one in Philadelphia, which kept going until 1845, although its building no longer stands. Another in New York City, possibly designed by Peter Harrison and built of brick, was revived for its purpose as a school in the early nineteenth century. As far as can be determined, all the Bray School buildings have disappeared except for the one at 47 Division Street in Newport, RI (sometimes known as Mrs. Brett's School), where the house, which at some point belonged to Peter Bours, has been beautifully restored for private occupation, and the one in Williamsburg VA (sometimes known as Mrs. Wager's School), now on the west side of Nassau Street, which belonged to Dudley Digges, and has been restored after being moved to this location by the Colonial Williamsburg Foundation for exhibition to the public. The first location of the school building was on the east side of the first block of North Boundary Street, close to the College of William & Mary, with its front door facing west. The school was somewhat affiliated with the College of William & Mary (although not to the extent of the College providing money for the school). The school's teacher in Williamsburg was Ann Wager, and her death occurred a few months before the British shut-down of money for the school. The Bray trustees in England many times stated that they expected local residents to cover much of the cost of operating the Bray Schools, but except in the cases of post-war Philadelphia and New York City, that never happened. The Williamsburg Bray School was deemed too small after it had been in business for only five years, so in 1766 the school was re-opened in a larger building on the same exact site to which the original building has now been moved. Information gleaned from the Williamsburg and Newport schools suggest that about 200 students were educated by each school over the years.

William & Mary retired English Professor Terry Meyers had been responsible for identifying the former Bray School building, just before the College planned to tear it down to build a new dormitory building. Thanks to persistence by Professor Meyers, the school building was saved, moved, and restored to its original appearance. However, Meyers did not drop the project. He continued to research the matter of educating Black children in colonial Virginia. He learned that as early as 1723, an enslaved man in Virginia wrote an inspired letter to the Bishop of London, the Right Reverend Edmund Gibson, asking him to produce the money needed to educate Virginia Blacks. The Bishop of London was traditionally in charge of all the churches in the colonies. Gibson was sympathetic to the request, but somehow failed to come up with the money. Next, visiting British portrait painter Charles Bridges wrote to Bishop Gibson in 1735 and again in 1738, to no avail. The Reverend William Dawson was made President of the College of William & Mary in 1743, after the founding president, the Reverend James Blair, had died. Dawson had previously written to Bishop Gibson in 1740 to ask for help in educating Black children. Whether with Gibson's assistance or not, Dawson managed to get no fewer than three schools established for Black education in greater Williamsburg, but it was evident that the schools required constant financial support, which was not forthcoming from local residents – a recurring theme with the Bray Schools. As a result, all of Dawson's schools for Black students had to close in a few years. The Bray School endowment provided most of the ongoing support for one school to be continuously operated until the Revolutionary War forced it to be permanently closed. Professor Meyers is to be congratulated for pressing ahead with his research, which was summarized in the *Virginia Gazette* of 31 August 2024.

The school in Newport may have had an interesting relationship with the slave Newport Gardner. Gardner, born in 1746 in Africa and brought to Newport at age fourteen in 1760, was educated by tutor along with the Gardner family's children. The lad was a polymath. He had never been exposed to the English language or to western music before his arrival, and yet in 1768 he wrote an English Country Dance, both tune and dance directions, that was published in London, the first of many. We know that Gardner was already teaching music by 1770, when he taught Andrew Law, who was otherwise an undergraduate in Providence at The College at Rhode Island (later renamed Brown University). It is likely that Gardner offered to assist with teaching at the Bray School around 1770, and that the offer was possibly accepted. After the Revolution, Newport Gardner could see the harm done by the lack of the Bray School, so after achieving his freedom, he set up his own school in 1791, somewhat affiliated with Trinity (Episcopal) Church, and apparently located in a still existing building at 28 School Street at the corner of Mary Street, not far from the location of the former Bray School. The elegant purpose-built wood-framed building has a belfry on top, and for a time was used in the twentieth century as Shiloh Baptist Church. Although the students of Gardner's school also included white children, it was primarily aimed at Black children, both slave and free, and even a few adults. The school taught penmanship, English reading and writing, French reading and writing, arithmetic, history, music, and dance (but probably not Latin or Greek). No doubt, girls were also taught sewing and knitting. Newport Gardner's former master's wife was a student for a time at the school, in music composition, performance, and dance.

The Rector of Trinity Church, the Reverend George Bisset, sent two lists of students attending the Bray School in Newport in 1771 and 1772 to the Bray Associates in London. The Black students can be expected to have been given the last names of their masters, so one can look today for descendants with those names. The owners of students there included Ayrault, Buckmaster, Cahoone, Chaloner, Cooke, Dickinson, Duncan, Dupuy, Freebody, Honyman, Hunter, Johnston, Lyndon, Mumford, Scott, Shearman, Sneal, Wanton, Whitehorne, Wickham, and Wilkinson, many of whom (but not all) were members of Trinity Church. In addition, three "Free Negroes" were listed for each year. Historian Marian Desrosiers of Newport found these lists, but she observed that they did not correlate much with the names of Black property owners in early Newport, bearing in mind that the student lists covered only two of the fifteen years for which the school was open. The early Black property owners had the following last names: Anderson, Armstrong, Babcock, Barker, Bonner, Brinley, Brown, Chaloner, Clark, Coggeshall, Collins, Davis, Dyer, Easton, Ellery, Elliot, Fayerweather, Flagg, Gardner, Hampshire, Handy, Hicks, Jack, Johnson or Johnston , Keith, Lyndon, Mason, Mein, Mowatt, Overing, Pease, Phillips, Potter, Rodman, Simmons, Stevens, Taylor, Thurston, Wanton, and Weeden. Many of these names are shared with leading Caucasian families of Newport, of English, Welsh, German, and French Huguenot origin.

In the spring of 1764, elected Governor Stephen Hopkins had founded what he called "The College at Rhode Island." Hopkins persuaded various merchants involved in Rhode Island's lucrative rum trade to help endow the college and pay for its first proper building in Providence. Such a tiny colony as Rhode Island could not normally have afforded to operate a college in the absence of the rum trade, which was a business not legally available to any other colony. The most impressive donation came from the four Brown brothers from Providence, John, Nicholas, Joseph, and Moses. The first three were Baptists, but Moses was a Quaker. Their principal business was the rum trade. Rhode Island's exceptionally liberal Royal Charter from 1663 gave that colony an enormous advantage over all the other North American colonies when it came to importing no-cost molasses from French Haiti, converting it into rum in Rhode Island, and re-exporting it to all the other North American colonies, for use mostly as a food-preservative (meat, fish, vegetables, fruit, and even flour could be preserved indefinitely submerged in barrels of dark rum). If the Brown brothers occasionally traded slaves (John, for example, is quoted that he saw no difference between importing slaves and import- ing jackasses), it was a very minor part of their business when compared to the molasses/rum trade. On the other hand, the Haitian molasses was provided only because of Haitian slave labor making it in the first place as part of making sugar for export to France, whereas it was then illegal to export molasses or rum to France, in the interest of protecting France's brandy industry. Brown University was among the first American institu- tions of higher learning to come to some kind of terms with the role of slaves in its early years as a college, thanks to the leadership of its African- American president, Dr. Ruth Simmons, 2000–2012.

ENDING SLAVERY AND THE SLAVE TRADE

In the 8 January 1768 edition of the Newport *Mercury* appears this anonymous comment, probably attributable to Martin Howard II, a prominent Rhode Island Loyalist lawyer: "If you say you have the Right to enslave [Africans] because it is for your Interest, why do you dispute the Legality of *Great Britain's* enslaving you?" This comment threw the entire independence movement, including the later Declaration of In- dependence itself, into a quandary by exposing its hypocrisy, so that the controversy was carefully covered over in most forums. After the Decla- ration of Independence in July 1776, former Massachusetts Royal Gov- ernor, Massachusetts-born Thomas Hutchinson wrote, "… only I could wish to ask the Delegates of Maryland, Virginia and the Carolinas, how their Constituents justify the depriving more than an hundred thousand Africans of their right to Liberty." A similar comment was written about the Declaration of Independence by the British Dictionary-writer, Dr. Samuel Johnson: "How is it that we hear the loudest yelps for Liberty among the drivers of Negroes?"

Some early stirrings against slavery began to be seen in Europe. For example, in 1738, Caribbean slave Jean Boucaux, then working for his master Verdelin in France, was able to get the court to free him and award him back wages, based on a royal decree by Louis X from 1315 that outlawed slavery in France (but not in her colonies). Portugal outlawed slavery inside its home country in 1761, but not in any of its colonies. On 22 June 1772, the Lord Chief Justice of the Court of King's Bench in London (the highest court in the land), William Murray Earl of Mansfield, ruled that slave James Somersett was free of his master Charles Stewart, although he said that the ruling did not necessarily apply to all the 15,000 slaves then in England. Mansfield wrote:

> The State of Slavery is of such a Nature that it is incapable of being introduced on any Reasons, moral or political, but only by positive Law, which preserves its Force long after the Reasons, Occasions, and Time itself from whence it was created, is erased from Memory. It is so odious, that nothing can be suffered to support it, but positive Law. Whatever Inconveniences, therefore, may follow from the Decision, I cannot say this Case is allowed or approved by the Laws of England; and therefore the Black must be discharged.

As a result of Justice Mansfield's ruling, Black people who met the other criteria for voting were permitted to vote in parliamentary elections from 1774 onwards, and music-composer Charles Ignatius Sancho did so in 1774.

Scotland soon followed suit, when Chief Justice Alexander Boswell Lord Auchinleck ruled in 1778 that the slave James Knight was free. He wrote: "It may be the Custom in Jamaica to make Slaves of poor Blacks, but I do not believe it agreeable to Humanity nor to the Christian Religion." Scotland had only about 50 slaves in the entire country at that time. Like Britain and France, the Netherlands outlawed slavery at home at an early date, while maintaining slavery in its colonies.

On the verge of the American Revolution, in 1773, the Massachusetts General Court (the legislature), undoubtedly encouraged by Justice

Mansfield's decision in London only the previous year, voted to free all slaves in the colony with instant effect, but the bill was vetoed by Loyalist Governor Thomas Hutchinson, who said that he was not opposed to the legislation, but merely wanted to give slave-holders a chance to prepare for it. Because the war broke out in the meantime, the bill was not taken up again. However, a Black sailor from the Island of Nantucket, Massachusetts, named Prince Boston (born 1750), was placed by his master in the crew of a whaling ship, and at the end of the voyage Prince's master tried to get his hands on Prince's wages. Prince brought suit in Massachusetts court in 1773 that he was entitled to the pay for which he had worked so hard, and the court agreed. Not only did the court see that Prince was paid, but they also awarded him complete freedom.

Former elected Governor Stephen Hopkins of Rhode Island (1707–1785) returned home on vacation from serving in the Continental Congress in Philadelphia, and successfully introduced a bill in the Rhode Island Legislature with the following preamble:

> WHEREAS, the Inhabitants of *America* are generally engaged in the Preservation of their own Rights and Liberties, among which that of personal Freedom must be considered as the greatest; those who are desirous of enjoying all the Advantages of Liberty themselves, should be willing to extend personal Liberty to others.

The bill was passed on 10 June 1774, and it outlawed the importation of slaves to Rhode Island, the first such law in America. Rhode Island had earlier passed a bill outlawing the importation of Indigenous people to serve as slaves in 1715. Before introducing the 1774 bill, Hopkins first talked to three Rhode Island abolitionist friends of his: the Reverend Dr. Samuel Hopkins (no relation; 1721–1803, the pastor of Newport's First Congregationalist Church on Mill Street at the corner of Spring Street); the Reverend Dr. Ezra Stiles (1727–1795, the pastor of Newport's Second Congregationalist Church on Clarke Street, and later one of the greatest presidents of Yale College); and wealthy Quaker merchant Moses Brown of Providence (1738–1836). That meant that seven years later, there would theoretically be no more involuntary slaves in Rhode Island, the first place in the New World to do that, although as a practical matter some slaves remained in Rhode Island because they had not yet satisfied the justices of the peace that they would not be a burden on the community. As a practical matter, no Black slaves had been imported to Rhode Island for sale since 6 June 1763, and the law was broken only by the French military when they were based in Rhode Island 1780–2. French forces had been sent from Newport to Virginia in early 1781 in order to try to capture Benedict Arnold, but while they were in Virginia they captured the Loyalist brig *Molly* on 19 February, transporting an unknown number of former Virginia slaves (men, women, and children) who had sought refuge with the British. The French brought these slaves to Newport, and after French officers had purchased a few of them, the rest were auctioned on 13 June 1781. One of these was named Robert, who was purchased by Wainwood's Bakery. In 1788, Robert brought suit in a Rhode Island court for his freedom after having served his seven years, and it was granted.

General George Washington, whose home and life in Virginia were heavily supported by the work of numbers of enslaved people, was opposed at first to allowing Black people, enslaved or free, to serve in the Continental Army (even though they had been serving in the Continental Navy since late 1775). However, he saw how the British had been successful in enlisting Blacks in their armed forces. He was also persuaded by correspondence from Rhode Island General James Mitchell Varnum, urging him to accept at least free Blacks, so Washington wrote to Rhode Island Governor Nicholas Cooke offering qualified approval. Cooke then notified the Rhode Island General Assembly, and in February 1778 they passed legislation stating:

> Every able bodied Negro, Mulatto, or Indian Man Slave in this State may enlist into either of the said two Battalions to serve during the Continuance of the War with Great Britain; that every Slave so enlisting, shall be entitled to, and receive all the Bounties, Wages, and Encouragements, allowed by the Continental Congress . . . that every Slave enlisting shall, upon passing Muster before Colonel Christopher Greene, be immediately discharged from the Service of his Master or Mistress, and be absolutely FREE, as though he had never been encumbered with any kind of Servitude or Slavery.

This Rhode Island law was very unpopular with many slave-owners, even though they stood to be reimbursed for the value of their slaves. Therefore, the law was repealed in just over three months, after somewhere between 100 and 200 slaves had gained freedom through it.

Rhode Island followed up a short while later in 1779 with another law forbidding the sale of Rhode Island slaves outside the state. In 1777, residents of the future state of Vermont voted to outlaw slavery there, but they had no recognized political entity yet in which to do so, because at least half of Vermont belonged to New Hampshire, and half was claimed by New York. On 1 March 1780, Pennsylvania voted to end slavery, but only gradually. MumBet (ca. 1744–1829), a New York-born female slave living in Massachusetts, petitioned the court to free her. The court did so in August 1781, thus setting the stage for ending slavery in Massachusetts. She then changed her name to Elizabeth Freeman. In 1783, the Massachusetts Supreme Court flatly outlawed all slavery in that state. Spanish Florida also maintained for a time Fort Moise not far from St. Augustine, where escaped British Caribbean slaves were permitted to live free.

By 1784, it was becoming apparent that the Rhode Island law freeing slaves after seven years of servitude was not working, probably because the justices of the peace were being too vigorous in enforcing the clause requiring that each slave have a well-paying job waiting. Therefore, on 1 March the General Assembly passed legislation speeding up the process, but only on a gradual basis. On the same day, neighboring Connecticut passed a similar but less complete law. The preamble to the Rhode Island law (likely written by Stephen Hopkins) stated:

> WHEREAS, all Men are entitled to Life, Liberty and the Pursuit of Happiness, and the holding of Mankind in a State of Slavery, as private Property, which has gradually obtained by unrestrained Custom and the Permission of Laws, is repugnant to this Principle, and subversive of the Happiness of Mankind, the great End of all civil Government.

One negative aspect of the Rhode Island slavery laws was that the Legislature felt that it had little or no authority about the behavior of Rhode Island residents when they were outside the colony, and thus Rhode Island merchants, such as the De Wolfe family of Bristol, were among the major importers of African slaves to Santo Domingo, Cuba, and other Caribbean colonies in the late eighteenth century and early nineteenth century. Rhode Island lawmakers attempted to remedy that problem by voting in October 1787 (two years after the death of Stephen Hopkins) that Rhode Island residents were barred from participating in the slave trade, no matter where, but the law was ignored by many traders, and was in any case difficult for the Rhode Island courts to enforce. This law spelled out that the slave trade was "inconsistent with Justice, and the Principles of Humanity, as well as the Laws of Nature, and that more enlightened and civilized Sense of Freedom which has of late pre-vailed." Rhode Island in time of peace had no navy or coast guard service, and even the Continental Navy went out of business in 1785 and was not replaced by the United States Navy until 1797, so Rhode Island residents were quite safe in conducting themselves as they saw fit while outside the state, in the absence of any enforcement mechanism for more than a dozen years.

During the American Revolution, British troops and officials set free thousands of slaves whom they encountered in America, partly as a strategy to win the war, and partly as a reflection of the fact that slavery had been ruled illegal in England in 1772. Virginia's last Royal Governor John Murray Earl of Dunmore took thousands from Tidewater Virginia to Halifax, Nova Scotia in 1776 (unfortunately, many of these ex-slaves died of smallpox and other diseases along the way). Most slaves that the British found in Boston in 1775, Newport RI, New York City, and Perth Amboy NJ in 1776, and Philadelphia in 1778 followed to Halifax, as well as those found in Wilmington NC, Charleston SC, Savannah GA, and St. Augustine, FL, but not those found in Bermuda, the Bahamas, the Carib-bean islands or British West Florida.

The Charleston slaves had a particularly unusual story: when Brit-ish soldiers arrived after capturing the city in May 1780, they found that the white female residents there refused to join their proposed weekly English Country Dance assemblies during the cooler months of the year. Therefore, British officials sent to London for a great many splendid ball-gowns in a variety of sizes, and outfitted most of the female slaves of the city in those gowns, so that the British could dance with them each week, often until as late as 4.00 am, much to the horror of the white resi-dents. The British ostentatiously picked up the female slaves in elegant coaches and returned them after the dancing in the same way [see Kate van Winkle Keller, *Dance and its Music in America 1528–1789*, (Hills-dale NY), Pendragon Press, 2007, pp.105–113]. The slaves, of course, all knew the dances as well as the white people did. Dance-Master and oboist Hezekiah Cantelo (1750s-1811) is known to have led dances for the British at Charleston. Once back in London, he published a book, *Twenty-four American Country Dances as Danced by the British during their Winter Quarters at Philadelphia, New-York & Charles Town*, Long-man & Broderip, London, 1785.

With various European countries and various US states outlawing slavery in the late eighteenth century, the handwriting was on the wall for slavery. Haiti's revolution in the 1790s and the early nineteenth century, established government by Blacks, if tenuously, and freed all slaves within its borders. British abolitionists were so numerous and powerful that they persuaded parliament to end the slave trade in 1808, and because the Royal Navy was charged with enforcement the British enforcement quickly spilled over to covering all other nations in the greater Atlantic region. At first the United States was upset about British bullying, but very quickly the US fell into line. Next, the independent republic of Mexico outlawed slavery in 1828. The British led the way in the English-speaking world with their Caribbean colonies, where they ended slavery in 1834. The French, after some stumbling early in the nineteenth century, finally ended slavery in their colonies in 1848, the same year as the Danes did in their Virgin Islands. The Dutch ended slavery in their colonies in 1863, and the United States ended slavery in all their lands (after a brutal and bloody Civil War, that was at least partly about slavery) two years later in 1865. Portuguese colonies ended slavery in 1869, except in Brazil, where it was still legal until 1888. The Spanish kept slavery going in Cuba until 1886. With the exception of Codrington College in Barbados, that was mostly aimed at providing clergy for the Anglican Church from the middle of the eighteenth century onwards, no English-speaking institution of higher learning existed in the Caribbean until the University of the West Indies was founded in 1948 at Mona, a suburb of Kingston, Jamaica. The University of Havana, Cuba was founded by Dominican clergy in 1728, but it was limited exclusively to [white] men studying for the priesthood, until it became a secular university in 1842. The oldest university in all of the Americas was founded in Santo Domingo in 1538, but it was reserved until the nineteenth century exclusively for [white] men studying for the priesthood, as was the University of Michoacan in Mexico, founded in 1540, and the University of Mexico, founded in 1551. None of them appear to have had any interest in educating Black or Indigenous people until at least the nineteenth century.

2

Music Composers

SISTERS TEODORA & MICAELA GINES, *ONCE ENSLAVED*, 1530–1598 (HISPANIOLA & CUBA)

Not much is known about Teodora Gines (1530–1598) and her sister Micaela. They are said to have been enslaved mulattas born in Santiago de los Caballeros in what is now the Dominican Republic, and they soon demonstrated an interest in music. They were freed in their twenties, and moved to Cuba, where they were associated with the orchestra at the Cathedral of Santiago (Saint James) de Cuba. Santiago de Cuba is located on the south coast of the eastern end of the island, not far from Guantanamo. Normally, women were not allowed to be part of cathedral musical accompaniment, but in this case male musicians were sufficiently scarce that the rules were bent in the favor of the two women. Micaela was apparently a violinist (but her instrument looked very different from today's violins because the violin had not really yet been invented, so perhaps it was a treble viol with a flat back, having up to six strings over frets. A treble viol could be played off the shoulder like a violin, or like a miniature cello hanging from a harness), and Teodora played both the vihuela (looks like a small guitar, but tuned differently) and the bandola (looks like a pear-shaped mandolin, but tuned differently). At the moment, no church music has been found that may have been written by these women, but a Cuban folk-song, believed to have been written about 1563, has survived in oral tradition, *Son de la Ma Teodora*. The song is in

the call-and-response format and is infinitely expandable as the perform-
er invents new lyrics, much as chantey-men often did on sailing ships.
This piece was finally published in the late nineteenth century. Cathedral
musicians were of course expected not to compose folk-songs, but either
no one of importance noticed, or once again the rules were bent. The
cathedral buildings in both towns were many times destroyed by hurricanes, earthquakes, and pirate attacks, and the replacement buildings
are different. Any documentation of the music of these two sisters would
have been destroyed by the hurricanes, earthquakes, and pirate attacks.

This entry was paraphrased from Wikipedia, with geographical and
historical additions by the author.

JUAN DE LIENAS, *NATIVE AMERICAN CHIEF*, FL. 1617–1654 (MEXICO, CENTRAL AMERICA, SPAIN, ITALY)

Juan de Lienas was a composer active in Mexico and Central America in
the second third of the seventeenth century. Very little is known about
him, but he is said to have been a Native American chief, possibly from
Guatemala, who was singled out for intensive education. Since he showed
an interest and talent in music, he was taken to Spain for some of his education, and possibly also to Rome, where he would have been exposed to
the music of Giovanni da Palestrina (1525–1594). We know that he was
married, and that much of his music was written for a female choir of the
Convent of Our Lady of the Incarnation, connected with the Cathedral
in Mexico City. Some of the Convent's music contains lines for tenor and
bass, but it is thought that these were likely played by nuns on viola da
gamba or bassoon, since men were never allowed contact with the nuns.

Two collections of De Lienas' music survive, a set of six choir-
books now in the Newberry Library in Chicago, and another collection
in Mexico City. His elegant polyphonic music is sometimes reminiscent
of Palestrina and of Francisco Guerrero and Cristobal de Morales, and
belongs more to the sixteenth century than to his own time. A number of
recordings of De Lienas' music have been made.

This entry is paraphrased from Wikipedia, with geographical and
historical additions by the author.

JUAN MATIAS DE RIVERA, *NATIVE AMERICAN*, CA. 1618–1665 (OAXACA, MEXICO)

Juan Matias de Rivera was a Native American from the Zapotec tribe in Oaxaca State, Mexico, born in San Bartolo Coyotepec. He was first employed as a bass singer before he was hired as the first indigenous chapel master of Oaxaca Cathedral. He directed the cathedral music to a high level of professionalism that would be maintained for the next century and a half. In the archives of the Archdiocese of Guatemala can be found: a mass for 4 parts, a *Cantate Domino* for 8 voices, and two villancicos (folk songs) for 8 voices: *Quien sale aqueste dia disfrazado*, and *Quien puebla de delicias*. Six works have been found in Oaxaca Cathedral, including a mass for 4 voices. In San Pedro Huamelula are *Nos autem gloriari*, *Gaudeamus*, and *Domine ad adjuvandum me festina*, as well as two masses, one for 4 voices and one for 8. In San Bartolo Yautepec the hymn *Ave Maris stella*, and the incomplete mass, *Missa Batalla* are found.

Beyond this, very little is known about this composer. His music is much more characteristic of the country than the music of Juan de Lienas, so it is likely that he never travelled to Spain or anywhere else in Europe.

This entry is paraphrased from Wikipedia, with geographical and historical additions by the author.

FRANCIS WILLIAMS, *FREE BLACK*, 1702–1771 (JAMAICA AND GREAT BRITAIN); [ECD].

Francis Williams was born in 1702 (or thereabouts) to John and Dorothy Williams, a free Black couple in Jamaica. John Williams, who had accumulated substantial property, had been freed as recently as 1699 in the will of his former master. Due to John Williams' wealth, Francis and his siblings were able to be provided with an excellent education in Continental Europe and England. It is said that Francis attended Cambridge University and may even have graduated there about 1723, but all of the university records were destroyed during an outbreak of scarlet fever in an effort to stamp out the disease, so no record of his being there survives. Some accounts say that Major General John Montagu, 2nd Duke of Montagu (1690–1749), had taken young Williams under his wing, because he wanted to see how well a Black person could do with a university education, but there is no documentary proof of that. Williams was naturalized as a British citizen in 1723, and took the oath of citizenship, which accorded him greater rights when he returned to Jamaica. He even attended as an invited guest of the great surgeon, William Chelselden, several meetings of the prestigious Royal Society (the world's leading scientific organization, both at the time and now), although when the surgeon also proposed him as a member, he was denied actual membership simply on grounds of race.

Williams established a free school at Spanish Town, Jamaica, for Black children, where he taught reading, writing, Latin, history, and mathematics, among other subjects. Every time that a new governor was inaugurated, Williams wrote a flowery Latin poem to celebrate the occasion (and provided an English translation in case the governor had forgotten his Latin). During the governorship of Edward Trelawney (1738–1752), Williams managed to be elected to the Jamaica Legislature, but the loud, bigoted complaints of both Trelawney and some other members of the legislature caused Williams to bow out gracefully, which leaves Matthias de Sousa of Maryland (a Roman Catholic originally from Portuguese Angola, via a few years in Barbados) the only Black to be elected to a colonial American legislature, and to serve in 1641. The Victoria & Albert Museum in London owns a folk-art portrait of Williams, shown about 1750 in his study at Spanish Town, Jamaica, with its black and white marble floor, wearing a white wig, and fancy velvet and silk clothes, surrounded by hundreds of books, and an elegant Jamaica-made mahogany arm-chair and tripod table, and two globes. Some say that the anonymous artist was mocking Williams by painting his hands and feet as such tiny appendages. Williams owned a plantation and several slaves (yes, many free Blacks owned slaves; remember that most slaves in that day were initially prisoners of war in one of hundreds of local West African tribal wars). Spanish Town, incidentally, was originally known as Santiago de la Vega, and served as the first capital of Jamaica, but in the middle of the eighteenth century, Peter Harrison of Rhode Island was hired to design splendid statehouses and governor's mansions for both Spanish Town and the commercial capital, Kingston, and the government alternated between the two locations, for many years.

A letter published in 1760 reported that one literate Black man in Jamaica, called John, was the captain of a fishing-boat (likely a schooner of about 60 feet long on deck). His master was said to have placed unlimited confidence in him, and the writer praised him for giving him in advance of his trip to England "a pretty good notion of the customs and

manners of England, and of the things which would be taught in school."
No doubt, John had learned all of that in Williams' school.

Williams was noted for his scholarship in many areas, likely including music, and it is believed that he wrote the words (but not the tune) to the song *Welcome, Brother Debtor* that first appeared in the ballad opera *The Prisoners' Opera*, produced in London in 1730 by Edward Ward. English Country Dances that Williams may have written include *Port Royal* (published by Neal in Dublin in 1726); *Barbados* (published by Johnson, Book III, in London in the 1740s); *The Negroe* (published by Johnson in 1751); *A Trip to Kingston* (Johnson, 1751); *Queensberry House* (Rutherford I 1756, and R. Bremner, 1757).

WELCOME, BROTHER DEBTOR

Welcome, welcome, brother debtor to yon poor but merry place,
Where no bailiff, dun, or fetter dare show their frightful face.
But, kind sir, as you're a stranger, down your garnish you must lay,
Or your coat will be in danger: you must either strip or pay.
Ne'er repine at your confinement from your children or your wife.
Wisdom lies in true refinement through the various scenes of life.
Scorn to show that least resentment, though beneath the frowns
    of fate.
Knaves and beggars find contentment; tears and cares attend the
    great.
Though our creditors are spiteful and restrain our bodies here,
Use will make a jail delightful, since there's nothing else to fear.
Every island's but a prison, strongly guarded by the sea.
Kings and princes for that reason prisoners are as well as we.
What was it made great Alexander weep at his unfriendly fate?
'Twas because he could not wander beyond ye world's strong
    prison gate.
The world itself is strongly bounded by the heavens and stars
    above.
Why should we then be confounded, since there's nothing free but
    love.

This entry is paraphrased from Wikipedia, with geographical and historical additions by the author.

CHARLES IGNATIUS SANCHO, *ONCE ENSLAVED*, 1729–1780 (CARIBBEAN & GREAT BRITAIN) [ECD]

Charles Ignatius Sancho was born on a slave ship on its way to the Caribbean. His mother died almost immediately after the ship arrived at the Spanish colony of New Granada (now essentially Colombia), and his father committed suicide shortly after that. The infant is said to have been baptized by the Bishop of Cartagena, hence his unusual middle name. The two-year-old orphan was taken to England and given to three spinster sisters who lived in Greenwich (about seven miles east of the City of London, on the other side of the Thames), and he was their slave for eighteen years. While there, he was taught to read and write, courtesy of the Duke of Montagu. At age twenty, Sancho ran away to the Montagu household at Blackheath (near Greenwich), where he spent two years as butler. After the Duchess of Montagu's death in 1751, Sancho started his own business as a shopkeeper, which also gave him the opportunity to read extensively, and to write and publish essays, music, books, and plays. He received in the Duchess' will an annuity of thirty pounds per year (about $12,000 in 2023 money), plus a year's salary.

Sancho married a Caribbean woman, Anne Osborne, on 17 December 1758, and she produced seven children: Frances Joanna, Ann Alice, Elizabeth Bruce, Jonathan William, Lydia, Katherine Margaret, and William Leach Osborne. Needing additional money to support his growing family, about 1762 until 1773, Sancho became a hired valet to George Montagu, a kinsman of his previous employer. At least two portraits were painted of him, one by the Scottish painter Allan Ramsay showing him as a young man, and one by Thomas Gainsborough in 1768.

Sancho directed many of his efforts at getting the slave trade outlawed, and then at getting slavery itself banned in Britain. He wrote to the Irish novelist Laurance Sterne in 1766, asking him to write essays against the slave trade, and Sterne's answer to him was soon incorporated into abolitionist literature of the day. The exchange, in turn, established Sancho as a man of letters, and he was soon on very close terms with the likes of actor David Garrick, violinist/composer Felice Giardini, clergyman William Dodd, sculptor Joseph Nollekens, and statesman and abolitionist Charles James Fox.

In 1774, Sancho, who was by now suffering from gout and other maladies, opened a shop at 19 Charles Street (now King Charles Street, running between Whitehall and Horse Guards Road) in Westminster,

London, ironically selling mostly goods produced by slaves, such as tobacco, sugar, spices, and tea. The then Duke Montagu assisted him in establishing the shop. Also in 1774, since as a property-owner Sancho met the qualifications to vote, he became the first Black to vote in a parliamentary election, a feat that he repeated in 1780. Sancho died from complications of gout on 14 December 1780, and was buried at St. Margaret's, Westminster, close to the houses of parliament. Slavery itself was essentially abolished in Britain in 1772, but the slave trade was not abolished for British citizens and ships until 1807.

Sancho wrote numerous essays, including *Theory of Music* (now lost) and letters to newspapers (sometimes signed "Africanus"), and a vivid account of the Gordon Riots of June 1780 (a violent demonstration by 100,000 extreme Protestants against Parliament's vote to extend the vote to Roman Catholics, which resulted in some parts of London being burned and looted). He also wrote two plays. After his death, Frances Crewe arranged to publish 160 of Sancho's letters. The edition sold remarkably well in several printings, and provided Sancho's widow with substantial royalties. Sancho wrote and published numerous English Country Dances, minuets, songs, and other chamber music between 1767 and 1779.

Sancho's Commentary on the Slave Trade

The grand object of English navigators, indeed of all Christian navigators – is money – money – money – for which I do not pretend to blame them. Commerce was meant by the goodness of the Deity to diffuse the various goods of the earth into every part, to unite mankind in the blessed chains of brotherly love, society, and mutual dependence. The enlightened Christian should diffuse the riches of the Gospel of peace with the commodities of his respective land. Commerce attended with strict honesty, and with Religion for its companion, would be a blessing to every shore it touched at. In Africa, the poor wretched natives, blessed with the most fertile and luxuriant soil, are rendered so much the more miserable for what Providence meant as a blessing: the Christians' abominable traffic for slaves, and the horrid cruelty and treachery of the petty kings encouraged by their Christian customers, who carry with them strong liquors to enflame their national madness; and powder and bad fire-arms to furnish them with the hellish means of killing and kidnapping.

The entire known output of Sancho's music compositions can be found in Josephine R. B. Wright, ed., *Ignatius Sancho (1729–1780, An Early African Composer in England,* New York & London, Garland Publishing, Inc. 1981. Sancho's English and French Country Dances included: Le Jour de May Cotillon, The Merry Wives of Westminster, Les Contes des Fees Cotillon, Christmas Eve, Le Douze de Decembre Cotillon, Nothing at All, Kew Gardens, La Loge de Richemont Cotillon, The Carravan, L'Homme et la Femme Cotillon, Les Nains Cotillion, The Friendly Visit, Just so in the North, Les Matadors Cotillon, Le Vieux Garcon Cotillon, La Maison de la Reine Cotillon, L'Etourderie de Catos Cotillon, Sir Harry Flutter, Richmond Hill, Marianne's Reel, Who'd a Thought it, Lady Mary Montagu's Reel, Culford Heath Camp, Ruffs and Rhees, Bushy Park, Lord Dalkeith's Reel, Lindrindod Lasses, Trip to Dilington, Strawberries and Cream, All of One Mind, The Royal Bishop, Dutchess of Deconshire's Reel, Mungo's Delight.

This entry is paraphrased from Wikipedia, with historical and geographical additions by the author.

JOSEPH BOLOGNE, CHEVALIER DE SAINT-GEORGES, *FREE BLACK*, 1745–1799 (GUADELOUPE & FRANCE) [ECD]

Joseph Bologne (sometimes spelled Boulogne) was born on Christmas Day 1745 at Baillif, Basse-Terre, Guadeloupe. Guadeloupe on the map looks like a butterfly, and Basse-Terre, despite its name, is actually the higher half, located to the southwest. His father Georges Bologne de Saint-Georges was a wealthy, married sugar planter on the Caribbean Island of Guadeloupe, and his mother Anne/Nanon Danneveau was a sixteen-year-old Senegalese slave woman belonging to his wife. At the age of seven, Joseph was taken to France by his father to be educated at a boarding school. The father legally acknowledged Joseph to be his son, and gave him his surname, before he returned to his plantation in Guadeloupe. Two years later, the senior Saint-Georges and Nanon both arrived in France, and lived with Joseph at 49 rue Saint-Andre' des Arts near the south bank of the Seine. At age 13, his father enrolled him in the leading military school, where he was expected to learn swordsmanship and horsemanship, but his progress was so great that when he graduated in 1766, he had already beaten many of the leading fencers in France. He was then made an officer of the King's bodyguard and a chevalier; otherwise, as an illegitimate son, he would have been ineligible to inherit his father's rank.

In addition to being a superb fencer and horseman, Saint-Georges was also a fine dancer, and he was welcomed to balls, salons, and boudoirs of high-ranking women. All this time, he had also been studying music, particularly playing the violin, taught in part by Francois-Joseph Gossec, and in 1764 the composer Lolli wrote two concerti for him to play as soloist. In 1766, Gossec wrote a set of six string trios for him. In 1769, Saint-Georges was the principal violinist in Gossec's new orchestra, Le Concert des Amateurs. Three years later, with Gossec conducting, Saint-Georges made a sensation by performing two concerti that he had written, and the following year Gossec made him conductor of the orchestra. The Concert des Amateurs was thought to be the best orchestra in all of Europe for performing symphonies, but in 1781 during the American Revolution the orchestra ran out of money, money which the nobility no longer possessed because they had helped to pay for the War for American Independence. When Saint-Georges made a plea for help, his friend the influential Philippe D'Orleans, Duc de Chartres reconstituted the same orchestra as Le Concert Olympique, reflecting the fact that Philippe was Grand Master of the Masonic Order in France. The orchestra performed in a variety of places, including the Hotel de Soubise (not an hotel in the modern sense of the word, but a family mansion), now home to part of the National Archives. Because Queen Marie Antoinette occasionally dropped in on these concerts, the musicians wore bulky court attire for every concert, just in case.

In 1776, Saint-George's name had been proposed to be the next director of the Paris Opera, but three leading ladies protested, so the offer embarrassingly had to be withdrawn. Saint-Georges nevertheless wrote six operas, for which the music was declared a great success, even if the libretti and narratives were not as good. Unfortunately, except for the overtures and one or two other pieces, the sheet music for all but one of the operas has been lost; the one survivor, *L'Amant Anonyme*, has been recorded. After the American Revolution, the Concert Olympique lost its preferred concert hall, which had to be massively rebuilt. Additionally, Saint-Georges lost his free residence, which he had generously shared for about ten weeks in 1778 with the 22-year-old Mozart while Mozart was visiting Paris. At the suggestion of Philippe D'Orleans, Saint-Georges took a trip to Great Britain in 1785. There, Philippe introduced him to the Prince-Regent (the future George IV) and many important people, some of whom were abolitionists. He performed at a number of concerts, and beat most fencers who wanted to fence with him, and formed joint plans with abolitionists to end the slave trade. He was soon on a fine footing with the leading abolitionists, such as William Wilberforce, John Wilkes, Charles James Fox, Josiah Wedgwood and the Reverend Thomas Clarkson. Before Joseph left England for the first time, Mather Brown painted his portrait. Another portrait was made of him in London in 1787 fencing against an apparent woman, the Chevaliere d'Eon, but after the death of that woman in 1810 it was revealed that the fencer had been a man all along. Saint-Georges returned to England shortly afterwards, and was there when the French Revolution broke out.

After recovering from a sudden illness, thought to have been men-ingitis, Saint-Georges took command of a branch of the National Guard to defend against a 1791 attack by the Austrians, and his unit was the only one to hold the line while the rest were routed by the Austrians. Then he wrote the music for a Requiem Mass (now lost) held at Lille. His friend Philippe D'Orleans identified with the Revolution, but it did him little good: he was sent to the guillotine in 1793, along with many other notables. King Louis XVI· was guillotined on 21 January at age 38, and Queen Marine-Antoinette, who had been a champion of the music of Saint-Georges, was guillotined on 16 October at age 37. Meanwhile, somewhat inaccurate news arrived in France that the Blacks of Haiti had revolted and butchered thousands of people there, so Saint-Georges joined a 1796 expedition to Haiti of 15,000 troops with the intention of abolishing slavery there. He and his friends formed the Saint-Georges Legion. However, he was quickly disheartened by the savagery of fighting between the Blacks and the Mulattoes, and between the wealthy whites and the low-income whites, so he returned to France in disgust. By now, at age 51, he was no longer needed by the army, so he founded yet an-other Paris orchestra, Le Cercle de l'Harmonie. In 1799, Saint-Georges was suffering from a perforated ulcer that he tried to hide from everyone, but he died in Paris from gangrene on 12 June 1799 at age 53.

Saint-Georges had written six operas (some of the opera overtures were also separately issued as symphonies), fourteen violin concerti, four Symphonies Concertantes for violin and orchestra, numerous pieces of chamber music for one to four instruments. He also wrote a handful of English Country Dances by themselves. However, in that period, French operas were required to contain periods of country dancing, so the music of the one surviving opera also contains a number of dance tunes but without the dance directions. His independent country dances include *A Trip to Guadeloupe* (Thompson II), *A Trip to Martinique* (Thompson II), *La Chasse* (Thompson 1780), *La Chasse Cotillion* (Longman), *La Belle Annette* (Cantelo) and *The Saint-George* (Cantelo). He has been widely hailed as "The Black Mozart," but that title does neither Saint-Georges nor Mozart justice; the two men were friends and close colleagues. Saint-Georges has been depicted in several motion-pictures, sometimes with questionable accuracy.

This entry is paraphrased from Wikipedia, with historical and geographical details assed by the author.

NEWPORT 'NKRUMAH MIEREKU' GARDNER, *ONCE ENSLAVED*, 1746–1826 (GHANA, RHODE ISLAND, LIBERIA) [ECD]

Newport Gardner was born Occramer Marycoo (Rhode Island spelling of Nkrumah, meaning ninth-born son, Miereku) at Anomabo on the coast of Ghana in 1746. The whole area was riven with frequent wars between tribes, so he was taken prisoner in 1760 and sold at age 14 to a slave merchant, who brought the lad to Newport, Rhode Island. It is important to understand that the ship on which he was taken to Rhode Island was small, probably not much bigger than 65 feet (20 metres) long on deck, carrying only a dozen or two slaves. Those hideous graphics of hundreds of slaves crammed into a large ship represented slaves being taken to tropical areas, like the Caribbean or South America.

Once he had arrived in Newport, which was the fifth largest town in colonial America, he was sold as a slave to 21-year-old Caleb Gardner. Caleb Gardner (1739–1806), later captain of a ship, sailed far afield to China and the East Indies after the Revolutionary War. As Caleb grew older, he became a major player in Newport's slave trade, and he continued his part in that trade long after the end of the Revolutionary War. He lived for many years in a waterfront house along low-lying Thames Street, which was subject to serious flooding in hurricanes and other storms, but late in life, he bought and lived in the impressive John Mawdsley House one long block uphill at 228 Spring Street, which had been enlarged from a 1680 house a little further up the hill on Prospect Hill Street.

The Gardner family educated young Newport as if he were their own child, and they were pleasantly surprised to see that he rapidly soaked up everything that they could teach. He was a veritable polymath. No one knows for sure whether he may have studied (or almost certainly later taught) at the Bray School located at 47 Division Street that had been founded in order to educate Blacks, whether enslaved or free. The Bray Endowment had been established in England in the 1720s by the Reverend Dr. Thomas Bray (1658–1730), and it eventually founded twenty-two schools from Nova Scotia to the Bahamas to educate Black boys and girls, both enslaved and free. The one in Newport was founded in 1760, and like many of the other Bray Schools, it was regarded as successful. However, when the Revolutionary War began in 1775, the British government cut off all financial contact between the Endowment and all the schools, which forced the schools to close. The Newport Bray School, restored as a private house known as the Peter Bours House, is one of only two Bray School buildings to have survived, the other being originally on North Boundary Street in Williamsburg, Virginia (now moved to the corner of Francis Street and Nassau Street). Gardner learned English and French, reading and writing (his penmanship was elegant, judging from a surviving letter at the Newport Historical Society), arithmetic, history, music composition, and English Country Dance.

Gardner probably studied music with composer Josiah Flagg (1737-ca. 1794), and possibly with William Sampson Morgan (fl. 1760–1780) and William Selby (1738–1798), all of whom were Episcopalian composers and organists spending time at Trinity Church in Newport. There, the Richard Bridge organ had been donated in 1733 by Irish philosopher-theologian the Very Reverend Dr. George Berkeley (pronounced Barkly; he's the man who asked, 'If a tree falls in the forest and there was nobody there to hear it, did it make a noise?), and the organ had been approved by George Frederick Handel. Congregationalist churches at this early date outlawed organs and harpsichords in church, so Gardner had to go to the Episcopal Church for his keyboard lessons. Historian G. C. Mason, writing a century later, asserted that Gardner had studied with Congregationalist psalmodist Andrew Law (1749–1821) who was then a student in Providence at The College at Rhode Island (later Brown University), but it is almost certain that it was the other way around: Gardner, who was three years older than Law, had already studied music in his mid-teens, and was therefore sharing what he knew with college student Law in Providence about 1770. Whether Law came to Newport for his lessons or Gardner sailed to Providence and back is unknown, but it is likely that Law spent his vacation time in Newport, because Gardner would have been too busy to travel. Gardner is also believed to have played the violin proficiently, and he probably used that instrument to accompany the English Country Dancers whom he taught. Newport Gardner is likely to have studied English Country Dance at the school of Mary Cowley on Thames Street near the intersection of Church Street, which she operated from about 1760 onwards. The dance school's location was not far from where the Gardners' house stood on the water side of Thames Street. If young Gardner was permitted to study at the Cowley School, letting an enslaved Black boy dance with white children is simply more evidence that at least some of the people of Newport were particularly open-minded.

In 1997, Harvard historian Dr. Eileen Southern identified the tune *Crooked Shanks* in her book, *The Music of Black Americans: A History* (3rd edition), W. W. Norton & Co., as having been written by Gardner. The tune was published in 1803 in *A Number of Original Airs, Duettos and Trios* as having been written by Gardner. This tune had previously been published in London for two English Country Dances, a 40-bar version for *The Seaside* (Bride, 1768, when Gardner was only 22 years old, only eight years after he had arrived in America!), and a 28-bar version for *Bill of Rights* (Thompson, 1770s), both appropriate names for dances coming from Newport. I believe that several other dances were written by Gardner: *Newport Assembly* (Thompson, 1780); *The Bells of Newport* (*Gentlemen & Ladies Companion,* 1798; tune: Murphey MS, 1790), *The Rose* (Three dance directions to same tune: Rutherford II; Thompson 1778; Muzzey MS ca. 1790), *Boston Assembly* (Griffiths 1794; tune: Pike MS; tune became popular Revolutionary War military march *On the Road to Boston*); *Ticonderoga* (Thompson 1778), *Hopkins' Fancy* (tune only, Mittell MS, 1799), *Hopkins' Whim* (Thompson 1780), *Lafayette Cotillion* (Griffiths 1788; tune: Adams MS); *Monsieur Lafayette* (Griffiths 1788, tune: Turner MS), *La Beaute'Cotillion* (Griffiths 1788; tune: Perkins MS), *La Petite Province Cotillion* (Griffiths 1788; tune: Carroll MS), *Rhode Island March Country Dance* (Griffiths 1794; tune: Shepley MS), and *Sea Flower* (Griffiths 1794; tune: Litchfield CT Historical Society MS); *Sea Flower* was the name of the Boston ship that brought the first fourteen slaves to Newport to arrive on an American ship in 1696, so Gardner obviously included that name on purpose.

Gardner was ordained a deacon under his Pastor, the Reverend Dr. Samuel Hopkins, in the First Congregationalist Church on Mill Street at the corner of Spring Street in Newport, where he had previously served as sexton (the 1729 building still stands, minus its handsome steeple, although the building is now converted to condos). Then, in 1824, the Black members decided to separate and establish their own Colored Union Church on Division Street, and Gardner as their leader transferred his membership there. This new church was an attempt to start an ecumenical movement of sorts. Newport by this time had congregations of Quakers, many different stripes of Baptists, Congregationalists, Methodists, Presbyterians, Moravians, and Episcopalians. With the exception of the Apostolic Succession of Moravian and Episcopalian clergy, and the Quakers having no clergy at all in those days, most people could not discern a ha'penny's worth of difference between all the denominations, so some sort of Union church could be seen to be useful.

All the rest of the music by Gardner (said to be numerous church pieces) is presumed lost, including the music for *Promise*, an anthem from the 1790s whose text survives.

Promise

These are the words of the Lord, the God of Israel: write in a book all that I have said to you, for this is the very word of the Lord: the time is coming when I will restore the fortunes of my people Israel, says the Lord, and bring them back to the land which I gave to their forefathers, and it shall be their possession. It is not fair to take the children's bread and throw it to the dogs, but even the dogs under the table eat the scraps of the children. (Jeremiah 30, 1–3; Mark 7, 27–28). If anyone should find the musical setting for this text, please notify the author of this essay.

According to the *Rhode Island Republican* of 4 January 1826, Gardner wrote and conducted a triumphal anthem at the Park Street Congregationalist Church in Boston in celebration of the departure of Gardner and about 36 of his followers aboard the ship *Vine* for Liberia, but that anthem is also believed to have been lost. The Park Street Church had been founded in 1804 and constructed with its extremely tall steeple designed by Peter Banner in 1809, still a Boston landmark.

Gardner was also on good terms with the Reverend Dr. Ezra Stiles, pastor of Newport's Second Congregationalist Church, built in 1735 on

Clarke Street, and still standing minus its steeple, and it, like the First Church, is now occupied by condos. Stiles, a 1746 graduate of Yale College, later made a name for himself by serving as President of Yale College from 1778 to 1795.

Under Rhode Island Common Law, which stated that slavery was to last for only seven years, but starting only at age 21, Gardner would have been eligible to petition a justice of the peace for his freedom on his 28th birthday in 1774. This was the same year in which Rhode Island was the first colony to outlaw the importation of slaves on 10 June. However, he did not petition for his freedom until 1791 at age 45. Apparently, he liked the relatively friendly arrangement he had with the Gardner family, and saw no reason to terminate it until he had amassed (thanks to having won a lottery) enough money to live comfortably on his own. Then, he moved to a new house that he bought at 25 Pope Street, with his wife Limas (died 1821) and their then seven children. If it is the wooden building that stands on the site today, it has been unrecognizably altered. Another house across the street is known as the Newport Gardner Bed & Breakfast, but that is not the right address.

Presumably influenced by his previous connection with the Newport Bray School only a few yards away on Division Street, Gardner opened another school in 1791, primarily to educate Blacks (both enslaved and free, children and adults) and a few whites, in penmanship, English reading and writing, arithmetic, French, history, music (both singing and composition), and English Country Dance, although probably not Latin or Greek. It is believed that the school in question was at least from 1799 onwards in the building at 28 School Street (of course it would be on School Street!) at the corner of Mary Street and Touro Street, whose founding had some connection with Trinity [Episcopal] Church three blocks away at the corner of Church Street and Spring Street. The 18th-century wooden schoolhouse with belfry on top in more recent years served as Shiloh Baptist Church. Some of the students at Gardner's school were white, including his former master's wife, who studied singing, composition, and English Country Dance in that school.

Gardner was a leader of the Back-to-Africa Movement, but the Newport flock whom he led back there were almost immediately bereft of Gardner, who died (like so many others) from lack of immunity to African diseases, only weeks after his arrival in Liberia in 1826 at the age of eighty. In the same way that the British had purchased in the 1780s the land known as Sierra Leone, with its new capital city of Freetown, for formerly enslaved American Blacks who had wanted to return to Africa, the United States acquired land in the 1820s next door to Sierra Leone that they called Liberia (Land of Liberty) for America's former slaves. Since the move was championed by President Monroe (himself a slave-holder), the capital city was thoughtfully named Monrovia. Even if the lad had remained in his native Ghana, it is likely that Gardner would not have had immunities to Liberian diseases, since Ghana and Liberia are several hundred miles apart.

Sierra Leone lurched along until deposits of diamonds were found, which provided some national income to assist the population. Liberia had no diamonds, and the former American Blacks found themselves in an almost perpetual civil war against the locals, who greatly resented the arrival of so many Americans. In the 1990s, crooked politician Charles Taylor (born 1948), who had graduated from Massachusetts-based Bentley University, returned from guerilla training in Libya, and had Liberia's democratically-elected president executed. In order to produce money to pay for his activities, he encouraged some disaffected people in Sierra Leone to rebel, and then led Liberian fighters to invade Sierra Leone. The Liberians left behind thousands of Sierra Leone residents who had been horribly mutilated and maimed, while Taylor carried off all the diamonds that he could. World-wide revulsion at Taylor led to an agreement that all diamonds that were for sale anywhere must carry a passport detailing their mine of origin. Since Taylor could not obtain such passports for his diamonds, he found a client willing to buy them at a steep discount: Al-Qaeda. Taylor went into exile in Nigeria, until the World Criminal Court in the Hague managed to bring him there for trial, and he is now serving a fifty-year sentence in prison. Liberia's next elected president, Ellen Johnson-Sirleaf, is widely praised for restoring order and credibility in her war-torn country.

Milestones of Newport Gardner's life, according to African Union Society records:

26 February 1778, birth of first child Prince Gardner

28 October 1779, birth of second child Dinah Gardner

December 1780, birth of third child Solomon Gardner

9 May 1781, marriage to Limas (mother of the three children) at 2nd Baptist Church, Newport

26 August 1781, admitted to full communion at 1st Congregationalist Church, Newport

2 April 1783, birth of 4th child Silvia, (who died 16 ½ months later)

4 June 1784, birth of 5th child Elizabeth

19 November 1785, birth of 6th child Jacob

15 November 1787, birth of 7th child, son Ahema

23 November 1789, birth of 8th child Amy

1791, won lottery, bought house on Pope Street, secured freedom, and moved in

6 October 1791, birth of 9th child Martha

20 January 1794, birth of 10th child Charles

2 September 1795, birth of 11th child Abraham

13 April 1798, birth of 12th child Ruben

19 May 1800, birth of 13th child Ann

1821, death of wife Limas

1824, founded Colored Union Church, initially on Pope Street, later on Division Street

December 1825, departed aboard ship *Vine* for Boston and then Liberia.

This entry is mostly a paraphrase of Wikipedia, but with Geographical, historical, and musical additions supplied by the author.

JULIUS 'MUNGO MACARONI' OTHELLO SOUBISE, *ONCE ENSLAVED*, 1754–1798 (ST. KITTS, GREAT BRITAIN & INDIA) [ECD]

Julius Soubise was born in slavery on the Caribbean Island of St. Kitts in 1754. At the age of ten, he was bought by Royal Navy Captain Stair or Alastair Douglas under the name of Othello. The captain gave him to an eccentric London relative, Catherine Hyde Douglas (1701–1777) the Duchess of Queensberry (*sic*). She gave him a new name Julius Soubise, inspired by her friendship with a French duke. She brought him up as if he were her own son, and her Scottish husband Charles Douglas, 3rd Duke of Queensberry (1698–1778) apparently approved.

One of the areas in which Soubise was trained was fencing, where his teacher was Domenico Angelo (a close friend of the Chevalier de Saint-Georges). Soubise soon became the duchess' fencing and riding master. Soubise became friends with many upper-class contemporaries, and joined some of their fashionable clubs. He even claimed to have been the Prince of Anamaboe in Ghana (a place to which he had never travelled, although perhaps his parents had come from there). He was widely known by the nickname of Mungo Macaroni. Mungo was the name of a badly-behaved Black slave in Isaac Bickerstaffe's 1769 comic opera *The Padlock*. Macaroni is a reference to an informal club established by British youths who had visited Italy and adopted unusual clothing and wig-styles seen on some Italian youths. His unseemly and outrageous antics even attracted the notice of Charles Ignatius Sancho, who cautioned him in a surviving letter in 1772 to consider how lucky he was to be an unusually privileged Black person, so he should conduct his life more responsibly. Soubise was also known to be an accomplished violinist and singer, and he took elocution lessons from David Garrick, which suggests that he acted at least occasionally on the stage.

Two days before the duchess died in 1777, Soubise took ship for India. Some say that it was to avoid a trial for rape in London. In Calcutta, he founded a fencing and riding school, which he advertised was open for both male and female students. Twenty-one years later, in 1798, Soubise was severely injured in an accident with a horse and died shortly afterwards. He was the father of at least two children, Mary and William Soubise, with an un-named mother.

Two satirical portraits of Soubise were published, one by Matthew and Mary Darly in 1772 as a dandy with the title 'A Mungo Macaroni,' and another by William Austin in 1773, showing him scoring a point in a fencing bout with the Duchess of Queensberry. He is believed to have written a handful of English Country Dances, including *Mungo* (published by Longman in 1770 and again by Bride in 1776), and *The Macaroni* (published by Griffiths in 1788; tune: Turner MS); *The Macaroni Dance* (Thompson 1774), possibly *The Negro Boy* (Mittell MS, 1799) and *Calcutta* in a 1790s MS); *A Trip to Bengal* (Straights, 1784); *A Trip to Calcutta*, probably by him, has been lost.

This entry is a paraphrase of Wikipedia, with geographical and historical additions by the author.

'CHEVALIER' JOSSE JEAN-OLIVIER DE MEUDE-MONPAS, *FREE BLACK*, BORN CA. 1756 (PARIS)

Not much is known about the life of Meude-Monpas. He was born a free Black in Paris about 1756, and was the youngest son of a Parisian master-goldsmith. He studied violin with Pierre Lahoussaye, and composition with the conservative Francois Giroust. In 1786, he issued a set of six violin concertos (scored for violin, viola, double-bass, 2 oboes, and 2 horns), of which No. 4 in D has been recorded. They are regarded as excellent examples of the music of their day. Meude-Monpas has no documented connection with the violinist and composer the Chevalier de Saint-Georges (who was a real Chevalier). No English Country Dances can be connected with Meude-Monpas, although if he actually wrote any operas, country dances were required by French law to be included in all operas to be performed on the French stage.

Meude-Monpas, who was definitely not a real chevalier, was a staunch supporter of Louis XVI (who was in turn Meude-Monpas' paymaster for his work as a violinist and composer). Like many other members of the court, he left France during the French Revolution. For a time, he served in a military corps under the Prince de Condé, known as the Black Musketeers (which had nothing to do with the color of their skins, but the fact that they rode on black horses). He is known to have been in Berlin in 1788, where his poetry received a bad review. Meude-Monpas wrote a short essay in 1790, in which he asserted that Emmanuel du Plessis le Duc d'Aiguillon had dressed up as a woman in order to participate in the Women's March on Versailles, which was protesting the high price of bread on 5 October 1789. The problem with that assertion is that Aiguillon had died a year previous to the event! Perhaps Aiguillon had dressed up for some earlier event. Meude-Monpas was also a frequent contributor to a counter-revolutionary newspaper, *Le Journal de la cour et de la ville*, nicknamed *Le Petit Gautier*. The date and manner of his death are not recorded.

This entry is a paraphrase of Wikipedia, with historical additions by the author.

THE REVEREND JOSE MAURICIO NUNES-GARCIA, *FREE BLACK*, 1767–1830 (RIO DE JANEIRO, BRAZIL)

The Reverend Jose Mauricio Nunes-Garcia was born in Rio de Janeiro, Brazil to two bi-racial parents. He lost his father at an early age, and his mother, noticing that he had an impressive aptitude for music, arranged her work so as to provide enough money for him to continue his musical education. In the 1790s, he was ordained a Roman Catholic priest, one of the requirements for ordination being that he had to own his own house, and fortunately a family friend donated a house! He is likely to have been one of the first Black people ordained as a priest since the early years of the Apostle Saint Thomas' church in south India around 50AD. Thomas is also known to have ordained women. Nunes-Garcia's early musical training had been by Salvador Jose de Almeida e Faria, who came from the gold-mining area of Minas Gerais, and some of the Minas Gerais style can apparently be detected in Nunes-Garcia's earliest music. He did not own a keyboard instrument, so he learned starting in 1779 by teaching local leading ladies on their own keyboards. After his ordination, he learned to play the organ, assisted by other organists. By 1783, at age 16, he wrote his earliest surviving work, an antiphon, *Tota pulchra es Maria*. In 1784, local musicians founded the Brotherhood of Saint Cecilia (the traditional guild of musicians), and he was allowed to be one of the founders. Throughout the 1780s, Nunes-Garcia wrote many lovely church anthems for choir and organ, and in 1790 he wrote the first work that made him famous, the *Funeral Symphony*. Even though he was appointed the city's [unpaid] public music instructor, the only instrument that he owned was a steel guitar. About this time, he was the first to perform music by Mozart in Brazil.

In 1807–8, Prince-Regent John (the same age as Nunes-Garcia) left Portugal in order to avoid Napoleon's invasion, and he took about 15,000 people with him to establish a new life in Brazil, Portugal's biggest colony. As both priest and musician, Nunes-Garcia was appointed Master of the Chapel Royal at Rio de Janeiro. At the time of his mother's death in 1816, John became King John VI of the Joint Kingdom of Portugal and Brazil, but even though Napoleon had been defeated, John decided to run his empire from Brazil instead of Lisbon. For the prince's impending arrival, Nunes-Garcia was asked to write a grand *Te Deum* for choir and large orchestra. The prince was impressed at the music but not by the players, so he transferred the best of the musicians to a church next to his mansion and called it the Chapel Royal, with Nunes-Garcia in charge of the music. Some members of the court from Europe conspired to have Nunes-Garcia ousted because he was Black, but the king over-ruled them. In 1809, the prince-regent officially made Nunes Garcia a Knight of the Order of Christ. Just before Prince John's arrival, Nunes-Garcia, despite his priestly vow of celibacy, began living openly in a marital relationship with the teenaged Severiana Rosa de Castro, born 1789. The couple had five children, Jose Apolinaro in 1807, Apolinaro Jose in 1808, Josefina in 1810, Panfilia in 1811, and Antonio Jose in 1813. The father officially acknowledged his children in 1828, two years after King John had been assassinated in Portugal. Brazil had been granted independence in 1822. Apparently, although his domestic arrangements were apparently fairly well known in official circles, he never encountered any serious trouble for being married at the same time as being a Roman Catholic priest.

Nunes-Garcia informed the prince-regent in 1810 that he was becoming ill from all the work he was required to do, so the royal composer from Lisbon, Marcos Portugal, was asked to come and take up many of the duties of Nunes-Garcia. Most reports say that the two musicians got along very well. When John's mother died in 1816, Portugal wrote the official *Requiem*, but Nunes-Garcia's mother also died that same day, so he wrote his own *Requiem* for the queen, inspired by Mozart's from 1791, and it is considered to be his masterpiece. Also in 1816, he wrote a motet for the consecration of the new Bishop of the Chapel Royal, which was well received.

Nunes-Garcia wrote perhaps 240 pieces of church music that survive and another 170 that are lost, but he also wrote a number of secular pieces, including one opera, *Le Due Gemelle* (the Two Twins), which was unfortunately destroyed in the 1825 fire at the Royal Theatre of Sao Joao in 1825. If the Portuguese followed the same rules as the French for structuring operas, some through-composed Country Dances would have been included. In 1809, he had written incidental music for two stage plays, one of which was called *The Triumph of America*, for which the sheet music survives. He also wrote two surviving overtures, and 12 divertimenti (lost). He wrote an impressive book, *Treatise of Harmony and Counterpoint* (lost). A European expert wrote in 1820 that Nunes-Garcia's music was "in nothing behind any European presentation."

After the king's return to Portugal, all the royal subsidies that had supported Nunes-Garcia's musical work were abruptly cancelled, so he had to scramble to make up for the lost income; the Lisbon court had also left the Bank of Brazil bankrupt, which caused no end of trouble. Nunes-Garcia wrote his last major work, the *St. Cecilia Mass* in 1826, and that still survives. A short time after Marcos Portugal's death in 1830, Nunes-Garcia felt his own death near, so he had a bed set up for himself on the ground floor, so as to cause as little problem for anyone else. He died a few days later in the presence of one of his sons and a house-slave.

This entry is paraphrased from Wikipedia, with historical, geographical, and musical additions by the author.

JOSEPH ANTONIO EMIDY, ?*FREE BLACK*, 1775–1835 (PORTUGAL, BRAZIL, GREAT BRITAIN) RN

Some disagreement exists about Joseph Emidy's origins. Some say that he was born in Guinea, Africa and enslaved as a child to some Portuguese, who took him to Brazil, and then back to Portugal. He himself stated that he had been born in Portugal of mixed race, but presumably he had spent some time in Brazil, where he may have studied violin intensively, before returning to Portugal. In Portugal, as a teenager he became the leading violinist in the Lisbon Opera Orchestra. In 1794, when Emidy was only nineteen years old, a press gang from Captain Sir Edward Pellew's 44-gun frigate *Indefatigable* sought out Emidy for his musical abilities, ambushed him, and brought him aboard the frigate for almost four years, where he was made to play sea songs, drinking songs, and chanteys, which he grew to hate. In 1798, Pellew (who was soon to become Admiral Lord Exmouth) brought his frigate to Falmouth, Cornwall (his home county), and gave Emidy his freedom, along with back pay and a not insignificant amount of prize money that he had earned by virtue of being in the official crew.

Rather than return to Portugal, where the future did not look rosy with the continued likelihood of invasion by Napoleon, Emidy remained in Falmouth. He made a living as a violinist and a music teacher. He taught keyboard, violin, cello, and flute. The larger city of Truro is only 11 miles (18 km) from Falmouth, so Emidy soon became a leader at the Truro Philharmonic Orchestra. He composed many pieces of music, including at least one symphony and several concerti, but so far, no copies have been found of any of them. No English Country Dances that he may have written have yet been identified.

In 1802, Emidy married Jane Hutchins, daughter of a Falmouth businessman, and they had eight children. They moved to Truro about 1815 at the end of the Napoleonic Wars. After a long career, Emidy died at Truro in 1835, and is buried at St. Keyne's Church (also known as Kenwyn Church in the Cornish dialect). He is memorialized by a stone with a long text in the churchyard, and a colorful boss added to the church ceiling in 2015.

This entry is paraphrased from Wikipedia, with geographical, historical, and musical additions by the author.

GEORGE AUGUSTUS POLGREEN BRIDGETOWER, *FREE BLACK*, 1778–1860 (POLAND & GREAT BRITAIN)

George Bridgetower was born at Biala Podlaska, Poland (about 90 miles/144 km east of Warsaw) in 1778. His father, who is thought to have come from Barbados, although he claimed to have been an African prince, worked for Prince Hieronim Radziwill until 1779, when he started working for Hungarian Prince Esterhazy. George's mother, Maria Anna Ursula Schmidt was from Swabia (now part of Germany) and was described as a Polish lady of quality, although it is thought that she later became a housemaid in the house of the lady who married Prince Radziwill. George was brought to London at an early age, and started performing as a violin soloist at the Drury Lane Theatre by age ten.

Since the young lad had demonstrated such considerable talent, he was taken to give well-received violin concerts in Paris, London, Bath, and Bristol in 1789. In 1791, the Prince-Regent (the future King George IV, who had previously taken an interest in the Chevalier de Saint-Georges) insisted on overseeing his musical education. The prince had him study under Francois-Hippolyte Barthelemon, the leader of London's Royal Opera, with Croat-Italian composer Giovanni Giornovichi, and also with Thomas Attwood (who had received his early education under Mozart, and who was now a professor at the Royal Academy of Music, as well as organist at St. Paul's Cathedral). Bridgetower performed at about 50 concerts at such London theatres as Covent Garden, Drury Lane, and the Haymarket Theatre in the decade from 1789 to 1799. The prince made sure to have the lad perform with his orchestra, both at Brighton and in London. In the spring of 1789, he performed to popular acclaim at the

Abbaye de Pentemont on the rue de Grenelle in Paris, with US Ambassador Thomas Jefferson and his family in attendance, presumably including Sally Hemings (the Black half-sister of Jefferson's late wife).

Bridgetower sought permission from the prince in 1802 to visit his mother and brother Frederick, a cellist in Dresden, and he gave some concerts there as well. In 1803, he visited Vienna, where he performed with Beethoven. Beethoven was so impressed by his talent that he wrote a special piece for him, the Violin Sonata No. 9 in A Minor (Op. 47). When Bridgetower accidentally said something less than polite to a woman who was a close friend of Beethoven, Beethoven washed his hands of him, and re-dedicated the piece to Rudolphe Kreutzer, who disdainfully refused ever to play the so-called Kreutzer Sonata, saying that in any case it was too difficult!

Bridgetower, back in England, continued his musical career with both teaching and performing. In 1807, he was elected to the Royal Society of Musicians. He attended Trinity Hall at Cambridge, where he was awarded his Bachelor of Music degree in 1811 at the age of thirty-three from Cambridge University. He married Mary Leech Leeke in 1816. Their daughter moved to Italy, and he visited her there. He died in 1860, and is buried at Kensal Green Cemetery in Kensington, London. Dominique-Rene de Lerma developed a list in 1990 of all of Bridgetower's known compositions in "Black Composers in Europe: A works list," *Black Music Research Journal* 10, pp.275–334. No English Country Dances by Bridgetower are known.

This entry is paraphrased from Wikipedia, with historical, geographical, and musical additions by the author.

ANONYMOUS NARRAGANSETT NATIVE AMERICAN ?JOSEPH COMMUCK, FL. 1790, (RHODE ISLAND)

The Narragansett Indians of Rhode Island had lived in peace with English settlers from the very first, when Anglican priest the Reverend William Blackstone founded Rhode Island in 1634 (two years before the better-known Roger Williams arrived). 'King Tom' Ninigret (1738–1770) was sent to England to be educated at Christ Church College Choir School at Oxford, but he had to return to Rhode Island after only a few years in order to take up his duties as the new Sachem, because his father had died. He had architect Peter Harrison design him a fine house (which of course was sarcastically called King Tom's Palace) and a church for the tribe at their reservation home at Charlestown in southwest Rhode Island. Tom was otherwise profligate with spending the tribe's money, so he was deposed. Members of the tribe seem to have enjoyed a fairly high level of intellectual life, some of that secured by a percentage of them crewing on Rhode Island ships trading with other parts of the Atlantic world.

One Narragansett, Thomas Commuck (1804–1855) moved away from Rhode Island, but assembled a book of 120 Christian hymns sung by Narragansett and other Native American groups, which he published in 1845 as *Indian Melodies*. The best-known tune today in the book is called *The Lone Pilgrim*. His father Joseph Commuck (fl, 1790) was a member of the tribe's governing council, and it is believed that his own interest in music is what got his son into music. Therefore, the English Country Dance *Cornplanter*, which was published in John Griffiths' second book of English Country Dances in 1794 (the tune appearing in the Carroll Manuscript of the same era) is likely to have been Joseph's creation. Cornplanter (ca. 1750–1836), not to be confused with Shawnee Chief Cornstalk from Lord Dunmore's War in 1774, was also known as John O'Bail/Abeel III because of his Dutch father. He was a Seneca chief in the Iroquois Confederacy. Although he refused (at least publicly) to learn any English, and always conversed through an interpreter, he fought on the British side in the American Revolution, but he later negotiated a treaty with George Washington for his tribe to live in perpetuity in certain tribal lands (the treaty has of course been broken many times since then). This dance tune, therefore, may be the first published tune written by a Native American. The fact that Cornplanter always stood tall against United States aggression no doubt made him a hero to many Native Americans.

This entry is paraphrased from Wikipedia, with geographical, historical, and musical additions by the author.

3

Architects, Sculptors, Master-Builders, Painters, Potters, and Silversmiths

ANTONIO FRANCISCO "ALEIJADINHO" LISBOA, *FREE BLACK*, ARCHITECT & SCULPTOR, 1738–1814 (OURO PRETO, BRAZIL)

Although the white residents of Brazil often took pride in "blood-purity," yet at the same time space was set aside for Black and mulatto residents who showed exceptional talent, such as the composer Jose Mauricio Nunes-Garcia (see above). At least four eighteenth-century Black and mulatto architects worked in eighteenth-century Brazil. Manuel Ferreira Jacome (ca. 1677–1736) worked in Recife for the last three decades of his life. Valentim de Fonseca e Silva (ca. 1745–1813) worked in Rio de Janeiro for the last fifty years of his life. There, the viceroy, ordered his favorite architect, whom he called Mestre Valentim, to rebuild the Home for Wayward Women after it had burned down in 1780. While it was being rebuilt, a fine painting was executed of various Black artists and architects, including Valentim and Leandro Joaquim, who was the viceroy's favorite painter. Jose Joachim da Rocha (ca. 1735–1807) practiced architecture in Salvador (about 600 miles/1000 km up the coast from Rio de Janeiro) for the last fifty years of his life. Probably each of these men deserves a monograph of his work, but they all pale beside the career of Antonio Lisboa

Very little is known about the actual life of Antonio Francisco Lisboa, nicknamed Aleijadinho because he was for many years seriously crippled. He apparently spent most of his life in the state of Minas Gerais in Brazil, an area made unusually wealthy because of its mineral mines, including gold-mines. He was born enslaved in 1738 (some people say 1730) in Vila Rica ("Rich-town"), which has since been renamed Ouro Preto ("Black-Gold"). His father, a builder, manumitted him at his baptism a few days after birth. He probably learned the rudiments of architecture from his father, and sculpture from his uncle Antonio Pombal, and otherwise was liberally educated at the local Franciscan boarding school. As an illegitimate son, he was not even mentioned in his father's will of 1767.

In 1768, he was commissioned to design the façade of the Church of Our Lady of Carmel at Sabara, possibly his first building. In 1772, he was made a member of the Brotherhood of Sao Jose de Ouro Preto, the official local guild of builders and architects. The guild members were then required to travel to Rio de Janeiro to work on a government project, and there Lisboa acknowledged his paternity of a son, Manuel Francisco Lisboa, but he never married the mother, who took the child and left Lisboa. From 1777 onwards, Lisboa showed signs of a serious illness, which deformed his body and caused him great suffering, although modern physicians have been unable to agree on a diagnosis for it. He lost most of his fingers and both feet, forcing him to move about on his knees, and his face started looking grotesque, although by 1796 he was still able to write clearly.

> A 1790 government report about Lisboa (now partly lost) described him as "the new Praxiteles," compared to the ancient Greek architect and sculptor who lived 395–330 BCE. *Superior to everything else and unique in stone sculptures in full relief or half relief and in regular outlines and ornaments of the best French taste is the aforementioned Antonio Francisco. In any piece of his that serves to enhance the most elegant buildings, one admires the invention, the natural or composed balance, the accuracy of the dimensions, the energy of the uses and customs and the choice and arrangement of the accessories with the believable groups that inspire the beauty of nature. So much preciousness is found deposited in a sick body that needs to be carried everywhere and [needs to have the working tools] tied to it in order to be able to work.*

Lisboa's architecture exemplified the best elements of baroque and rococo styles, but depending not at all on precedents in Portugal. Nearly all his churches were framed by a pair of towers (which in France and French Canada is called the Sulpician form). It is often said that no other architect in any era did as much to put Brazil on the map with excellent architecture. One problem with his work, though, is that many other hands altered many of his works, so it is not always possible to decide which parts are by Lisboa and which is by others. Among his best works are the church of Sao Francisco de Assis at Ouro Preto, begun 1766, and the somewhat similar church of Sao Francisco de Assis at Sao Joao del-Rei, begun in 1772. Quite different is the church of Bom Jesus de Matosinhos at Congonas. The Church of Santo Antonio at Tiradentes (literally "dentist") is another of Lisboa's designs, among many others.

Lisboa is equally heralded for his sculptures, some in wood, and some in stone, of Christ and numerous saints, as well as Roman soldiers, some of them inside the churches, and some of them displayed in the Museum of the Inconfidencia at Ouro Preto, which was built to mark the unsuccessful revolt against the colonizers in 1789; the Portuguese government insisted on running the gold mines at full speed at any cost in order to satisfy their greed, and this resulted in political and social agitation and conspiracy. Other museums also house his sculptures. Serious tourists in Brazil ought to plan to spend many days in Minas Gerais seeing the incomparable works of Lisboa.

This entry is paraphrased from Wikipedia, with architectural, geographical, and historical comments by the author. The author was further informed by his architectural history research resulting in forthcoming books about two leading architects of the period, who have until now escaped notice: Elizabeth Wilbraham (1632–1705) and Peter Harrison (1716–1775)

SCIPIO MOORHEAD, *ENSLAVED*, PAINTER, FL. 1760S-1770S (BOSTON, MASSACHUSETTS)

Scipio Moorhead was an enslaved African-American who lived in Boston. He was the slave of Irish-born Congregationalist minister the Reverend John Moorhead (1703–1773), pastor of what is now known as the Arlington Street Church, Boston. The minister's wife Sarah, who was an art teacher, encouraged Scipio to develop his obvious talents at drawing and painting. The famous Black poet, Phillis Wheatley, dedicated a poem to him in her 1773 book of poems, "To S. M. a young African Painter, on seeing his Works." An advertisement appeared in a Boston newspaper that same year, which included "negro artist… A negro of *extraordinary genius*," which is likely to have been referring to Scipio.

The frontispiece of Wheatley's 1773 book of poetry shows an engraving of Wheatley seated on a stylish chair at a round table, writing with a quill pen, and it is very likely that the portrait was the work of Moorhead, although there is no proof of that. Some people have suggested that the portrait was the work of John Singleton Copley, but the proportions of the chair are not in line with Copley's other works.

Scipio was sold at auction in January 1775 as part of an estate sale, but what happened to him in the years following the sale is not recorded. Massachusetts eliminated slavery in the 1780s, but it is not known whether Scipio was still living in Massachusetts at that time, or whether he was still alive at all. So far, other than the engraved portrait of Phillis Wheatley, not a single painting has been plausibly identified as having been painted by Scipio, whether in a private collection or a public museum, but it is possible that one or more may yet be identified in the run-up to the USA's 250th birthday.

This entry is paraphrased from Wikipedia, with artistic and historical comments by the author.

CHARLES PAQUET/PACQUET, *ONCE ENSLAVED*, MASTER-BUILDER, CA. 1758-CA. 1820 (LOUISIANA)

Charles Paquet was born in French Louisiana about 1758. He was the son of Jean-Baptiste Paquet, a free mulatto, who cultivated indigo, and his mother was apparently a slave belonging to Leonard Mazange. He was also possibly connected to Claude Pacquet, Director General of the Compagnie du Senegal dans les Iles, in Martinique, and other family members in Quebec. Shortly after the child's birth, France sold what they called Western Louisiana to the King of Spain in 1762, because the French national treasury was almost empty, and Eastern Louisiana (essentially today's Alabama and Mississippi) had been captured by the British. So, the lad grew up in a Spanish political system, but it made little difference because most of the people owning and running things in this area were still French-speaking.

Jean-Baptiste Paquet married a free woman of color, Marie, before the early 1780s. She had at least four children at that time, all grown up. Charles was born earlier of a woman who was apparently a slave. The earliest reference to Charles was a 1787 document that describes him as both a carpenter and a brick mason. This is the contract in which Charles agreed to build a house for Robin de Logny, the house that became known as Destrehan Plantation House. Charles is described as a free mulatto, but he was actually still owned by his mother's owner, Leonard Mazange. Charles had already been told that his father was buying his freedom, so the contract anticipated that he would soon be free. Charles made his mark on a 1790 document, stating that the house was satisfactorily completed and that he had been paid in full what he had been promised (a cow and her calf, a quantity of grain, a similar quantity of rice, and a slave trained in carpentry). It is evident that at this time Charles was not able to read or write, or even sign his name.

Jean-Baptiste's will specified that Charles was to marry Marie's daughter Madelaine, and that he should also care for his grandmother, Angelique Perret, for the rest of her life. Either Charles or Madelaine must have objected to the proposed marriage, because it did not take place, and Madelaine married somebody else in 1801. Charles owned some land covered in mature bald cypress trees, and he operated a portable water-powered sawmill. The normally-accepted way of setting up the sawmill was to dig a hole in the levee into which the water-wheel was inserted, and then the hole was filled in when all the trees had been sawn into posts. In 1808, Charles hired two slaves to help him with the sawmill to cut 60 cypress posts, but he may not have known that the men were runaways. He was sentenced to pay a $124 fine as a result.

In the 1804 census, Charles was listed as married to a slave, and they had two female slaves living with them, who could have been Charles' daughters. In the 1810 census, Charles and family were listed as still living in the same place, but no one with Paquet as a last name appears in the 1830 census.

Destrehan Plantation House on River Road about 20 miles from New Orleans belonged to Marie-Celeste Robin de Logny and her husband Jean-Noel Destrehan. It is two stories tall under a high hip roof (that contains an additional story with a few dormer windows). The ground floor was built of brick with brick columns to support a porch all around. The main living area was the upper floor with its wrap-around porch. The porch is seven bays wide, but the upper floor of the house is nine windows wide. The roof was supported by turned cypress columns above each of the brick columns, but in the nineteenth century the brick lower columns plus cypress upper columns were replaced by giant wooden columns, which alters the whole appearance of the house. The Historic American Buildings Survey (HABS) makes available its elevation of Destrehan from before the change. The house, which is open to the public, was originally very similar to many other Louisiana plantation houses, such as Homeplace, Ormond, Parlange, Pitot, Saint-Joseph, Marigny (destroyed), and Whitney, before the giant columns were installed. Some of these houses were built after and some before Destrehan, so it is indeed possible that Paquet had designed and built some of them as well. Charles was obviously the building's master-builder, carpenter, and mason, which is by itself impressive, but owing to the similarity with all those other plantation houses it may be a slight stretch also to call this illiterate man an architect. Destrehan Plantation has sponsored the publication of a little booklet that spells out all that can so far be found about the life of Charles Paquet.

This entry is paraphrased from Wikipedia and from the information supplied by the staff at Destrehan Plantation, with architectural and historical comments by the author.

JOSHUA JOHNSON/JOHNSTON, *ONCE ENSLAVED*, PAINTER, CA. 1760-CA. 1824 (BALTIMORE, MARYLAND)

Joshua Johnson was born the son of a white man, George Johnson, and an un-named slave woman owned by William Wheeler, a farmer near Baltimore. In 1764, George purchased the child Joshua for half the price of an adult field slave. George acknowledged Joshua as his son, and agreed to free him if he entered and completed a seven-year apprenticeship with blacksmith William Forepaugh, or failing that, when he turned 21. Joshua received his freedom in 1782. By 1796, he was advertising himself as a portrait painter, and possibly supplemented his income by painting chairs, after the fashion of the time. In 1785, he married in the Roman Catholic Church his first wife, Sarah, with whom he had two sons and two daughters. The two daughters died young, as did his wife, and in 1803 he married his second wife, Clara.

Some experts claim they can see connections between Johnson's painting style and Charles Peale Polk, and Ralph Earl I & II. Johnson himself claimed in an advertisement that he was "self-taught," and derived his knowledge of art from "nature and industry."

Johnson is known to have moved between many Maryland locations, presumably in order to be near his sitters. Unlike many portrait painters of his day, Johnson seems to have been fond of including groups of people in a single portrait, including at least one with a dog as well. Many of his paintings are held in private collections, but some can be found in the National Gallery of Art in Washington DC and the Corcoran Gallery at The George Washington University, also in Washington DC. Other Johnson paintings can be seen at the Maryland Center for History and Culture, and the Baltimore Museum of Art.

This entry is paraphrased from Wikipedia.

THOMAS W. COMMERAW, *ONCE ENSLAVED*, POTTER, 1772–1823 (NEW YORK CITY)

Thomas Commeraw was born in New York City in slavery, but he was given his freedom at age seven in 1779. He started working in ceramics at least as early as 1797. His first wife Mary died in a dysentery epidemic in 1813, and he quickly married a second wife, Ann. In 1819, Cornelius Bogert was granted a judgement against them in the equivalent to the later state supreme court, and the court then seized their two lots on Corlears Hook near the East River between Cherry and Lombardy Streets, where his pottery kiln and shop were located.

At that point, the Commeraw family left New York to travel with the American Colonization Society to Sierra Leone. He wrote a letter back in 1820, describing the land as rich and fertile, but the Society forced Commeraw and his associates to move to another piece of land, in the belief that the British government might want to confiscate the valuable land. After all, the British had established the colony exclusively for the benefit of former slaves from the former British colonies in North America, and not for later arrivals in America, so some administrators in Sierra Leone took a dim view of newcomers from America. In the meantime, his wife had died, leaving three small children to be supported and raised. Commeraw and the children returned to New York after only two years away.

He lived only a short time after his return, and what happened to the children is not recorded.

Two trained potters had come to New York before 1797 from Westerwald, Germany (a hilly area near Bonn and Koblenz, not far from the Rhine River, with a strong tradition of stoneware pottery), Johan Willem Crolius and Johannes Remmey, who were married to two sisters. They dominated New York stoneware production for many years, starting with their first kiln on Pottbaker's Hill. They created works with a salt-glaze, cobalt-blue paint, and incised floral details, very similar to what Commeraw would later make. Crolius, whose kiln was located just twenty minutes' walk away from the slave market, operated with the help of numerous enslaved people, some of whom could be hired by the day. Numbers of these slaves became quite proficient at making salt-glaze stoneware, and it is possible that one or more of them were the method of transmission to Commeraw of the secrets of making stoneware.

Commeraw's pottery was mostly limited to handsome storage jars, decorated with incised and painted blue tassels, scallops, leaves, and petals. His pieces were often signed in incised capital letters. Commeraw's works can be seen at the Metropolitan Museum of Art, the Brooklyn Museum, the Smithsonian National Museum of American History in Washington DC, the Winterthur Museum of Art in Delaware, the New-York Historical Society, the Grolier Club in New York City, and the New York City Archaeological Repository. Commeraw's pottery is not necessarily outstanding, but it should be viewed in the light of the fact that for the most part the British would not permit any kind of pottery to be made in America before about 1770, when small porcelain manufactures were establish in Charleston SC and Philadelphia, and the Moravians were allowed to make decorated redware pottery in Bethlehem PA and what later became known as Winston-Salem in North Carolina.

This entry is paraphrased from Wikipedia, with historical and geographical details added by the author.

PETER BENTZON, *FREE BLACK*, CA. 1783- CA. 1850, SILVERSMITH (SAINT CROIX, PHILADELPHIA)

Peter Bentzon (may also be occasionally listed as Benson) was born about 1783 on the Danish Virgin Island of Saint Thomas. He was sent to Philadelphia for his education in 1791. In 1799, he was apprenticed to a

Philadelphia silversmith, and he completed his apprenticeship in 1806, at which time he returned to Saint Croix in the Virgin Islands, where he started his own silversmith's shop. The Napoleonic Wars ended in 1815, and so Denmark reclaimed ownership of the island from the British the following year. However, since the Danes had stricter regulations for free people of color than the British or Americans had, Bentzon moved his family and shop to Philadelphia. In 1829, he moved back to Saint Croix for two decades, but returned to Philadelphia in 1848, where he died about two years later. Bentzon marked all his work with his initials or his name. His work can be found in a variety of museums around the United States, including the Smithsonian's National Museum of African American History and Culture, the African American Museum in Philadelphia, the Philadelphia Museum of Art, the Colonial Williamsburg Foundation, the Winterthur Museum in Delaware, and others. Fewer than forty pieces have been identified to date, most of which were silver spoons.

Evidently, many silversmiths taught enslaved Black apprentices to assist in their shops, but very few of them made useful records of that. Abraham Petrie was listed as a silversmithing slave to Alexander Petrie in Charleston SC when Alexander died in 1768. Newport Anthony was advertised to have been the trained goldsmith/silversmith slave of Isaac Anthony in Newport RI when he ran away in 1749; any record of whether he was ever found and retrieved has not been found. At least one Native American silversmith worked in America in the colonial period, and went by the name of Slender Maker of Silver.

Similarly, many furniture-making shops, such as that of Thomas Elfe in Charleston SC and that of Gilbert Ash in New York City, or Samuel Loomis, Benjamin Burnham or Eliphalet Chapin of Connecticut, must have had enslaved trained apprentices, but at the moment no such slaves have been identified. The famous Goddards and Townsends in Newport RI were all Quakers, and Quakers were generally opposed to slavery, although of course not opposed to training apprentices.

This entry is paraphrased from Wikipedia, with historical details added by the author.

4

Writers, Poets, Business People, Actors, and Clergy

WRITER AYUBA SULEIMAN 'JOB BEN SOLOMON' DIALLO, *ONCE ENSLAVED*, 1701–1773 (SENEGAL. MARYLAND, UK, FRANCE)

Ayuba Suleiman Diallo was born in the Bondu region of Senegal in 1701. He studied the Qur'an extensively. He married two women who had previously been his slaves (some Muslims were permitted to be married to as many as four women at a time), and fathered several children. He and his family owned several slaves who had been prisoners of war, and they bought and sold slaves much of the time. While on a trip to the coast to sell slaves, Diallo and his translator were seized and sold to factors of the Royal African Company. They were placed aboard a slave ship commanded by a man named Pike, who sailed to Annapolis, Maryland.

Diallo was bought by Mr. Tolsey of Kent Island, Maryland, and made to work in the tobacco fields. He was called Job Ben Solomon in America, which is a rough translation of his actual name. Then he was promoted to watching over cattle. He used to go into the woods to pray, but one time he was teased by a child for doing that, so he ran away. He communicated his desire to pray, and his master made allowances for that. Diallo impressed a lawyer and an Anglican priest, the Reverend Thomas Bluett.

Tolsey permitted Diallo to write a letter in Arabic to his father, and the letter was viewed in London by James Oglethorpe, a director of the Royal African Company. Oglethorpe, who later was one of the founders of Georgia (where he had temporarily ruled permanent slavery to be illegal), forwarded the letter and purchased Diallo for forty-five Pounds. Once in England, Diallo suspected that people were getting ready to sell him once again, so he got in touch with Bluett, who took him in, introduced him to many important people, including members of the royal family, and the Montagus, and secured him a safe passage home.

When he arrived home in 1734, he found that one of his wives had given up on seeing him again and had married another man, and that his father had died. Civil war had ravaged his part of the country. Nevertheless, Diallo was able to rebuild his business, including buying and selling slaves. Meanwhile, Bluett had published Diallo's Memoirs in both English and French.

In June 1736, Diallo was captured by the French and held for a year. He wrote letters to Oglethorpe in London to ask permission to be taken to London, but was turned down. Letters from his family in Senegal eventually secured his release. He continued in his efforts to have the people in London release his friend the translator, and with the help of Bluett, the translator was sent home to Senegal. The rest of Diallo's life was much less exciting, and he died in 1773. A portrait was painted of Diallo by William Hoare of Bath in 1733; it now belongs to the Qatar Museums Authority, which have loaned it temporarily to the Jamestown-Yorktown Foundation in Virginia.

This entry was paraphrased from Wikipedia, with historical details added by the author.

WRITER UKAWSAW 'JAMES ALBERT' GRONNIOSAW, *ONCE ENSLAVED*, CA. 1705–1775 (NIGERIA, BARBADOS, NEW YORK, NEW JERSEY, MARTINIQUE, CUBA, UK)

Gronniosaw was born in Bornu in what is now northern Nigeria in about 1705. He was the grandson of the king of Zaara. When he was about fifteen, a marauding tribe took him as a prisoner of war and sold him to a slave dealer in Ghana. The dealer sold him to a Dutch captain for two yards of check cloth. An American in Barbados bought him and resold him for fifty Pounds to a Dutch Reformed Church minister, the Reverend Theodorus Jacobus Frelinghuysen, who was based in New Jersey.

Gronniosaw was taught to read and write, and brought up as a Christian. His reaction was to say that he wanted to return to Africa, but that was not possible. He tried to commit suicide because he thought he was a failure as a Christian. The minister died suddenly and freed Gronniosaw in his will. Gronniosaw stayed on to work for the widow, who died soon after, and for the children, but they all died within four years. He had assumed the English name of James Albert.

Gronniosaw planned to travel to England and meet other pious people like Frelinghuysen, but he sailed instead to the Caribbean, where he signed on as cook for a privateer ship, and then he enlisted in the 28th Regiment of Foot in order to earn money for the trip to England. He served in Martinique and Cuba before he was discharged and provided with enough money to pay for his trip to England.

At first, he settled in Portsmouth, but he had to move to London when he was swindled out of his money. There he married Betty, a young English widow who was a weaver and had a child. She bore him at least two more children. She lost her job in an economic downturn, so they moved to Colchester. They were saved from starvation by Quaker lawyer Osgood Hanbury (grandfather of abolitionist Thomas Buxton), who hired Gronniosaw for construction work. Unfortunately, construction work is seasonal, so yet another Quaker stepped up to help, Henry Gurney (grandfather of Thomas Buxton's wife Hannah Gurney), who kindly paid their back rent, as they moved to Norwich. A daughter died, but the local clergy refused to bury her because she was not baptized. She was buried eventually.

The family moved to Kidderminster, Worcestershire, in the English Midlands, where Betty found a good job as a weaver. On Christmas Day 1771, Gronniosaw had their remaining children baptized by an associate of the Countess of Huntingdon: six-year-old Mary Albert, four-year-old Edward Albert, and newborn Samuel Albert, and the next newborn child was also baptized, James Albert II. The Countess of Huntingdon also sent him a generous financial contribution.

While he was in Kidderminster, Gronniosaw spent time with a Mrs. Marlow so he could dictate to her his life story. This was published in Bath in 1772 as *A Narrative of the Most remarkable Particulars in the Life of James Albert Ukawsaw Gronniosaw, an African Prince, As related by himself*. This is the first published slave narrative written in English by an African man in England. Gronniosaw died on 28 September, 1775 at Chester, not far from Liverpool.

This entry is paraphrased from Wikipedia.

WRITER JUPITER HAMMON, *ENSLAVED*, 1711–1806 (LONG ISLAND, NEW YORK), POET, PUBLISHED 1761

Jupiter Hammon (no relation to Briton Hammon) was born into slavery at the Lloyd Manor on the north shore of Long Island, New York, about one third of the way along the coast from the western end of the island. He served the Lloyd family his entire life. Perhaps in return for his cooperative attitude, the family saw that he was educated through a program administered by the Anglican Church. He learned to write both prose and poetry, and eventually published in both forms. His first piece published was written on Christmas Day 1760 and published a few months later, a poem entitled "An Evening Thought: Salvation by Christ, with Penitential Cries." This made him America's first Black published poet. In addition to these literary works, he was also known as a preacher.

Jupiter Hammon's Works, two of them found only recently, in 2011 and 2015:

"An Evening Thought" (1761)

Untitled, unpublished (1770)

"An Address to Miss Phillis Wheatley (1778)

"An Essay on the Ten Virgins," a lost work (1779)

"A Winter Piece" (1782)

"A Poem for Children with Thoughts on Death" (1782)

"An Evening's Improvement" (1783)

"The Kind Master and Dutiful Servant" (1783)

"An Essay on Slavery," unpublished (1786)

"An Address to the Negroes in the State of New York (1787)

Hammon was a great admirer of the Black American poet Phillis Wheatley, although he never met her. In his last work, he wrote: "If we should ever get to Heaven, we shall find nobody to reproach us for being

Black, or for being slaves." He also wrote that while he personally (at age 76) had no wish to be free, he did wish that others, especially "the young negroes, were free." He seemed to think that the best way to end slavery was to do it gradually. His essay was widely republished.

This entry is a paraphrase from Wikipedia.

BUSINESSWOMAN ELISABETH SAMSON CREUTZ ZOBRE, *FREE BLACK*, 1715–1771 (SURINAME, NETHERLANDS

Elisabeth Samson was born in 1715 in Paramaribo, the historic capital city of Suriname, otherwise known as Dutch Guiana. Most modern Americans have never heard of Paramaribo, which stands only 400 miles north of the equator and is essentially a Colonial Williamsburg waiting to be discovered. It also stands not far from the largest snakes in the world, the anaconda, a boa constrictor that can be found up to 35 feet long (10.7 metres), although residents of the city can live their entire lives without ever seeing such a snake. In the colonial period, Paramaribo was one of New England's most popular trading partners. The St. Louis Art Museum in Missouri has a painting by John Greenwood, *Sea Captains Carousing in Suriname*, showing several important Rhode Islanders drunk in the 1760s. The local cemeteries in Paramaribo contain headstones of many New England sailors of the eighteenth century. In the seventeenth century, the Dutch and the English came to a treaty whereby the English became the new owners of the formerly Dutch colonies of New York and New Jersey, and the Dutch were confirmed in their ownership of far more valuable Dutch Guiana. During the American Revolution, the Netherlands by accident found itself on the side opposite the British, so the British felt free to conquer Dutch Guiana. At the new peace treaty, the Dutch were allowed to keep the part now known as Suriname, and the British kept the more westerly part, now known as Guyana. The principal city in the British section was once called Stabroek/Stabroeck, and it has since been renamed Georgetown and serves as the capital city of Guyana.

Elisabeth was the youngest of nine children of a Black female slave named Nanoe who was brought from the Caribbean Island of St. Kitts about 1700, and had been given her freedom just before Elisabeth was born. Elisabeth was brought up free by her much older step-sister Maria and Maria's Swiss planter husband. When the husband died, Maria married another man. Elisabeth learned to read and write (both Dutch and English) and do arithmetic in those two households, and was baptized at age ten. At age 21, Elisabeth was caught up in a scandal of slandering someone important, and was sentenced in court to be banished. She travelled to the Netherlands to appeal the verdict, which was overturned in 1739, so she happily returned to Paramaribo at age twenty-four.

Elisabeth gradually acquired Black slaves, and she purchased two coffee plantations, the first of many. She began a relationship with Carl Otto Creutz from Germany. Creutz was awarded in 1749 by the governor a 1000-acre plantation, known as Clevia, for his services in negotiating a peace treaty. Elisabeth contributed her 200 slaves to operate the plantation, as well as a cattle ranch called La Solitude, and two city houses with 44 house slaves. Although the two never actually got married, they were given a document in 1751 that testified that they had joint ownership of the property as if they were married.

Creutz died of malaria in 1762, so Elisabeth temporarily inherited all their joint property. The property was to go to Creutz's brothers when she died, but she came up with 155,000 Florins to buy out the brothers, or about $3 million today. In 1764, she wanted to marry Christopher Braband, the white organist of the Dutch Reformed Church who rented an apartment in one of Elisabeth's houses. She wrote to the appropriate authority seeking permission (Blacks were not generally permitted in Suriname to marry whites). The local authority wrote to authorities in the Netherlands, who ruled that Dutch law did not exclude such marriages, but during the three years that it took to obtain that decision Mr. Braband died. Just under two years later, Elisabeth married a very much younger white man, Hermanus Daniel Zobre, who had just arrived from the Hague, the first legal marriage in Suriname of a Black and a white person together. Elisabeth died only four years later in 1771. Zobre was not a good financial manager, so he ran the estate into the ground, and Elisabeth's impressive business success was obscured for many years until the published research of Cynthia McLeod, begun in 1988.

Elisabeth's handsome wooden clapboarded house, close to the governor's mansion (now the President's mansion), is on the side of the hill leading down to the river at 22 Wagenwegstraat in Paramaribo. It is five bays long and five bays wide, with five stories in height under a high gable roof and over a full basement. Ms. McLeod has established a foundation to preserve and restore the house. Readers are urged to visit Paramaribo and the house: you will not regret it.

This entry is paraphrased from Wikipedia, with geographical, historical, and architectural comments by the author.

WRITER BRITON HAMMON, *ENSLAVED*, CA. 1727- CA. 1775 (MARSHFIELD, MASSACHUSETTS), RN, 1760

No relation to Jupiter Hammon (see above), Briton Hammon was born into slavery in Massachusetts for the family of then militia Captain John Winslow, who incidentally was involved in a failed 1740 attack on Cuba, where Hammon found himself imprisoned a few years later. At about the age of twenty, Hammon was given leave by his master to work in the crew of a sailing ship bound for Jamaica. However, the ship was wrecked on the coast of Florida. Some of the crew made it to shore, but they were attacked and killed by local Indians, who also killed the crew left aboard and burned the remains of the ship. Briton was the only one not killed. Instead, the Indians fed him well. Then a Spanish ship arrived from St. Augustine, and the captain bought Hammon for $10, saying that if further men were ship-wrecked he would gladly pay the same amount for each of them. Hammon was delivered to Havana, Cuba.

There Hammon lived in the governor's castle, where he was one of many slaves serving Governor Francisco Cajigal de la Vega. After about a year, he was confronted in the street by a Spanish Navy press-gang, which put him in jail over-night. When, as an Englishman, he refused to serve on a Spanish warship, he was thrown into a dungeon for more than four years. He asked numerous prison visitors to tell the governor about him, all to no avail. A Mrs. Betty Howard passed word about him to a visiting Boston ship's captain during a time of peace between Britain and Spain. The captain then visited Hammon in the prison, and brought word of him to the governor. The governor had Hammon returned to the castle to continue serving him for about a year.

During this second time of serving the governor, Hammon attempted three times to escape by sneaking aboard an outward-bound ship, but each time he was returned to the castle. The governor offered the Roman Catholic Bishop Pedro Agustin Morell de Santa Cruz several slaves, including Hammon, to carry the bishop about on a litter on his visitations to churches all over Cuba. Once again, Hammon was thrown into prison for refusing to serve on a Spanish Navy ship, and he had to remain there for more than four years. In 1758, still in time of peace (the French had forced a new war on the British in the mid-1750s, but the Spanish did not jump into that war until 1762. In 1762, the British captured both Cuba and the Philippines in retribution for Spain's unprovoked attack on Gibraltar, and they traded their captured territory for East and West Florida), a British Navy lieutenant heard about his plight and managed to spirit Hammon and several others aboard a relatively small British warship bound for Britain.

In the course of the voyage home, the British ship was attacked by a larger French warship. In the sharp engagement, the British lost seventy men killed, but the French lost even more. Hammon was wounded both in the arm and in the head, so he spent time at Greenwich Hospital, near London, recovering, and was officially discharged from the Royal Navy. After working again for a few weeks at a job he did not name, he caught a serious fever and had to remain in bed in London for six weeks, by which time he had exhausted all his money. By a most amazing coincidence, Hammon was reunited after thirteen years with his Massachusetts master, now Major General John Winslow of Massachusetts forces, who happened to be visiting London. According to the story, they were both delighted to have found each other, and they sailed back to Massachusetts together.

Hammon then wrote a book about his amazing adventures, which was published in 1760, the first book ever published in America written by a Black man: *A Narrative of the uncommon Suffering and surprising Deliverance of Briton Hammon, servant to General Winslow*. It apparently sold quite well, but Hammon is not known to have written any further books. Hammon and Winslow died within a few months of each other.

This entry was paraphrased from Wikipedia, with historical and geographical details added by the author.

WRITER BROTEER 'VENTURE SMITH' FURRO, *ONCE ENSLAVED*, CA. 1729–1805 (SENEGAL, BARBADOS, RHODE ISLAND, NEW YORK, CONNECTICUT)

Broteer Furro was born about 1729 in the Savannah region of Senegal in West Africa, but when he was only six and a half years old, 6000 marauding tribesmen attacked his village and took him as a prisoner of war to Anomabo in Ghana, where the boy was sold into slavery. In spring of 1739, a ship sailed to Barbados with 260 captives. During the voyage, sixty captives were killed by an outbreak of smallpox. Robinson Mumford of Rhode Island purchased the lad for four gallons of Rhode Island rum plus a piece of calico. Mumford took him with him to his country residence on Fisher's Island near the eastern end of Long Island, New York. He adopted the name Venture because Mumford had described his purchase as having been a business venture.

Mumford found the lad to be entirely trustworthy, but he forced him to do heavy manual labor, and to suffer severe punishments. Mumford's son was particularly brutal to him. When Furro was twenty-two, he married an enslaved woman named Meg or Margaret. In 1754, he and Meg initially participated in an attempt to run away with three others owned by Mumford, but it soon became obvious that that what the others wanted was the money that the Furros had saved up, so Furro organized a group of people to hunt down and recapture the fugitives, which was much appreciated by Mumford.

Later in 1754, the Furros had a daughter named Hannah. Only one month later, Furro was sold to Thomas Stanton of Stonington, Connecticut. However, a year later, Stanton also purchased Meg and Hannah. Smith started saving money from outside jobs in order to buy freedom for his family, but one day he found Stanton's wife and his own wife in a brawl. When he tried to break it up, Stanton's wife tried to beat him with a switch, so Furro threw it in the fire. At that point, Stanton hit Furro with a boat oar. Furro went to the local magistrate to complain, but once they were out of sight of the courthouse Stanton and his brother started beating Furro, until he got the upper hand. In the meantime, Meg produced two additional children, Solomon in 1756 and Cuff in 1761. Furro was sold twice more, the second time to Colonel Oliver Smith in 1760. Smith agreed to allow Furro to purchase his freedom, which he was able to do in early 1765. Because this last owner undertook to sell him, Furro adopted the last name of Smith: Venture Smith.

He then purchased his sons. Solomon was then hired out to Charles Church, but Church ordered the lad to take a whaling boat on a cruise. He never returned from the cruise, having died of scurvy. Furro was then able to purchase his wife, who was pregnant. If she had given birth before the sale, he would have had to pay for the additional child as well. He named the new son Solomon in memory of the son lost at sea. Furro had many financial reverses over the coming years, some out of prejudice against Black people.

In 1775, he bought a farm at Haddam Neck on the Salmon River, Connecticut, not far up the Connecticut River from Old Saybrook, and gradually increased its acreage. In addition to the farm, he made money from fishing, whaling, and trading in the Long Island Sound area. In 1798, Furro, who was going blind and losing a lot of strength, dictated his life experiences with a view to having the work published by *The Bee* in New London. He titled it: *A Narrative of the Life and Adventures of Venture, a Native of Africa: But Resident above Sixty Years in the United States of America.*

This entry was paraphrased from Wikipedia, with geographical and historical details added by the author.

WRITER THE REVEREND SAMSON OCCOM, *NATIVE AMERICAN*, 1723–1792 (CONNECTICUT, UK, & NEW YORK), (PRESBYTERIAN)

Samson Occom was born to Joshua Tomacham and his wife Sarah in the Mohegan nation near New London, Connecticut. About age 16, he was impressed by the teachings of Christian evangelical preachers who were part of the Great Awakening. He began in 1743 to study theology for four years at the Latin School run by Congregationalist minister, the Rev. Eleazar Wheelock, where he also learned to read and speak Latin, Greek, and Hebrew. From 1747 to 1749, he worked under and studied with the Rev. Solomon Williams in New London.

Occom received a call to be a teacher, preacher, and judge among the Montaukett Native Americans in the eastern part of Long Island, New York. There he married a Montaukett woman, Mary Fowler. He also helped numerous Pequot Native Americans to adopt European-style houses, lifestyle, dress, and culture. He was officially ordained in 1759 by the Presbytery of Suffolk County, New York. They promised that he would be paid the same salary as white clergy, but it never happened. He occasionally received small payments from the church thousands of miles away in Scotland, but he lived for most of his life in substantial poverty.

In 1761 and 1763, he preached to members of the Six Nations of the Iroquois in upstate New York, but when he won but few converts, he returned to New London to teach the Mohegan. He was seen to be a leader who strengthened relations between the Native Americans and the colonists. In 1764, Occom took a stand opposing the sale of tribal lands, asking the governor to return the lands to the Mohegans.

Wheelock, meanwhile, had established an Indian charity school at Lebanon, Connecticut in 1754. Wheelock persuaded Occom to travel to Britain to raise money for the school, while Wheelock promised to care for his wife and children while he was away. Occom sailed from Boston just before Christmas 1765. He remained in Britain, preaching almost 400 sermons and teaching large crowds everywhere. He managed to raise over 12,000 Pounds for Wheelock's school, of which King George III donated 200 Pounds, and the Earl of Dartmouth gave over fifty Pounds. However, when Occom returned, he found that Wheelock had not cared in the slightest for his wife and children. Moreover, Wheelock had moved to New Hampshire, where he used the money raised by Occom to establish Dartmouth College. At the new college, white boys, not Indians, would be educated. When Occom complained about the apparent betrayal, Wheelock threatened to have his ordination revoked, a threat he redoubled when it turned out that Wheelock was on the side of the colonists in the Mohegan land controversy. Some of the colonists spread vicious, false rumors about Occom that he was an incurable alcoholic, and that he had sought ordination only for show. Wheelock picked up those rumors and spread them himself.

Occom felt moved to write a ten-page manuscript in 1768, *A Short Narrative of My Life*, located in the Dartmouth College Archives, but not published until 1982. In 1774, Occom assembled a book, *A Choice Collection of Hymns and Spiritual Songs*, published in New London. The book contains 109 hymn texts, mostly by other authors, but including six by Occom; the book contained no music. Also in 1774, Occom worked together with his relatives to establish a place in upstate New York for Christian Indians of New England and Long Island to relocate. The Revolutionary War put an end to that plan, so in the meantime they settled in Stockbridge, Massachusetts. After the war, they moved to Brothertown NY, and then joined with Oneida and two Lenape groups to found New Stockbridge NY. In the 1820s, New York insisted that the Brothertown and New Stockbridge Indians all move to Calumet County, Wisconsin, where they founded a new Brothertown. The Oneida had been the only major tribe to fight on the American side in the Revolution, so they were very put out that their land was sold for development while they had to move west to what is now Wisconsin. In the two centuries since then, the Oneida have reversed their fortunes by establishing and operating gambling casinos. With some delicious irony, when the Museum of the American Revolution in Philadelphia was unable to raise all the money needed to complete it in 2017, the Oneidas donated the huge sum required, but with the stipulation that they got to write the captions in the museum. The captions clearly state that one of the major purposes of the Revolutionary War was for real estate speculators to use the war as a smokescreen behind which they could rip off enormous tracts of Indian lands.

This entry was paraphrased from Wikipedia, with historical and geographical details added by the author.

DIPLOMAT & ACCOUNTANT WILLIAM ANSAH SESSARAKOO, *ONCE ENSLAVED*, CA. 1736-CA.1770 (GHANA, BARBADOS & UK)

Wealthy and powerful Muslims were permitted to have up to four wives, of whom they often designated one to be the primary wife. John Corrente was essentially the most powerful member of the Fante royal family in Ghana, with enormous wealth that he had gained by selling prisoners of war from interior tribes into permanent slavery, usually in the Americas. Corrente astutely observed how the various Europeans trading to Ghana were able to be easily manipulated. In order to curry favor with the French, he sent his eldest son and heir from his favorite wife to be educated at schools in France in the early 1740s. When Corrente was impressed at how that had worked well, he decided to send another son from a different wife, William Ansah Sessarakoo, to receive a similar education in Great Britain, at the invitation of the Royal African Company. The Royal African Company, which had initially been established in order to trade for ivory and gold along the Ivory Coast and the Gold Coast (the Ivory Coast, French-speaking, is still known as Cote d'Ivoire, and the Gold Coast is now known as Ghana), quickly understood that it could make a lot more money by transporting permanent slaves to colonies in the Americas. The company, which had a trademark of an African elephant with a howdah or castle on its back, had its principal offices near the south bank of the Thames across from the City of London in a district that is still today called Elephant & Castle, and the river landing there was known as Elephant's Stairs. As a child, William had spent much of his time at Fort Elmina or Cape Coast Castle, renamed Fort William in the nineteenth century, where thousands of slaves were dispatched to the New World, and so he was already fluent in English.

The Royal African Company paid for William's voyage to London from Annamaboe (modern Anomabu) in 1744, but William and his family were left to make the actual arrangements. They made the arrangements with Captain David Bruce Crichton for passage on the ship *Lady Carolina*. But Captain Chrichton appears to have died when he reached Barbados, and no other people in charge had any idea that William was supposed to be conveyed to London. William was therefore thought to have belonged to the cargo of slaves that the ship was taking to Barbados. People back in Ghana heard no more news from William, so they began to assume that he must have died on the voyage, or perhaps have been killed in a French or Spanish attack on William's ship. Because the family blamed British carelessness for William's presumed death, they made sure that British slave traders in Ghana were given the run-around and not permitted to load many slaves for British colonies.

Sometime later, a Fante trader doing business in Barbados stumbled across William in bondage there and instantly recognized him. He returned to Ghana and told John Corrente, who issued orders that William should be immediately freed and sent to London, where he arrived in 1748. Officials in Britain were hugely embarrassed by what had transpired in Barbados, and wished to make amends. As William stepped ashore, he was greeted as Prince William Ansah Sensarakoo, the Royal African, and fitted for elegant British clothing commensurate with his rank. George Montagu-Dunk Earl of Halifax was President of the Board of Trade, and because he wanted to reverse the unpleasant political and economic cloud that was covering British-Ghanaian relations, he saw to it that William was treated with the utmost respect and privilege. The prince was even presented to George II, who was flush with happiness at British forces having fended off Bonnie Prince Charlie's French-financed invasion in 1745–6, and defeated both the Spanish and French in the war that had just ended (known widely as the War of Austrian Succession, although that name had been a disguise for France's brazen but failed attempt to solve her almost bankrupt status by trying to conquer all of Britain's colonies in India and the Americas).

In between all his glittering social engagements, William furthered his education. People witnessing him were impressed at his fine manners and gentle, gracious attitude. He had an obvious understanding of British culture. William was even baptized as a Christian in 1749. Most accounts of William's stay in England refer to his attending the theatre, where he saw *Oronooco*, a play by Thomas Southerne, based on the 1688 novel of the same name by the woman writer Aphra Behn. The play told a story about an African prince who had been captured into slavery, where he organized a slave rebellion that failed, and he was executed afterwards. William was so moved by this story, which was somewhat of a mirror to his own experience, that he fled the theatre in tears, much to the confusion of the audience. A book of William's experiences in Britain was published in 1749 (with two subsequent editions in 1754), *The Royal African, or, Memoirs of the Young Prince of Annamboe*, and it became a best-seller. His portrait was painted in oils by Gabriel Mathias in 1750, and an engraving was published in *The Gentleman's Magazine & Historical Chronicle* from the painting – the same magazine in which the book had been serialized. More modern accounts of William's life were written by Sheldon Cheek and by Wylie Sypher.

Around 1750, William returned home to Annamaboe, where his father was delighted to see him again. He obtained a job from the British governor of Cape Coast Castle as a writer (a term used to describe someone who kept the business accounts; for example, in the 1770s, the British East India Company built the largest building in the world in Calcutta, the so-called Writers' Building, full of hundreds or even thousands of men keeping the company's trading accounts, still standing, but now used for different purposes). In 1761, the governor attacked the genial William with his fists as a result of a misunderstanding. The governor had believed that William was his father's heir, and so he had treated him exceptionally well, but then he found out that William was not the heir. The governor dismissed him from his job and ordered him not to enter the fort again. The rest of William's life is essentially unrecorded, but it is believed that he died around 1770, in his thirties.

Many people today do not understand that African slavery was not based on Europeans or Americans coming to Africa and stealing African residents. Instead, it was based on hundreds of interior tribes in Africa waging almost permanent war on each other, resulting in a pool of thousands of prisoners of war, who were sold to coastal African brokers, and these brokers then sold them as permanent slaves to Europeans and Americans. That does not of course excuse the practice, but it does explain it. William exemplifies a bit of irony about the situation: his father, as a coastal chief or king, managed the slave trade for that part of Ghana and served as the region's broker. William, who hung out at the fort and thus learned fluent English, was part of what his father did. Suddenly, William was accidentally swept into being a slave in a British colony (a nasty and unexpected experience), until he was rescued. After a short stint of education in England, William returned to Ghana, where he once again took part in the management of the slave trade, by serving for almost decade at the fort as a "writer" or accountant. The French have a saying, which in translation goes: the more things change, the more they remain the same. That seems to describe the ups and downs of William's career.

This entry was paraphrased from Wikipedia, with historical and geographical details added by the author.

THE REVEREND PHILIP QUAQUE/KWEKU/ QUAICOE, *FREE BLACK*, 1741–1816 (GHANA & UK), (ANGLICAN)

Born into the Fante tribe in Ghana in 1741, and named Kweku, he was one of three thirteen-year-old boys selected by the Rev. Thomas Thompson (the first Anglican missionary to West Africa) to be taken to England for education. Thomas Cobbers, one of the three boys, died after only four years, and William Cudjoe suffered a mental breakdown and died in 1766. Kweku, who took the Christian name of Philip, was baptized at St. Mary's Islington in 1759, and studied theology at the University of Oxford, and received his MA degree. In 1765, he was ordained a priest in the Church of England. He was one of the first Black men ordained in a church with Apostolic Succession since the early years of the Apostle Saint Thomas's church in south India about 50AD. The same year as his ordination, he married Catherine Blunt, an English woman, and they set out for Ghana the following year.

The Royal African Company employed him as chaplain at the slave fort of Cape Coast Castle, but he quickly confronted an embarrassing problem: he had forgotten how to speak most of his native Fante language! Therefore, at first, he reserved the school he established in his house for the growing numbers of Mulatto children of both sexes in the area of the fort, although he later relented and admitted African children. His wife Catherine died fairly soon after they arrived, and he married twice more, each time to African women. In 1784, he sent his two children to London for education.

Kweku found his job as a missionary extremely difficult. It was difficult for the Africans to drop the concept of polytheism and embrace just one God. He also found himself trying to mediate conflicts between the representatives of the various European countries who were involved in trading for goods and slaves along the coast, and the spill-over of the American Revolution made things even more difficult. Nevertheless, he was able to perform hundreds of baptisms, many among adults. He made frequent reports to the Society for the Propagation of the Gospel in Foreign Parts, his sponsors in London, but in all his fifty years on the job, including a period of serious illness, they sent him only three letters.

Kweku observed in his letters that many Africans despised Europeans, and even though he was of course African-born they also regarded him as too Europeanized. Kweku also entered into correspondence with two Congregationalist pastors in Newport, Rhode Island (the Rev. Dr. Samuel Hopkins of the First Meeting House of 1729, and the Rev. Dr. Ezra Stiles of the Second Meeting House of 1735, both of which wooden buildings still stand in greatly altered condition), who had managed to raise the money to train two former slaves to send back to Africa as missionaries. Black poet Phillis Wheatley in Boston raised some money for the project. John Church Quamino and Bristol Coggeshall Yamma left Newport as special unenrolled students at the College of New Jersey (now called Princeton University) under the direct supervision of President John Witherspoon. However, the American Revolution disrupted their studies and the missionary plan had to be either postponed or abandoned. Kweku had tried to talk the two ministers out of the plan because he said that Africans were not the slightest bit interested in welcoming missionaries from overseas, even if those missionaries had been born in West Africa. Kweku took the trouble to find Quamino's mother and assure her that he was intending to come to see her soon. Quamino of course had to earn money in order to live, so he signed aboard an American privateer ship during the War of Independence, but he died in a battle against a British ship in August 1779. Yamma moved to Providence, and announced after the war that he was still interested in pursuing the mission work in Africa, but he died in Providence in the 1790s with the plan still not accomplished.

This entry was paraphrased from Wikipedia, with historical details added by the author.

WRITER THE REVEREND DAVID GEORGE, *ONCE ENSLAVED*, CA. 1742–1810 (VIRGINIA, SOUTH CAROLINA, GEORGIA, NOVA SCOTIA, SIERRA LEONE) (BAPTIST)

David George was born about 1742 in Essex County, Virginia, along the south bank of the Rappahannock River to African parents John and Judith Chapel. George witnessed his mother receiving a horrible beating, so he ran away and moved to South Carolina. He was captured and helped by a Creek Indian Chief named Blue Salt. George's former owner tried to purchase him back from Blue Salt, but was turned down. George worked for several years for Creek and Natchez tribes.

George escaped and ran away again, and this time he encountered George Galphin, a Scottish trader, who had many African slaves, quite a few of whom had intermarried with Creek. George worked for Galphin at Silver Bluff in inland South Carolina. Galphin's children, using mostly the Bible, taught George to read and write.

During this time, George met and married Phyllis, who was part Creek. Together they had four children born in what is now the United States. They had two additional children born in Nova Scotia, followed by four more born in Sierra Leone.

In 1773, George met a childhood friend and former slave, George Lisle, who had become a Baptist. Brother Palmer was a white Baptist missionary who possibly founded the Silver Bluff Baptist Church in Aiken County, South Carolina. George and Phyllis and eight other slaves were baptized at Silver Bluff, and in 1775 or perhaps earlier George and eight other slaves formed one of the first African-American Baptist congregations in the United States. George became the first pastor of that church. An old picture of the church building shows that it was a reasonably large, square, two-story, clapboarded building, five bays on a side, with a gable roof. The building no longer stands, and the congregation moved a few miles away to a new location. Another claimant for the first Black Baptist congregation in America is the First Baptist Church in Williamsburg, Virginia, founded by Gowan Pamphlet.

When the British captured Savannah, Georgia it was common knowledge that the British were offering freedom to any North American slaves who registered with them, so George and his group moved to Savannah. There they worshipped at the First African Baptist Church, founded in 1773 by slaves. Its pastor was former slave George Lisle (also spelled Leile), who had been ordained in 1775. When the British departed Savannah, they transported David George, his wife Phyllis, and three children (Jesse, David, and Ginny), along with George Lisle, to Shelburne, Nova Scotia. This was part of a war's end evacuation of about 3500 former slaves to Nova Scotia, joining a few thousand others who had been evacuated earlier. George founded a Baptist church in Shelburne that welcomed both Blacks and whites, but a group of whites resented George's leadership, so in July 1784 a racist mob rioted and burned down the houses of many Blacks, including George. Most of the Blacks then moved to the Black settlement of Birchtown, where George became an influential leader.

Several years later, many Blacks chose to leave frigid Nova Scotia and accept British help in establishing a new colony in Sierra Leone with its capital city of Freetown. George and his family were part of this migration, as was Lisle. George founded the first Baptist Church there. George was elected Tythingman, a position of power in Sierra Leone at that time. George wrote and published a memoir of his life, *An Account of the Life of Mr. David George from S. L. A. given by himself.*

This entry was paraphrased from Wikipedia, with geographical details added by the author.

WRITER FRANCIS 'QUASHEY' BARBER, *ONCE ENSLAVED*, CA. 1742–1801 (JAMAICA, UK) RN

Born in 1742–3 enslaved in Jamaica as Quashey on the sugar plantation belonging to the Bathurst family, he was a descendant of slaves of the warlike Coromantee tribe from Ghana. When he was about ten years old, his owner, Colonel Richard Bathurst took him to England. Bathurst's son (also called Richard) was a close friend of Dr. Samuel Johnson of Dictionary fame. At about this moment, Johnson's wife Elizabeth died, and this sent Johnson into a serious depression, which the now renamed Francis Barber later described vividly to the diarist James Boswell. The Bathursts sent Barber to Johnson as his valet, arriving only two weeks after Elizabeth's death in 1752. Two years later, the elder Bathurst died, and he freed Barber in his will, also leaving him a small amount of money. Johnson himself was an unabashed opponent of slavery, both in England and in her colonies.

Barber was hired by an apothecary in Cheapside (a street near St. Paul's Cathedral), but about 1758 he heard that he could obtain steady work by enlisting in the Royal Navy. He joined the crew of the brand-new 32-gun frigate *Stag* as a landsman. The frigate patrolled extensively around the coasts of Great Britain, from Leith, Scotland to Torbay in southwestern England. Even though Barber had enlisted of his own free will, Johnson was under the impression that he had been swept up by a press-gang and forced to serve, so he asked his friends with influence at the admiralty to get him freed. Tobias Smollet was able to accomplish that task in October 1760, by calling in a favor from his friend Mr. Wilkes. Smollet, incidentally, was a well-known Scottish poet, author, playwright, and surgeon, who travelled widely in Europe.

Dr. Johnson, who could not understand why anyone would willingly serve in the Navy, famously proclaimed, "No man will be a sailor who has contrivance enough to get himself into a jail; for being in a ship is being in a jail, with the chance of being drowned." At another time, Johnson said, "A man in a jail has more room, better food, and commonly better company."

After being discharged from the Navy (against his wishes), Barber made his way to Dr. Johnson's law offices in the Inner Temple in London, and was hired by him. He lived with Johnson at his house in Gough Square, a short walk from the Inner Temple. At one point, Johnson sent Barber to study at a school at Bishop's Stortford, Hertfordshire, about 25 miles northeast of London. By studying writing, reading, history, and arithmetic, Barber could then be of much greater assistance to Johnson. He was also of great help to Johnson's famous biographer, James Boswell, as he could fill in some of the parts of Johnson's life that happened before Johnson and Boswell first met. Boswell frequently mentions Barber in his book *Life of Johnson*. No doubt, Barber was a great help to Johnson in the tiresome detail work involved in assembling his *Dictionary*. How much of that great work was written by Barber can never be known, of course, but one can be confident that his contribution was not small.

Two versions of a portrait of a handsome Black man (thought to be Barber) were painted, either by James Northcote or by his master Sir Joshua Reynolds. Recent experts lean more towards Reynolds as the artist, but one expert has suggested that the painting may not after all have represented Barber, but Reynolds' own servant. One of the paintings is on display at Dr. Johnson's house, which is now a museum.

On one occasion when Barber returned home from the three years of school in Hertfordshire, although he was in his mid-thirties, he was followed by a white teenage female haymaker. When a few years later, he married Elizabeth Ball, she was believed to be about seventeen years old. Barber was observed several times to exhibit extreme jealousy towards any man who had conversation with her.

Johnson asked one of his three biographers, Sir John Hawkins, how much he should leave Barber in his will. Sir John replied that a nobleman would give 50 Pounds a year, to which Johnson asserted that he would be "noblissimus" and give him forty percent more, but require Barber to move to Lichfield, Staffordshire, where he himself had been born. Sir John was appalled at Johnson's supposedly unnecessary generosity to a Black man.

Barber and his wife and two children did indeed move to Lichfield after Johnson's death in 1784, but Barber was not a good money manager, so he frittered away all his legacy. He sold off all his Dr. Johnson memorabilia, and opened a village school in nearby Burntwood. Barber and his wife Elizabeth had a son, Samuel II, who became a Methodist lay preacher, and a daughter Ann, who collaborated with her mother to operate a school after Barber died in 1801 from unsuccessful surgery at the Staffordshire Royal Infirmary. Barber's descendants still farm near the cathedral town of Lichfield.

This entry was paraphrased from Wikipedia, with geographical and historical details added by the author.

WRITER OLAUDAH 'GUSTAVUS VASSA' EQUIANO, *ONCE ENSLAVED*, CA. 1745–1797 (NIGERIA, BARBADOS, VIRGINIA, MONTSERRAT, PENNSYLVANIA, SIERRA LEONE, & ENGLAND) RN

Born in the Igbo village of Essaka near the coast of Nigeria. When he was about eleven years old, a roving band from a rival tribe kidnapped Olaudah and his sister. About six months later, ownership of him as a slave had changed several times, but he was taken on a European slave ship headed for Barbados with 244 other African slaves. He and a few others were then sent to Virginia. He was bought by tobacco planter, Mr. Campbell, who quickly sold him to Lieutenant Michael Henry Pascal of the Royal Navy, who renamed him Gustavus Vassa after the sixteenth-century Swedish king. Pascal trained Vassa as his valet, both in England and in war against France. Vassa kept a journal, and wrote, reporting what he saw at the capture of Louisbourg, Nova Scotia in 1758, the Battle of Lagos in 1759, and the capture of Belle Ile in 1761. Some of that time, he served on the 100-gun battleship *Royal George*, the Royal Navy's largest ship in those days. His job in battle was to carry gunpowder up from the magazine to the cannons on the gundeck. Here is a sample of what Vassa wrote about that experience:

> *The engagement now commenced with great fury on both sides. L'Ocean immediately returned our fire, and we continued engaged with each other for some time. During this time, I was frequently stunned with the thundering of the great guns, whose dreadful contents hurried many of my companions into awful eternity. At last, the French line was entirely broken, and we obtained the victory, which was immediately proclaimed with loud huzzas and acclamations. My station during the engagement was on the middle-deck, where I was quartered with another boy to bring powder to the aftermost gun. And here I was witness to the dreadful fate of many of my companions, who, in the twinkling of an eye, were dashed to pieces, and launched into eternity. Happily, I escaped unhurt, though the shot and splinters flew thick about me during the fight. Towards the latter part of it my master was wounded, and I saw him carried down to the surgeon. But though I was much alarmed for him, and longed to assist him, I dared not leave my post.*

When he did not need Vassa, Pascal sent him to live with his sister-in-law, where he learned to read and write. He was also baptized in 1759. In 1762, Pascal sold Vassa to Captain James Doran of the merchant ship *Charming Sally*, who took him to the Caribbean Island of Montserrat. There he was sold to Philadelphia Quaker merchant Robert King. King promised him freedom whenever he could pay him back the 40 Pounds that he had paid for him, and employed him in paperwork concerning his ships and stores. King taught Vassa to write more fluently, and encouraged him to trade both for his own account and for his owner. He sold glass tumblers, fruit, and other goods in voyages between Georgia and Caribbean islands. Vassa purchased his freedom in 1766, but King asked him to continue working as a business partner, which he declined to do, saying that it was too dangerous for him as a free Black man who could so easily be re-enslaved in the more southerly colonies.

Instead, he worked as a deckhand on various ships. In 1773, he worked on the Royal Navy corvette *Racehorse*, which had been greatly altered after her capture from the French under the name of *Le Marquis de Vaudreuil*. She was accompanied by the corvette *Carcass* on an exploration mission to the Arctic that had been encouraged by Sir Joseph Banks as a counterweight to Cook's explorations in the Pacific (at that time, Banks wanted to do anything he could to pull the rug out from under Cook, who he believed had slighted him), under the overall command of Captain Constantine J. Phipps. The expedition was notable for many things, one of which was measuring an ocean depth of 4100 feet, a record that stood for many years. Two of the midshipmen in the crew would make names for themselves: Nicholas Biddle of Philadelphia later became the Continental Navy's most respected captain, and Horatio Nelson (who courageously defended himself against a snarling polar bear by swinging his musket as a club) later became Britain's greatest naval hero. A crewman shot and wounded a walrus, which returned with some of its fellows and attacked the longboat, wrecking one of its oars. On that voyage, Vassa worked with Dr. Charles Irving, who had invented a method of distilling seawater, and later grew rich from it, as well as astronomer and mathematician Israel Lyons.

Irving talked Vassa into joining him for many years in a project to select and manage African slaves on plantations in what is now Nicaragua, but the venture eventually failed, and Vassa arrived back in England in 1777. By the 1780s, he was living in London, and became involved in the abolitionist movement. As early as 1783, Vassa gave details of the slave trade to leading abolitionists like Granville Sharp. In that same year, Vassa was the first to tell Sharp and the others the story about the hideous massacre aboard the slave ship *Zong* on her voyage from Africa to Jamaica, and it galvanized the movement. In October 1785, Vassa was selected as one of eight delegates to present an 'Address of Thanks' to the Quakers for their having stood up for those Blacks who had been unlawfully held in bondage. Many of the abolitionists begged Vassa to write his exciting life's story and get it published, while he was being financially supported by the wealthier abolitionists, among whom was the influential Countess of Huntingdon.

Finally, in 1789 his book was published, *The Interesting Narrative of the Life of Olaudah Equiano, or Gustavus Vassa, the African*. The book, which went through nine editions in his lifetime, was also published in Russia, Germany, the Netherlands, and the United States. It was extremely popular and influential, although of course Vassa's experience of being enslaved was vastly different from the experience of most slaves. He travelled about England, Scotland and Ireland giving lectures and promoting the book, which sold so well that he no longer needed financial support from abolitionists.

In 1792, Vassa married Susannah Cullen, an English woman, and they had two daughters, Anna Maria Vassa and Joanna Vassa. They lived at her home village of Soham, Cambridgeshire. He also worked for the establishment of a refuge for British poor Blacks in Sierra Leone, and he was appointed Commissary for their supplies in 1786. However, the leaders there resented his protests against financial mismanagement, and they sent him all the way back to London. Susannah died in 1796 at age 34, and Vassa died just over a year later. His death notices appeared in many British newspapers, as well as American papers.

This entry was paraphrased from Wikipedia, with historical and geographical details added by the author.

THE REVEREND GOWAN/GAVIN VOBE PAMPHLET, *ONCE ENSLAVED*, CA. 1746–1809 (? WEST AFRICA, VIRGINIA) (BAPTIST)

Pamphlet's date and place of birth, and parentage are unknown. Even the name Pamphlet seems to be a name he chose for himself later in life, probably to replace his previous last name. Since he was a slave, it is almost certain that his mother was a slave. He worked for the widow Jane Vobe, who was the owner of the prestigious King's Arms Tavern at Williamsburg, Virginia. He is likely to have worked in the tavern, although possibly also in Mrs. Vobe's house. After the capital of Virginia was moved from Williamsburg west about 60 miles to Richmond in 1780 during the American Revolution (so that the legislature of America's richest colony could not easily be subjected to conquest by British troops sailing up the James and York Rivers), Williamsburg had no commercial reason to continue as a city. Even though she had patriotically renamed the tavern as The Eagle, with the legislature no longer being in town, there were still no people visiting Williamsburg to stay in her rooms or eat and drink in her tavern. Therefore, Mrs. Vobe moved to the Manchester section of Richmond in 1785, and took Pamphlet with her, but she died in 1786, only three years after the end of the war. Mrs. Vobe, incidentally, was committed to the idea of educating Blacks. She had four of her slaves baptized at [Episcopal] Bruton Parish Church, and she sent two slave children to be educated at the Bray School in Williamsburg, which was founded in 1760, but forced to close when the British would not permit any more British money to be spent in rebellious America. Twenty-two Bray Schools were established from Nova Scotia to the Bahamas, and they were all forced to close. The school buildings in Williamsburg and Newport, Rhode Island are the only ones that still stand.

Pamphlet was inherited by Vobe's son David Miller, and he freed Pamphlet, who returned to Williamsburg. The reason that he returned was that, with Mrs. Vobe's permission, he had been ordained in 1772 as a Baptist pastor, the first Black man to be ordained in English America in any faith. Pamphlet felt called to establish Williamsburg's First Baptist Church, which continues in a different building today. At first, the church started small, because large gatherings of Blacks were prohibited for fear of slave uprisings. In addition, the two major faiths that were popular in Virginia, the Episcopal and the Presbyterian Churches, were suspicious of any new churches being established, and so they tried to make things difficult for Baptists. The Baptist Church was not actually illegal in either British Virginia or post-independence Virginia, but things were still difficult for Baptists, even after Thomas Jefferson was able to push through the Virginia Legislature the Virginia Statute for Religious Freedom in 1786. Pamphlet was even confronted in 1783 by the General [Baptist] Association, who actually had no authority over the Williamsburg church, but they tried unsuccessfully to prevent a Black man from preaching to Baptists.

Pamphlet is believed to have started assembling his flock shortly after his ordination in 1772, but the parish was numerous enough for it to be officially "constituted" with 200 members in 1781, the same year as the victory over General Charles Cornwallis and his British force of about 8000 men at Yorktown only twelve miles from Williamsburg. In 1791, Pamphlet successfully petitioned the so-called Dover Baptist Association (an almost entirely white organization based in the Richmond area) for permission to attend their annual meeting, representing the First Baptist Church of Williamsburg. Pamphlet attended most of their annual meetings for the rest of his life. The First Baptist Church of Williamsburg had grown to about 500 members, both enslaved and free, by the mid-1780s. Some people claim that Pamphlet's church was the first Black Baptist congregation in America, but rival claimants exist in Silver Bluff Baptist

Church in South Carolina and First African Baptist Church in Savannah, Georgia, all three founded about the same time.

This entry was paraphrased from Wikipedia, but with geographical and historical details added by the author.

THE REVEREND ABSALOM JONES, *ONCE ENSLAVED*, 1746–1818 (PENNSYLVANIA & DELAWARE) (ANGLICAN)

Absalom Jones was born in slavery to Abraham Wynkoop in Sussex County, Delaware in 1746. Sixteen years later, Wynkoop sold the mother and Absalom's siblings to a neighboring farmer, but kept Absalom and moved with him the short distance to Philadelphia, where he opened a shop. Wynkoop permitted Absalom to study at Anthony Benezet's School, where he learned to read, write and do arithmetic.

When Absalom was still enslaved at the age of 24, he received permission to marry Mary King, who was a slave of S. King, one of Wynkoop's neighbors, and the wedding was performed by the prestigious Reverend Jacob Duche, an Episcopal priest. Eight years later, he had earned enough money from work and donations so he could purchase his wife's freedom, which would mean that any children she had would also be free. Of course, Absalom wanted his own freedom as well, and Wynkoop delayed that until 1784. At that time, Absalom chose the last name of Jones for himself.

Around 1780, some Episcopalians, inspired by the teachings of the Rev. John Wesley and the Rev. George Whitefield, felt moved to break away into a new church, which they called the Methodist Episcopal Church. In 1784, The Reverend Thomas Coke and the Reverend Francis Asbury officially established the new separate faith in America. They founded St. George's Methodist Episcopal Church in Philadelphia, which was open to people of all races. Absalom Jones and his friend Richard Allen were among the first African-Americans to be licensed to preach by the Methodist-Episcopal Church.

However, the congregation of St. George's still practiced racial discrimination. They encouraged their Black members hold services at a much earlier hour than the white members, so Jones and Allen founded the Free African Society about 1790, which they thought of as a non-denominational mutual aid society for newly-freed slaves. The following year, they started holding religious services there. In 1792, St. George's announced in one of their services that from now on Blacks would have to worship only upstairs in the galleries (balconies), so Jones and Allen walked out with all the Black members following them.

After that, Jones and Allen, although still friends, split over what policy to follow. Jones wanted to found a Black congregation within the Episcopal Church, and his petition to do so was warmly received. Church authorities even gave him the plans for a church building that had been drawn by the celebrated architect Peter Harrison before the Revolution to be the chapel for "The College at Philadelphia," later known as the University of Pennsylvania. The college had decided that it did not need a chapel after all. The brick building had a gable roof, and two stories of compass-headed windows five bays long, so it had substantial galleries in the expectation of a large congregation eventually. It was designed also to have giant Ionic pilasters at all the angles, but they were omitted in order to save money, as was a cupola on the roof to hold a bell. Construction of St. Thomas's Church began in 1792, and it opened its doors on 17 July 1794. Jones was ordained a deacon in 1795 and the first Black priest in North America in 1802 by Bishop William White of Philadelphia. Unfortunately, the congregation found it advantageous to move to a new location in the nineteenth century, and this beautiful and historically significant church building was destroyed. When St. Thomas's opened, its founders and vestry published a pamphlet that was widely circulated, explaining "The Causes and Motives for Establishing St. Thomas's African Church of Philadelphia." They explained that they intended "to arise out of the dust and shake ourselves, and throw off that servile fear, that the habit of oppression and bondage trained us up in."

In the meantime, Allen had founded his own separate denomination, the African Methodist Episcopal Church (AME). Using a former shop building of no architectural pretensions, he and his followers opened Mother Bethel AME Church in 1794. The building was replaced in the nineteenth century by a much larger building that still stands. Allen was ordained a minister in 1799 by Francis Asbury, who in turn had been appointed a bishop of the Methodist Church (with no Apostolic Succession). Allen was elected the first bishop of the AME Church in 1816. The formerly enslaved John Gloucester established the first African Presbyterian Church in Philadelphia in 1807.

Jones died in 1818.

This entry was paraphrased from Wikipedia, with historical and architectural details added by the author.

PREACHER HARRY 'BLACK HARRY' HOSIER, *ONCE ENSLAVED*, CA. 1750–1806 (SOUTH CAROLINA, NORTH CAROLINA, VIRGINIA, MARYLAND, DELAWARE, PENNSYLVANIA, NEW YORK, & MASSACHUSETTS) (METHODIST)

Little is known of the early life of Harry Hosier. He was born into slavery near Fayetteville, North Carolina, and may have been sold to an owner near Baltimore, Maryland. While he was still in North Carolina, he met one of the founders of the Methodist Church, the Reverend Francis Asbury about 1780, and served as Asbury's carriage driver.

Asbury was extremely impressed: his totally illiterate driver could memorize long passages from the Bible verbatim. Asbury wrote, "If I had Harry to go with me and meet the colored people, it would be attended with a blessing." Hosier delivered his first sermon, entitled 'The Barren Fig-Tree.' to the Black Methodist congregation in Fairfax County, Virginia in 1781. The few white people present were amazed. Dr. Benjamin Rush, a Signer of the Declaration of Independence, announced that the sermon was the greatest he had ever heard. Blacks came from a great distance to hear him, but strangely his principal audiences were white. In 1784, he delivered a sermon in Delaware, the first time an all-white congregation would hear a Black preacher. He called on audiences to reject slavery and champion the cause of the common working man. Asbury tried to get Hosier to accompany him everywhere that he travelled, because news of Hosier's coming would draw much larger crowds than Asbury alone. Asbury's associate Thomas Coke wrote that Hosier was "one of the best preachers in the world," and at the same time "one of the humblest creatures I ever saw."

Hosier was present with Richard Allen in Baltimore at the official founding of the Methodist-Episcopal Church of America on 2 January 1785, but because they were Blacks, they were not permitted to vote on any of the items involved in the founding. When Hosier reached Boston, he spoke to an open-air crowd of over 1000 people. In spite of all the foregoing, Hosier was not included in the group of Black Methodist preachers who were ordained in 1799, possibly because he was still mostly illiterate. Near the end of his life, Hosier was found to be drunk and picking through garbage in abject poverty, although he did recover for a time and continue his ministry. He died in 1806. We are told without evidence that a Black preacher in this same era also named 'Black Harry,' who was sent by Dutch officials down to the Caribbean Island of Sint Eustatius (close to St. Kitts), but who was sent back to the United States because of local objections, was not the same man.

This entry was paraphrased from Wikipedia, with historical details added by the author.

WRITER, PREACHER/TEACHER JOSEPH JOHNSON, *NATIVE AMERICAN*, 1751–1777 (CONNECTICUT, RHODE ISLAND & NEW YORK)

Joseph Johnson was a member of the Mohegan Tribe, who studied at Moor's Indian Charity School. He was one of the principal organizers of the Brothertown movement, whereby members of seven Christian Algonkian-speaking Indian tribes in southern New England and various other tribes from other language groups could live together in Christian harmony in upstate New York in a town on land purchased from the Oneidas. Johnson was a New Light Congregationalist, and preached and taught and wrote accordingly. In 1768, he was sent away due to drunkenness and other bad behavior from the school where he was teaching. He taught for a while in Providence, Rhode Island, and even joined the crew of a whaling ship. Then he opened a school in Farmington, Connecticut, which he used as a base from which he could organize the Brothertown project. He died in his mid-twenties several years before Brothertown became a reality.

Johnson was a prolific writer, and his papers are well preserved. He even managed to be published shortly before his famous father-in-law. He married Tabitha Occom, daughter of the Reverend Samson Occom. Tabitha continued living at Mohegan even after Brothertown had taken off, and none of their children lived more than temporarily at Brothertown. Johnson, like Occom, David Fowler, Hezekiah Calvin, and other Native American intellectuals, could never reconcile the Christian teachings of the Reverend Eleazar Wheelock with Wheelock's scandalous treatment of Native Americans. Johnson died before he could actually be ordained. He is not to be confused with the Joseph Johnson, a Black sailor in the Royal Navy, who wore a square-rigged ship as his hat in London in 1817, as a prop for his begging routine after his discharge from the Navy when he had lost his left leg below the knee from fighting Napoleon's forces.

This entry was paraphrased from Wikipedia, with historical additions by the author.

WRITER THE REVEREND LEMUEL HAYNES, *FREE BLACK*, 1753–1833 (CONNECTICUT, VERMONT, & NEW YORK) (CONGREGATIONALIST)

Lemuel Haynes was born in West Hartford, Connecticut, but his parentage on both sides is considered a mystery, perhaps in order to hide someone's peccadilloes. He seems to have been a Mulatto, but whether it was his father or his mother who was Black, there is no record. When he was still a baby, an arrangement or "indenture" was arranged that he be placed in the care of David Rose, a blind farmer in Granville, Massachusetts, and his wife Elizabeth. As he grew older, he could help the family with running the farm. The arrangement was to end on Lemuel's 21st birthday.

Haynes joined the local militia, which was called up right after the alarm at Concord and Lexington in April 1775. Shortly after Concord, troops from New Hampshire, Massachusetts, Rhode Island, Connecticut, and New York under the command of Colonel Benedict Arnold captured Forts Ticonderoga and Crown Point (and a few days later Fort Saint John) from the British, and not long after that Elizabeth Rose died. In 1776, Haynes and his militia unit were ordered to garrison Fort Ticonderoga. While in the fort, he contracted typhus, so he was discharged and sent home. He went to the Rose homestead, which was the only home he had ever known.

His career of fighting in the Revolution was therefore ended, but in his writings, he hammered on the theme that the Revolution was not truly over until slavery was ended. He wrote extensively opposing the slave trade and slavery. He argued that slavery denied Black people their natural rights to "life, Liberty and the pursuit of Happiness." He pointed out the bitter irony of slave-owners pursuing liberty from Great Britain while denying liberty to so many people on American soil. This was part of a pamphlet, *Liberty Further Extended*, intended to be published, but it remained undiscovered in a Harvard University archive until 1983. He also preached sermons, and wrote on theological themes.

In 1779, he began intensive study with two Congregationalist ministers in Connecticut, the Rev. Daniel Farrand and the Rev. William Bradford, to learn Latin, Greek, theology, and homiletics. He helped Farrand with work on his farm, and Bradford found him a job as a teacher. In late 1780, he was granted a license to preach locally, and, at the same time, he started missionary work in the wilds of western New Hampshire, which soon became the independent state of Vermont. Haynes received his ordination in 1785, the first African-American to be ordained in the United States. For three years, he worked at Hemlock Congregational Church in Torrington, Connecticut, but then he moved to West Parish Church in Rutland, Vermont. He remained as pastor of this mostly white church for thirty years, while it grew from forty-two members up to more than three hundred and fifty.

In 1783, Haynes married a Massachusetts girl, Elizabeth Babbitt, a young white school-teacher. They had nine children: Elizabeth, Eunice, Louis, Electa, Lemuel II, Sarah, Olive, Pamela and Samuel Woodbridge (the latter named after the Hartland, Vermont minister who had married them).

Haynes continued to speak and write about the evils of slavery. Many white people at the time felt that the best solution would be eventual repatriation of American Blacks to Africa, and some Blacks agreed with that position, sending many of their colleagues to the British Colony of Sierra Leone, or later to the American Colony of Liberia. However, Haynes felt that freed slaves should be harmoniously integrated into the already polyglot population of the United States, and that God's plan called for that.

In 1818, the Rutland Church Council dismissed Haynes, but nobody knows why. He took a temporary position in Manchester, Vermont, and finally in 1822 at South Granville, New York, which is where he died in 1833 at the age of eighty. He had written his own epitaph: "Here lies the dust of a poor hell-deserving sinner who ventured into eternity trusting wholly on the merits of Christ for salvation. In the full belief of the great doctrines that he preached while on earth, he invites his children, and all who read this, to trust their eternal interest in the same foundation."

This entry was paraphrased from Wikipedia, with historical additions by the author.

WRITER PHILLIS WHEATLEY PETERS,
ONCE ENSLAVED, 1753–1784 (WEST AFRICA,
MASSACHUSETTS & UK), POET

Phillis was born somewhere in West Africa about 1753. Rampaging members of a rival tribe seized her when she was about seven or eight. They sold her to a middle man who transported her aboard the slave ship *Phillis* to Boston. John and Susanna Wheatley in Boston bought her. They taught her to read and write, and when they saw that she had a talent for poetry, they encouraged her to develop that talent. By age twelve, she was reading ancient classics in their original Greek and Latin. She also enjoyed reading the poetry of Milton and Pope.

Phillis was taken on a trip to London to see about having her poetry published. Her book, *Poems on Various Subjects, Religious and Moral* was published in London in September 1773, the first of many editions. Phillis was introduced to many important people in London, including Frederick Bull, the Lord Mayor. Her audience with George III had to be cancelled because she was due to leave for Boston. The Countess of Huntingdon, whom she did not meet, kindly subsidized her book.

Back in Boston, the Wheatley family gave Phillis her freedom in November 1773. Phillis then met and married John Peters, a Black grocer who had no money. John was imprisoned for debt in 1784. With a sick infant to care for, Phillis worked as a scullery maid at a boarding house, but she caught pneumonia and died in December 1784, aged thirty-one, right after giving birth to a daughter, who died the same day, and the infant son died soon after.

Not only did Phillis write poetry, but she also wrote letters to people like the Reverend Samson Occom, and British philanthropist John Thornton. She sent a copy of her poem, *To His Excellency, George Washington* to the general in 1775, and he invited her to visit him in Cambridge, Massachusetts, which she did. Thomas Paine republished that poem in the *Pennsylvania Gazette* in April 1776. She had previously written in 1768 *To the King's Most Excellent Majesty*, in which she praised the King for repealing the Stamp Act. In 1770, she wrote a tribute to the Reverend George Whitefield.

One poem tackled the subject of slavery, *On being brought from Africa to America:*

> *Twas mercy brought me from my pagan land, taught my benighted*
> *soul to understand*

*That there's a God, that there's a Saviour too: once I redemption
  neither sought nor knew.
Some view our sable race with scornful eye: "Their colour is but a
  diabolic dye."
Remember, Christians: Negroes, black as Cain May be refined and
  join th'angelic train.*

Phillis was required to defend her authorship of her poetry in court in 1772 before a group of important men, including John Hancock and Governor Thomas Hutchinson. She convinced them that she had indeed written the poems, and they signed a statement to that effect. However, that was not enough to get her poetry published in Boston, but the London public was excited to read her works. In 1778, African-American poet Jupiter Hammon, then living in Hartford, wrote a poem and sent it to her. French philosopher Voltaire wrote that Phillis had proved that Black people could write poetry, and Continental Navy Captain John Paul Jones asked a fellow officer to take some of his personal writings to "Phillis the African favorite of the Nine [muses] and Apollo."

As recently as September 2023, the Smithsonian's National Museum of African-American History and Culture acquired a previously unknown and unpublished manuscript by Phillis, including a four-page poem entitled *The Ocean*.

This entry was paraphrased from Wikipedia, with historical and geographical additions by the author

WRITER JAMES ROBERTS, *ENSLAVED*, CA. 1753- CA. 1850 (MARYLAND, LOUISIANA, WASHINGTON DC)

James Roberts was born in 1753 on the Eastern Shore of Maryland (the Eastern Shore is the large tongue of land that encloses the Chesapeake Bay; the bay was formed out of the estuary of the Susquehanna River by a giant meteor strike about 35 million years ago). His owner at the time of the Revolutionary War was Colonel Francis De Shields, and he fought next to De Shields in several battles. Once the war was over, De Shields worked for George Washington in Philadelphia, and Roberts accompanied De Shields as his servant. De Shields died, so Roberts expected to be set free. Instead, he was sold to William Ward, who tore Roberts away from his family and sold him at auction in New Orleans to Calvin Smith.

While he worked for Smith, he saw his own cousin brutally whipped and placed in the stocks, and die only one week after he had arrived at that property. In 1815, Major General Andrew Jackson came to Calvin Smith's plantation to enlist 500 slaves on the eve of the Battle of New Orleans, and Roberts was one of those men. It is worth explaining why the battle happened in the first place. The War of 1812 was widely claimed to have been fought because American sailors had been impressed to serve on British warships. While that did indeed happen, the numbers were very small. The real reason for the war is that real estate speculators in Congress thought that a quick war would net them huge areas of land in Canada, where the top incentive was control of the lucrative trade in beaver furs, but American attacks on Canada were unsuccessful. Even the American burning of the British capital of Ontario, York (since renamed Toronto), had repercussions when the British arrived to burn Washington DC in punishment for that. Finally, in late 1814 all parties took part in a European peace conference. The British diplomat in charge worried that Congress would not ratify the treaty, so he suggested that British forces should try to seize New Orleans. One reason for that was that New Orleans had been Spanish until Napoleon conquered Spain, which he said entitled him to do anything he liked with Spanish overseas possessions. Since New Orleans had been French before it was sold to the King of Spain in 1762, Napoleon wanted its ownership restored to France, along with the vast hinterland known as Western Louisiana. When Napoleon found out that the French people of New Orleans rejected his legitimacy, and that Haitian independence would not be easily reversed, he sold Western Louisiana to the United States – the Louisiana Purchase. The Spanish, who were in 1814 Britain's ally, asked for help in getting their territory back, so that was an additional reason for the British to try to capture New Orleans. One British hope was that by capturing New Orleans they could re-establish the right they had formerly had under the Spanish to sail up the Mississippi and Missouri Rivers and thus trade with the vast interior of the continent, but losing the Battle of New Orleans meant that this wish was unattainable.

The British fielded 8000 men under Major General Sir Edward Pakenham. Facing them was the United States Army of 5600 men, including 500 slaves and several hundred Choctaw. The British had been responsible for defeating Napoleon, so they should have won this battle easily, but sloppy management caused a British defeat, in which they lost 291 killed (including Pakenham himself), 1262 wounded, and 484 captured, versus American losses of 13 killed, 39 wounded, and 19 captured. The battle occurred fifteen days after the peace treaty had already been signed in Europe, so if the British had indeed won, they would have been obliged to return New Orleans anyway, although they might have been able to gain the right to sail up the Mississippi as they had in prior times. Many Americans may be familiar with the folk-style song, the Battle of New Orleans, written by Jimmie Driftwood in the 1930s, and sung by Johnny Horton.

As for Roberts, he had a finger chopped off in the battle, and he received a serious wound to the head. Jackson had promised before the battle that all the enslaved soldiers would be given their freedom, but after the battle he pretended that he had never said anything of the kind, and merely paid for all the slaves to drink as much liquor as they pleased at the Kentucky Tavern.

Roberts wrote a slave narrative, in which he said: *It is not for me to foretell the end of oppression in this country, but one thing is certain, virtue, sobriety, temperance, economy, education, and religion, will fit you for any emergency whatever, and are the best qualifications for free men. That their attainment may be your constant pursuit and most earnest endeavor, is the prayer of one now ready to depart.*

In another part, he wrote, quoting verbatim the words of General Jackson.

> *Never suffer negroes to have arms; if you do, they will take the country. Suffer them to have no kind of weapons over ten inches long. Never allow them to have a piece of paper with any writing on it whatever. You must examine your slaves very closely, for the time is coming when the slave will get light; and if ever his mind is enlightened on the subject of freedom, you cannot keep him. One slave bought from the East will ruin a multitude of those raised here. Before a slave of mine should go free, I would put him in a barn and burn him alive. Gentlemen, take me at my word; for if you do not, you will be sorry for it before many years. Never arm another set of colored people. We have fooled them now, but never trust them again; they will not be fooled again with this example before them. If you do, you will repent of it but once.*

This General Jackson was the same man who was responsible as US President for the infamous Trail of Tears, in which about 60,000 Cherokee, Choctaw, Creek, Chickasaw, and Seminole were forcibly marched off their eastern lands all the way to Oklahoma, with huge numbers dying

along the way, between 1830 and 1850. Bear in mind, that Jackson's deputy at New Orleans had been Brigadier General Pushmataha, the Choctaw
Paramount Chief, but he died before the forced resettlement began.

All Roberts was permitted to do after the night of drinking (in which
he did not drink) was to return to the Smith Plantation and continue to
work for him in between physical abuse for him and for others working
there. In 1856, Roberts wrote to President Pierce in Washington DC to
request an interview about the possibility of his receiving a pension for
the wounds he had received at New Orleans. Pierce replied that Black
men like Roberts were worth nothing more than a horse or a sheep, so
it would be disgraceful to take [Roberts'] pension that Calvin Smith was
still receiving and give it to Roberts himself.

This entry was paraphrased from Wikipedia, with historical and
geographical additions by the author.

WRITER THE REVEREND JOHN MARRANT, *FREE BLACK*, 1755–1791 (NEW YORK, SOUTH CAROLINA, GEORGIA, FLORIDA, NORTH CAROLINA, NOVA SCOTIA, & UK) (HUNTINGDONIAN/METHODIST) RN

John Marrant was born free in New York City in 1755. He had an older
brother, two older sisters, and a younger sister. His father died when John
was just four. They moved to St. Augustine, Florida (which became British in 1763; the British had captured Cuba in wartime, and traded Cuba
for both East and West Florida). He started school in Florida, but then
because of war they moved to Georgia. He continued in school until age
eleven. His mother remarried in this time, and an older sister married in
Charleston. In Charleston, he developed an interest in music, and in only
two years he became proficient at both French horn and violin, while at
the same time serving part of an apprenticeship with a carpenter.

At age 13, he and a friend went to listen to the Reverend George
Whitefield preach, and suddenly he was in a dramatic conversion, falling
on the floor and being unable to move for a time. He refused medicines,
but recovered through studying the Bible. His family treated him as if he
had a mental illness, so he ran away into the forest, where he encountered
a Cherokee hunter. He accompanied the Cherokee man for two months,
gathering furs to trade. When they arrived at the Cherokee's home town,
he was denied entry, and instead told that he was sentenced to death

for being in the wrong place. His prayers to God changed the heart of the executioner, who got the sentencing judge to introduce him to the Cherokee king, and the king pardoned him. They all heard Marrant pray in both English and Cherokee. He lived with the Cherokee for two years, and also visited other regional tribes, such as the Catawba, Housaw, and Creek. He converted many Native Americans to Christianity.

He wore Cherokee-style clothing. When he returned to his family, at first, they did not recognize him. He found work on various plantations as a free carpenter, and conducted missionary work among the slaves, which was accepted at some plantations but not at others, until the beginning of the American Revolution.

At the outset of the Revolution, he was impressed into the Royal Navy. He served first on the 8-gun corvette *Scorpion*, and later aboard *Princess Amelia*, 80 guns, where his skills as a musician were in great demand. He was present at the British capture of Charleston in 1780, and in 1781 he fought the Dutch at the Battle of Dogger Bank in the North Sea, where he was wounded. After his ship had wandered to many places, he was finally placed in the Naval Hospital at Plymouth, where a doctor announced that he didn't think Marrant would ever be capable of serving in the Navy again. After he was discharged from the Navy, Marrant worked for a clothing merchant in London, where he met the Reverend George Whitefield again, and related how he was converted. Whitefield introduced him to Selina Hastings, the Countess of Huntingdon, who sponsored a sect that practiced a combination of Calvinism and Methodism. It separated from the Church of England in 1783. Marrant was ordained in this church in Bath, and then left at the request of his brother to preach to the Blacks in Nova Scotia.

During the Revolution, it had been British policy to offer Blacks their freedom at every city that they occupied: Boston, Newport, New York, Perth Amboy, Philadelphia, Norfolk, Wilmington, Charleston, Savannah, and St. Augustine. Therefore, several thousand free but somewhat disgruntled Blacks found themselves after the war in Nova Scotia. Many of them congregated in Birchtown not far from Digby on the western side of the colony, before a large proportion of them departed for the new British colony specially set aside in 1787 for former slaves in West Africa, Sierra Leone with its capital of Freetown. Marrant preached in Nova Scotia to Black communities and white communities and also the Mi'kmaqs. Some congregations were upset that their members were going out to hear the preaching of some new fellow, but others were delighted.

While Marrant was in Nova Scotia, he did not receive the money that the Countess had promised to send him, and then he was laid low by smallpox for six months. Eventually, in 1787 he moved to Boston, where he became the chaplain of the African Masonic Lodge. In a speech to the Lodge, he described Black people as "an essentially distinct nation within a Christian universalist family of mankind." In 1788, he returned to Birchtown to marry Elizabeth Herries, whose parents were Black Loyalists, and he returned with her to Boston. Margaret Blucke (wife of Black Loyalist leader Stephen Blucke, who had succeeded Titus "Tye" Corlies in resisting the rebels in New Jersey) wrote and asked him about his children. This may mean that Marrant had been previously married to a woman who was deceased.

Marrant then returned to London, where he worked a short while as a Methodist minister, but on 15 April 1791, he died in the Islington district of London at age only 35. His writings were published in three parts. One book published in 1785 is *A Narrative of the Lord's Wonderful Dealings with John Marrant, A Black*, as transcribed by the Rev. William Aldridge. A sermon that he delivered to the African Masonic Lodge in Boston in 1789 was immediately published, stressing the equality of all men before God. Finally, his last published work was *A Journal of the Rev. John Marrant from August the 18th 1785 to the 16th of March 1790*. Here is an excerpt from the first book:

> *I was in the engagement with the Dutch off the Dogger Bank, on board the* Princess Amelia, *of 84 guns. We had a great number killed and wounded; the deck was running with blood; six men were killed, and three wounded, stationed at the same gun with me; my head and face were covered with blood and brains of the slain: I was wounded, but did not fall, till a quarter of an hour before the engagement ended, and was happy during the whole of it. After being in the hospital three months and 16 days, I was sent to the West-Indies on board of a ship of war, and, after cruising in those seas, we returned home as a convoy. Being taken ill of my old wounds, I was put into the hospital at Plymouth, and had not been there long, when the physician gave it as his opinion, that I should not be capable of serving the king again.*

This entry was paraphrased from Wikipedia, with historical and geographical additions by the author.

WRITER JOHN 'QUOBNA OTTOBAH CUGOANO' STUART, *ONCE ENSLAVED*, CA. 1757-AFTER 1791 (GHANA, GRENADA, & UK)

Quobna (Kwabena = 'born on Tuesday') Ottobah (Ottobuah = 'second-born') Cugoano was born at Ajumako in Ghana to a Fanti family. When he was thirteen, an armed force from an enemy tribe kidnapped him and many other children, and they sold them to a middle man. They were transported from Cape Coast Castle to the Caribbean Island of Grenada, which had only recently been captured from the French by the British. Grenada is the most southerly island in the chain down the eastern side of the Caribbean. There, or perhaps on the neighboring island of St. Vincent, he was put to work on either a sugar plantation or more probably a spice plantation. In 1772, when he was fifteen, he was purchased by a Scottish plantation owner by the name of Campbell, who made him a household slave (a big improvement over being a field hand). Campbell took Cugoano to England with him, where Campbell was surprised to learn that Cugoano was now free due to a recent court ruling. The court ruling was not intended to have been a general ruling at the time, but it was soon interpreted that way. Cugoano selected a British name for himself, John Stuart, and was baptized as a Christian at elegant and fashionable Saint James' Piccadilly in London on 20 August 1773.

The next decade seems to be a blank, but in 1784, Stuart was hired as a servant by Richard and Maria Cosway, both artist friends of Thomas Jefferson. The Cosways lived for many years in an apartment in Schomberg House on the south side of Pall Mall in London, close to Saint James' Palace. Through the Cosways, he was introduced to influential people of the day, including the Prince of Wales and the cutting-edge poet William Blake. Stuart and other educated British Africans formed the Sons of Africa, an abolitionist group, whose members wrote to newspapers in condemnation of slavery and the slave trade. In 1786, he played a central role in rescuing Henry Demane. Henry, a Black man, was kidnapped and was about to be sent back to the Caribbean and slavery, but Stuart contacted the well-known and influential abolitionist Granville Sharp, who was able to have Henry removed from the ship before it sailed.

In 1787, Stuart wrote and had published under his African name the book, *Thoughts and Sentiments on the Evil and Wicked Traffic of the Slavery and Commerce of the Human Species*. The book was intended to be read by British subjects, and he made sure that copies were sent to

George III, the Prince of Wales, and Edmund Burke (an important Member of Parliament). George III and his chief advisors remained opposed to ending the slave trade at this time, so the trade continued for another two decades. Stuart was by then a committed Christian, and he wrote the book in that light. In it, he called for the immediate end of slavery and the setting free of all enslaved people. The book states that a slave's duty is to escape from slavery, and, if necessary, force ought to be used to prevent further enslavement.

In 1791, Stuart published a shorter version of the book, this time addressed to the Sons of Africa. He expressed support for the British attempt to found an African colony for freed slaves, known as Sierra Leone, with its capital city of Freetown. It was founded in 1786. Some people had supported the idea as a way of dealing with London's large number of "Poor Blacks," many of whom were freed slaves from America who had ended in London after the Revolutionary War, but the original idea for Sierra Leone had been promoted by other American freed slaves who were stuck in chilly Nova Scotia with nothing productive to do. They had asked the British Government to find and purchase a piece of land in West Africa, which, perhaps surprisingly, they did. Stuart also called for schools to be established in Britain to educate British Blacks, somewhat echoing the efforts of the Reverend Dr. Thomas Bray, whose campaign in Britain starting in the 1720s had resulted in 22 Bray Schools being established in America from Nova Scotia to the Bahamas; the Bray Schools were however all stopped in 1775 when the British government refused to allow another penny to be sent to war-time America, and today only two former Bray School buildings survive in Newport, Rhode Island, and Williamsburg, Virginia.

The Cosways, and Stuart with them, moved to 12 Queen Street, Mayfair, in the angle between Hyde Park and Green Park, and only a few blocks from Schomberg House. At that point, he told the Cosways that he intended to sail to Nova Scotia and try to recruit more settlers for Sierra Leone, not realizing that nearly all the Nova Scotia Blacks had already sailed to Sierra Leone. Whether or not he did so remains unknown. No historical record of him has appeared after 1791, so it is likely that he died about that time, or sailed to Sierra Leone himself, a colony in which records were but poorly kept.

This entry was paraphrased from Wikipedia, with geographical and historical additions by the author.

THE RIGHT REVEREND RICHARD ALLEN, *ONCE ENSLAVED*, 1760–1831 (DELAWARE, PENNSYLVANIA, MARYLAND) (AFRICAN METHODIST EPISCOPAL)

Richard Allen was born in 1760 in Delaware on the country property of Philadelphia Quaker lawyer Benjamin Chew, but only a few years later Richard and his family were sold to plantation-owner Stokeley Sturgis of Dover, Delaware. Not long after, because of financial problems, Sturgis sold Richard's mother and the youngest two of the five children to another owner. Richard and his older brother and sister started to attend meetings of the local Methodist Society. Richard, who mostly taught himself to read and write, joined the Methodists at age seventeen, and began to preach to other slaves, which annoyed many slave-holders. Meanwhile, Sturgis began to be convinced that owning slaves was wrong, so he gave his slaves an opportunity to purchase their freedom at a reduced rate. Richard performed additional work in order to earn the necessary money, and he purchased his freedom in 1780. At the same time, he invented a last name for himself, Allen.

Allen married his first wife, Flora, in 1790, but she died of a lengthy disease ten years later. Allen then moved to Philadelphia, where he married Sarah Bass, a freed slave from Virginia who had moved to Philadelphia as a child. They had six children: Richard II, James, John, Peter, Sarah, and Anne.

Allen was officially given a preacher's license at the December 1784 conference in Baltimore that formally founded the Methodist-Episcopal Church. Allen and Harry 'Black Harry' Hosier were the only two Blacks in attendance. In 1786, Allen became an official preacher at St. George's Methodist Church in Philadelphia, along with Absalom Jones. They resented the white members of the congregation, who insisted on segregating worship services. Blacks were welcome to have their services very early in the morning. Or if they wanted to attend services with the whites they would have to sit only in the galleries (balconies). This was intolerable for both Allen and Jones, so they started meeting outdoors with their congregation, and working at odd jobs in order to pay family expenses. They formed the Free African Society. Allen and Jones found the money to pay for a piece of real estate in 1787. Jones decided to seek ordination in the Episcopal Church, and he founded St. Thomas's church in 1792, reserved mostly for Black parishioners (with an elegant brick design by Peter Harrison before the Revolution that had been originally intended as the chapel for what became the University of Pennsylvania). He became the first Black Episcopal priest, ordained by Bishop William White in 1802.

In 1793, Philadelphia was hit by a major outbreak of Yellow Fever. Some white people suggested that since it was a tropical disease Blacks were obviously immune to it (which of course was nonsense). Nevertheless, Allen and Jones organized hundreds of Blacks to look after the afflicted whites, partly out of Christian charity, and partly as a demonstration to show that these Blacks were as committed Christians as anyone else.

Allen did not feel comfortable in the long traditions of the Episcopal Church, but he also did not feel welcome in the recently-formed Methodist Church, so he decided to found his own new church but in the Methodist tradition. He called it the African Methodist-Episcopal Church, or AME Church for short. He moved a disused shop building to the land that the Free African Society had bought, and called that building Mother Bethel AME Church in 1793 (Beth-El is Hebrew for 'place of God'). In the nineteenth century, a much larger building was built on the same site, and it still stands today as the mother church. Allen was ordained by Methodist Bishop Francis Asbury in 1799 as the first minister or elder in the AME Church. Allen continued to have good relations with the Methodist Church, so when the AME Church attracted congregations in other communities, it was time to set up a more formal structure. Allen was elected the first bishop of the AME Church in 1816, and was ordained once again by Francis Asbury, this time as the AME Church's first bishop. Allen died in 1831. Former slave John Gloucester founded the first African Presbyterian Church in Philadelphia in 1807. The first African Episcopal Church in Philadelphia was St. Thomas' in 1792–4, founded by the Reverend Absalom Jones, also a former slave, as noted above.

This entry was paraphrased from Wikipedia, with geographical, historical, and architectural additions by the author.

WRITER THE REVEREND BOSTON KING, *ONCE ENSLAVED*, CA, 1760–1802 (SOUTH CAROLINA, NEW YORK, NOVA SCOTIA, SIERRA LEONE) (METHODIST)

Boston King was born in South Carolina as a slave. His father was a slave from Africa who knew how to read and write, and his mother was familiar with herbal preparations from the Native Americans, although whether that means that she was a Native American or not is unknown. King was apprenticed as a carpenter. Boston first joined the British at Charleston in 1780 when he was about twenty. After a bout with smallpox, he travelled to New York, twice evading capture by the Americans.

In New York, he met and married Violet, an enslaved woman from North Carolina, who had also joined the British. At the end of the war, they were among about 3000 Black American ex-slaves who were given certificates of freedom. Their names were entered in the *Book of Negroes*, and were evacuated with the British to Nova Scotia for resettlement there.

King, who was by this time a master carpenter, found work in Birchtown, a community near Shelburne set aside for mostly Blacks. The Black Loyalists had a particularly difficult time in Nova Scotia. The paperwork for their land grants seemed to take forever, as did supplies, and the soil was generally too poor for farming; the good farming soil was in the Annapolis Valley on the west side of the province, but that land had long since been spoken for, mostly by white settlers. Next, King was appointed a Methodist minister to a congregation at Preston in the Halifax area.

Although their condition was noticeably better, in 1792 they still felt drawn to emigrate to the new colony of Sierra Leone in Africa, with its capital city of Freetown. Unfortunately, Violet caught malaria and died soon after they arrived.

King was employed to preach to the native Africans in Sierra Leone, in spite of the fact that he did not know how to speak or understand their languages. Then he opened a school. In 1794, the Sierra Leone Company sent King to England to learn how to be a teacher and missionary at the Methodist-Kingswood School near Bristol. While in England, he wrote his autobiography, which was published in London in 1798, *Memoirs of the Life of Boston King*. King returned to Sierra Leone in 1796 so he could teach reading, writing, and arithmetic to settlers of all ages, and also to act as a missionary to local native peoples. He was sent to the Sherbro people on the coast about 100 miles south of Freetown. While there, he and his second wife both died in 1802. He was survived by two sons and one daughter. A second edition of King's autobiography was published in Canada, *The Life of Boston King, Black Loyalist, Minister, and Master Carpenter*.

This entry was paraphrased from Wikipedia, with geographical and historical additions by the author.

WRITER DIDO ELIZABETH BELLE DAVINIER, *ONCE ENSLAVED*, 1761–1804 (LONDON), LORD MANSFIELD'S UNOFFICIAL SECRETARY.

Dido Elizabeth Belle was born in 1761 in the Caribbean to an enslaved woman and Scottish Captain John Lindsay of the 28-gun Royal Navy frigate *Trent*. When Lindsay returned to England in 1765 after the end of the war, he brought the little girl with him, along with her mother. The story of Belle's beginnings is a trifle murky, but it seems that Lindsay's ship in 1760 captured a French ship transporting slaves to the Caribbean. One of those was 14-year-old Marie Belle, and 24-year-old Lindsay managed to get her pregnant (today, that situation would be characterized as statutory rape, but not so much in 1760).

Not having any closer relatives in England, he asked his uncle William and Aunt Elizabeth (the Earl and Countess of Mansfield) to look after the mother and daughter at their mansion Kenwood House. The following year, the little girl was baptized at the church of St. George's Bloomsbury (5 miles/8 km south of Kenwood). Dido was brought up as an educated woman in tandem with her same-age half-cousin Lady Elizabeth Murray, whose German mother had died. When the two girls were about sixteen years old, the Scottish portrait artist David Martin painted a beautiful double portrait of them (about 1777) in the style of Johann Zoffany, in which neither girl is shown to be in any way inferior to the other. When Dido was thirteen years old in 1774, her father officially set her mother free as a slave and sent her to Pensacola in British West Florida, where he gave her a piece of land that was hers to keep, only provided that she should build a house on it of at least a certain size within ten years. It is worth pointing out that Spain had reconquered both halves of Florida before those ten years had expired.

While Dido was resident in the Murray household, The Earl of Mansfield was the Lord Chief Justice of England, and in 1772 he ruled in favor of James Somersett, a Black slave who wished to be set free so he could not be compelled to return to slavery in the Caribbean. Some people felt that Dido's presence in the household, even though she was just eleven years old, set an example to the Earl showing that this Black girl was every bit the equal of her white half-cousin. Mansfield went to great pains to point out that the Somersett case was a ruling only about this particular Black man, but as a practical matter other people claimed that slavery in England was outlawed from that moment onwards. Only two years after the Somersett ruling, Black businessman Charles Ignatius Sancho became the first Black man ever to vote in a British Parliamentary election.

All that to the contrary notwithstanding, Dido certainly felt the pain of racial discrimination in the home. She was not allowed to take meals with the family (at least when company was being served), and she was not permitted to attend parties and balls at other houses, and yet she was also not permitted to take meals with the servants. She was not even invited to go riding with her uncle if that ride might end in visiting other people, but in evenings when company came for dinner, Dido was encouraged to join the ladies afterwards for coffee. Dido was also given clothing to wear and bedroom furnishings the equal of what were provided her cousin Lady Elizabeth. Dido's financial allowance was, on the other hand, less than one-third of what Lady Elizabeth received.

However, Lord Mansfield (who for whatever reason did not feel welcome to interfere in the domestic arrangements handled by his wife) found that Dido's assistance with his work was essential. He employed her as he would a legal secretary or clerk to take dictation from him, and write his correspondence for him. Nearly every day, he had her on his behalf organize things that he needed, in the same way that a 21st-century executive secretary or executive assistant could be expected to do. Dido also took over the management of the dairy and poultry yards at Kenwood when she was not needed in Mansfield's office.

Life at Kenwood continued much as before for many years, punctuated by major events. First, Lady Mansfield died in April 1784 after a long illness, but her place was soon taken by two aunts. Next, Lady Elizabeth married wealthy George Finch-Hatton and thus moved away from Kenwood. Dido's father, by this time Rear Admiral Sir John Lindsay, died in 1788, without having any legitimate heirs. Lindsay had married Mary Milner in 1768, but their marriage was childless. In his will, he split his estate between two more recent illegitimate children, who had been born of different mothers, John and Elizabeth Lindsay, but strangely left nothing for Dido. Finally, Lord Mansfield himself died in March 1793, and although he left a fortune to Lady Elizabeth, he left a much smaller but useful sum to Dido.

Later that same year, on 5 December 1793, Dido at age 32 married a French resident of London at St. George's, Hanover Square, Jean-Louis Charles Davinier, who worked for many years as a steward or valet to John Craufurd. They had three sons, the twins Charles and John in 1795, and William Thomas in 1802, all baptized at St. George's, Hanover Square. William worked for the East India Company in its London offices, and Charles worked for the same employer in India. Charles became an officer in the British Army in India in 1811, eventually being promoted to Lieutenant-Colonel in the Madras Native Infantry in 1855. Dido died in 1804 at the age of forty-three, only two years after the birth of William. In the same way that a modern executive secretary does not customarily claim credit for important things that he or she may have done for the boss, one should not claim anything of the sort for Dido for having organized the Lord Chief Justice's life and written his correspondence, and yet that is essentially what she did, according to a variety of witnesses. A heavily fictionalized version of Dido's story was made into a motion picture called "Belle" in 2013.

This entry was paraphrased from Wikipedia, with historical additions by the author.

WRITER ROBERT WEDDERBURN/WETHERBURN, *ONCE ENSLAVED*, CA. 1762-CA. 1835 (JAMAICA AND UK) RN

Robert Wedderburn (or Wetherburn, as it was sometimes spelled) was born in Jamaica about 1762. His mother Rosanna was a slave, but his father James was a white medical doctor initially in Kingston, and later the owner-operator of a sugar plantation. Eventually, James returned to Great Britain, but before he departed, he freed Robert and his older brother, also named James. James I had also fathered several other children by a variety of Black slave women. James I had a white heir in Britain named Andrew Colville, whose own paternity was obviously open to question, so Andrew wrote in the British press, presumably in self-defense, that these two Black men were not related to James I, and for good measure he wrote nasty things about Rosanna. Rosanna, for her part, had a "violent and rebellious temper," so she was sold away to another plantation, and Robert had to be raised by his maternal grandmother, who went by the name of Talkee Amy. Although his father complained probably justifiably that Robert was incredibly lazy, it is evident that Robert was as properly educated as it was possible to be in Jamaica at that time.

Robert enlisted in the Royal Navy at age 16 in the middle of the American Revolution. He thought that living conditions and food in the Navy were dreadful, so when he found his ship moored in England in 1779, he badgered the captain into letting him resign from the Navy (which was quite a feat to bring off in the middle of wartime!), and he settled in the neighborhood in London around the elegant church of St Giles-in-the Fields. This was a particularly diverse neighborhood, home to people from every corner of the British Empire. It is said that he was not beyond being involved in petty theft, but he also apprenticed himself to a tailor in order to learn a useful trade. It was indeed a trade from which he could find employment anywhere at any time. After a few years, he became a journeyman tailor, which means that he was accomplished enough to open his own shop, but not enough to teach others.

After a time, Robert was married, and his wife was pregnant, but the national economy after the American Revolution caused marginal people like Robert to be thrown out of work. Therefore, he travelled to Inveresk, Scotland, to ask his father's family for financial help, but other than the cook serving him a mug of beer and a footman giving him one coin, he received nothing. Back in London, he fell into petty theft, and even had a stint at running a brothel (brothels in those days were equally as illegal as theft).

Robert was walking through the district known as Seven Dials (not far from St Giles) in 1786 when he heard a Wesleyan preacher talking. As a result, he became a Methodist. With the enthusiasm that often accompanies a recent conversion, Robert wrote and managed to get published a tract called *Truth Self Supported: or, a Refutation of Certain Doctrinal Errors Generally Adopted in the Christian Church.* The little book contains no mention of slavery, but in its flavor, it suggests that Robert had a subversive and radical attitude towards religion and politics.

Robert was influenced by William Wilberforce in his drive to eliminate slavery; he was influenced by Robert Owen in the area of social reform, and he was influenced by the radical Thomas Spence in the areas of land reform and the equality of the sexes. Well-known caricaturist

George Cruikshank issued two engravings that depicted Robert Wedderburn, one in 1817 showing him with rapt attention to a speech by Robert Owen at the City of London Tavern, and one in 1819, thought to be showing him making a speech of his own at the New Union Club. After the official leaders of the Spencean Society were arrested on a charge of high treason, Robert became the new leader of the club. He published fierce tracts in favor of a republican, possibly violent, revolution to redistribute property, both in Britain and in the British Caribbean Islands. A book he wrote in 1824 with the help of George Cannon was published by William Dugdale, *The Horrors of Slavery*, exactly a decade before the British ended slavery for good in their Caribbean Islands. It should be noted that this was the era in which the absurdity of the House of Commons having half its members elected by districts that had only one or two voters was being widely pointed out. A petition signed by 750,000 citizens asking for parliamentary reform was rejected out of hand by the House of Commons. The climax of the moment was the so-called Peterloo Massacre in Manchester in 1819 (only four years after Napoleon had been defeated at Waterloo), in which 60,000+ peaceable and unarmed demonstrators were charged by cavalry and other military units, resulting in at least 18 dead and perhaps 600 seriously wounded. The military, it seems, had decided in advance to strike the women demonstrators with the most fury so as to teach them a lesson; it was one thing that qualified Blacks were allowed to vote in Parliamentary elections from 1774 on, but it was completely unthinkable that women should ever be granted the right to vote or to hold office! It is not clear whether Robert personally participated at Peterloo, but his close associates did so.

Robert's radical political views were foremost in his head, but he still worked at developing his religious views, which continued to evolve. By this time, he had become a Unitarian, so he opened a Unitarian chapel on Hopkins Street in Soho (a district close to St Giles). After that, he started to question all Christian ideas, and became a Deist or a Free-thinker. In this, he was influenced by Richard Carlile, the Free-thinker, who had been one of the organizers of the demonstration at Peterloo, Manchester.

All the political, social, and religious activism was useful in its way, but Robert also continued various illegal activities, including petty theft, and running a brothel, so he was forced to serve at least two terms in prison, one in Dorset, and another at the Giltspur Street gaol in the City (perhaps a mile or two from St Giles). The Giltspur Street institution was normally for debtors, but in this case, when Robert was 68 years old, it was for "theft, blasphemy, and keeping a bawdy house."

When he was released about two years later, Robert sailed to New York City, but while he was there, he was involved in a case of fraud, and the New York *Evening Star* of 6 January 1834 described him as "a tailor and breeches maker, field preacher, anti-bank deposit politician, romance writer, circulating librarian, and ambulating dealer in drugs, deism, and demoralization in general." He returned to London immediately, where he was recorded as present in a chapel service in March, the last reference known to his life.

This entry was paraphrased from Wikipedia, with historical additions by the author.

BUSINESSMAN JAMES FORTEN, *FREE BLACK*, 1766–1842 (PHILADELPHIA AND UK)

James Forten was born free on 2 September 1766 in Philadelphia, one of two children. His father was a sailmaker, who unfortunately died in an accident when the boy was about six. James started to work to help his mother and sister, his first job being a chimney sweep. He attended the free African school run by the Quakers. His mother wanted him to continue in school, but he left so that he could work full-time.

In 1781, he signed on in the crew of the brand-new Pennsylvania Navy 24-gun frigate *Royal Louis* under Rhode Island Captain Stephen Decatur I. The first cruise was successful, netting the lad some prize money to share with his family, but on the second cruise they encountered the British 32-gun frigate *Active*. After most of the American ship's cannon crews had been killed or wounded, the ship was forced to surrender. British Captain John Beazley kindly offered James the chance to be educated in England alongside his own son Henry, but James said, "I have been taken prisoner for the liberties of my country, and never will prove a traitor to her interest." So, instead, James was made to suffer imprisonment aboard the infamous prison-ship *Jersey*, moored off the Brooklyn shore in New York Harbor.

After seven months, James was freed on a prisoner exchange, in which he promised not to fight for the rest of the war. He walked back to Philadelphia to the delight of his mother and sister. He signed on in the crew of a merchant ship, which was one of the first American ships to trade with Britain at the end of the war. He spent more than a year working in a British shipyard, before returning to Philadelphia in 1790. There, he began an apprenticeship with sail-maker Robert Bridges, who had been his father's employer and a family friend. He was so adept that he was quickly promoted to foreman. When Bridges retired in 1798, James was in a position to purchase the business. He invented a tool for man-handling the large sails around the loft, so that by 1810 James had built up one of the most successful sail-lofts in all of North America, and he became one of the wealthiest residents of Philadelphia, Black or white.

James was married twice. His first wife, Martha Beatty, died in 1804 after only a few months of marriage. The second in 1806 was Charlotte Van Dine (Duyne?), who bore him nine children. All were well educated, and all were active abolitionists. James was additionally active in concerns of Black adults, namely that they were generally not permitted to vote, nor to serve on juries. He watched many Blacks being caught up in the movement to resettle in Sierra Leone, or later in Liberia, or in Haiti, but he became opposed to such movements, saying that if the United States were run properly in accord with its founding principles there would be no need for Black people to leave. He worked closely with Bishop Richard Allen of the African Methodist Episcopal Church that had been founded in Philadelphia, and at a large meeting of 3000 men hosted by that church they voted unanimously against overseas colonization. Word of that vote was quickly spread with great effect to politicians up and down the coast.

This entry was paraphrased from Wikipedia, with naval and historical additions by the author.

BUSINESSMAN, PHILANTHROPIST PIERRE TOUSSAINT, *ONCE ENSLAVED*, 1766–1853 (HAITI, NEW YORK)

Pierre was born into slavery in 1766 in Haiti. His mother was Ursule, and they lived on the Artibonite Plantation, near Saint-Marc on the west coast, that belonged to the Berard family. His father's name is not known. He was raised as a Roman Catholic. Pierre was educated by the Berard family tutors, and his job was a house-slave.

The senior Berards returned to France, taking Pierre with them, and leaving the plantation in the hands of their son Jean. As it appeared that the French Revolution was brewing, Jean Berard and his second wife moved to New York City in 1797, taking Pierre and his sister Rosalie and three other slaves with them.

In New York, Jean Berard arranged for Pierre to be apprenticed to one of New York's leading hairdressers. Then Berard returned to Haiti, where he died of pleurisy. Meanwhile, Pierre was becoming very successful as a hairdresser, so he voluntarily took on the support of Madame Berard, now that no further money was coming from Haiti. She married another refugee from Haiti, Monsieur Nicolas. On her deathbed, she made her husband swear he would free Pierre. Pierre had been so impressed by one Haitian leader, Toussaint, that he adopted that as his last name.

Toussaint made so much money from his hairdressing business that he was able to buy his sister Rosalie's freedom. They both still lived in the same house, which was by then called the Nicolas House. Toussaint was awarded his freedom in 1807.

Toussant had connections in the French émigré community in New York, and he met people who knew the Berards in Paris. They began writing letters back and forth, particularly Aurora Berard, his godmother. It turned out that the Berards had lost their entire fortune during the French Revolution. Aurora's father had died in prison, and her mother died shortly afterwards. Her siblings had married in France. Toussaint also corresponded with friends in Haiti.

In August 1811, Toussaint married Juliette Noel after first purchasing her freedom. She was twenty years younger than he. For four years, they continued to live at the Nicolas House, paying rent. His sister Rosalie unfortunately died of tuberculosis, so Toussaint and his wife took in Rosalie's daughter Euphemia and adopted her. They made sure that she was fully educated and that they paid for her music lessons. Euphemia died young of tuberculosis. Juliette died in 1851, and Toussaint died in 1853 at age 87. They had moved for a while into the southern United States.

Toussaint had made a habit of charity among the poor of New York, and he was particularly good at helping new immigrants because he spoke excellent English and French. He even was noticed for crossing barricades to nurse cholera patients during a quarantine. As a result, the Roman Catholic Church started to take the steps necessary for declaring him a saint, a process that is on-going.

This entry was paraphrased from Wikipedia with historical additions by the author.

WRITER OMAR 'MORRO' 'PRINCE OMEROH' IBN SA'ID, *ENSLAVED*, CA. 1770–1864 (SENEGAL, SC, NC)

Omar ibn Sa'id was born about 1770 in a wealthy inland family in what later became known as three separate countries, Senegal, Mauritania, and Mali, somewhere along the river that forms the boundaries between those countries. Omar was given the life of an Islamic scholar, studying for 25 years with leading Muslim teachers. He became well-versed in writing, mathematics, astronomy, theology, and business. Without any warning, his region became embroiled in one of Africa's frequent conflicts, and Omar was made a prisoner of war. In 1807, he was sold as a slave, and shipped across the Atlantic to Charleston, South Carolina. There, he was purchased by a man for whom Omar had no respect, and Omar observed that the man seemed to respect no one, but behaved cruelly to his slaves.

As a result, Omar took with him his few belongings, as well as a sufficient supply of food, and he ran away. He travelled over rudimentary roads about 220 miles to Fayetteville, North Carolina, perhaps planning to travel still further, but he was captured and placed in jail. While he was in the jail, he found a piece of coal, and wrote with it on the wall of his cell an Arabic inscription, which drew the attention of his next owner. He was purchased from the jail by James Owen, whom Omar described as gracious. The Owen family were impressed at Omar's advanced education, and they took the trouble to provide him with an English translation of the Qur'an.

The poet Francis Scott Key, who had recently written his poem *The Star-Spangled Banner* in 1813, heard about Omar, and sent him an Arabic translation of the Bible, which Omar welcomed. All Muslim scholars at that time revered and studied extensively the Old Testament. They also revered the parts of the New Testament that describe Jesus (Issah in Arabic) as important to Muslims, because they regarded Jesus as second only to Mohammad as an Islamic prophet. More than a few North Carolina residents attempted to convert Omar to Christianity, and some even believed that they had succeeded, but Omar's own writings contradict that theory. Omar was given several opportunities to return to his home in Africa, but he declined to accept the offers, because he said that he feared that it would be impossible to find his family, if indeed there were any members left alive.

Having both the Bible and the Qur'an in both Arabic and English no doubt facilitated Omar's learning to write and to speak English, but when he wrote essays, he wrote all fourteen of them in Arabic. Perhaps his most significant writing is an 1831 account of his life, *The Life of Omar ben Saeed, called Morro, a Fullah slave in Fayetteville, N.C. Owned by Governor Owen.* This document begins with a quotation from the Qur'an that claims that God alone (and not other humans) may own humans. Then it continues, describing some of the events of his life. He was always generous-spirited in describing the Owen family. While he claimed that he was always a steadfast Muslim, he was also appreciative of other God-fearing people. This is the only known American slave narrative written in Arabic, and it has belonged to the Library of Congress since 2017. It has recently been translated into English.

Omar's other writings mostly deal with Islamic topics, and most of them can be seen in the North Carolina Collection in the Wilson Library at the University of North Carolina at Chale Hill. Omar also wrote a wide-ranging letter in Arabic to Major John Owen in 1819, brother of James Owen, and this is in the collections of the Andover-Newton Theological Seminary at Newton Centre, Massachusetts. The Islamic Mosque in Fayetteville renamed itself in 1991 in honor of Omar: Masjid Omar ibn Sayyid. Inspired by the experiences of Omar, Rhiannon Giddens and Michael Abels wrote an opera, *Omar*, which had its first performance at the Spoleto Festival at Charleston SC in May 2022, and won the Pulitzer Prize for Music in 2023. Omar was still technically enslaved at the time of his death in his mid-nineties in 1864 in Bladen County NC.

This entry was paraphrased from Wikipedia with historical additions by the author.

WRITER JOHN JEA, *ONCE ENSLAVED*, 1773-AFTER 1817 (NIGERIA, NEW YORK, BOSTON, NEW ORLEANS, SOUTH AMERICA, UK)

John Jea was born in Nigeria in 1773 to parents Hambleton Robert Jea and Margaret Jea. When he was only 2 ½ years old, his entire family was kidnapped by a marauding band of tribesmen, and sold into slavery. They were taken to New York City, where they were purchased by a Dutch couple, Oliver and Angelika Triebuen. The Triebuens were very conservative members of the Dutch Reformed Church. They did not believe in introducing slaves to Christianity, but rather saw sentencing the children to attend church services was a useful punishment for bad behavior. As a result, John Jea conceived an initial hatred for Christianity.

However, as a teenager, Jea suddenly embraced Christianity, finding in it grounds to accuse his enslavers of gross hypocrisy. His master told him that Black people have no souls, and that he would die "like the beasts that perish." Although he saw himself as "treated worse than a beast of burden," he publicly thanked God for blessings received. Triebuen gratefully sold Jea to another owner, and he was sold several other times in quick succession. He finally convinced the last owner to free him for being such a devoted Christian. He thought that his literacy had been a major factor in his emancipation, and tried to convince other slaves to become literate.

In the 1790s, Jea began a series of voyages to Boston, New Jersey, New Orleans, and South America, and he preached the Gospel everywhere he went. He fathered a child by a Native American woman named Elizabeth, but before he could actually marry her, she was executed for having murdered her child, or at least that is how the story was told to Jea. His next attempt at matrimony involved a Maltese woman named Charity, but she died only a short time later.

From 1801 to 1805, he was living in Liverpool, England. He used a Methodist style of preaching, but was careful not to say much about the evils of slavery in a city that had made so much money out of the slave trade. Then he took a job as a cook aboard a series of ships sailing around the coasts of North America, the Caribbean, South America, even as far away as [modern] Indonesia, and Ireland. While he was in Britain, he ventured into publishing. In 1816, he published his autobiography, *The Life, History, and Unparalleled Sufferings of John Jea, the African Preacher.* At about the same time, he also published a hymnbook, *A Collection of Hymns, Compiled and Selected by John Jea, African Preacher of the Gospel,* 1816. It contains 334 hymn texts, including no fewer than 29 written by Jea himself. The hymnbook, of course, contains no musical notations.

This entry was paraphrased from Wikipedia, with historical and geographical additions by the author.

ACTOR WILLIAM 'BILLY' WATERS CA. 1774–1823
(NEW YORK AND LONDON) RN

William 'Billy' Waters was born in New York City about 1774. The identities of his parents are not recorded, so it is not known whether he was Black or of mixed race. John Murray the Earl of Dunmore was the last royal governor of Virginia, and he was often regarded as somewhat of a fool. However, Dunmore, who saw his standing in Virginia fast eroding due to the greed of the Virginia tobacco planters for additional land (tobacco ruins the soil it is planted in, and so every eight years, planters had to move further west, but Dunmore was ordered by London not to allow the planters to seize Ohio because that land belonged to the Indigenous people), issued a brilliant decree. All the slaves of Virginia planters could gain their freedom, originally by signing up to fight in his army, and a few days later he changed it to merely by registering with him at his new capital city of Norfolk, Virginia. Thousands of Blacks presented themselves in short order. He could not house them ashore because the planters would simply send an army to reclaim them, so he rented an increasing number of merchant ships anchored in the harbor. Unfortunately, some of the slaves brought smallpox with them aboard the ships, and perhaps half of the Blacks died of that disease. On New Year's Eve 1775–6, the planters burned Norfolk to the ground, sparing only the hospital – even all the churches were deliberately destroyed, and the planters publicly blamed Dunmore for the fire. Dunmore therefore felt obliged to sail his fleet to Halifax, Nova Scotia. After that point, the slaves who were resident in every North American city or town occupied by British forces (Boston, Newport, New York, Perth Amboy, Philadelphia, Wilmington NC, Charleston, Savannah, and Saint Augustine) were awarded their freedom and transported to Halifax when the British evacuated those cities. Some of the Blacks remained in Canada, and some moved to Great Britain, but others persuaded the British government to establish a new colony especially for freed slaves at Sierra Leone, West Africa, with its new capital city of Freetown.

Therefore, thanks to the example set somewhat accidentally by Dunmore, we can be reasonably sure that William and his parents and any siblings sailed from New York between August and November 1783, when the British evacuated that city. The family stopped briefly in Halifax, Nova Scotia before sailing on to Great Britain. Most Blacks in Britain lived in London. William would have been nine years old at that time, and it is likely that he had received a more or less adequate education in New York. When William was about 16, if it had not happened before that age, he would have been ordered to find employment. It is likely that his voyage to Nova Scotia and the second voyage to England made a good impression on the lad, so that when he had to find a job, he found it presumably with the British East India Company. The East India Company sailed ships back and forth between London and Bombay or Madras or Calcutta, India, or Canton, China, or Bengkulu in modern-day Indonesia. Their ships resembled 36-gun frigates, but with blunter bows and a high stern. The ships carried both cargo and passengers. The wealthier passengers, mindful of their comfort under the tropical sun, invented the word POSH, meaning the most expensive cabins were on the *port* side going *out* and *starboard* side going *home*, and thus less broiled by the tropical sun. There is no proof that William was employed by the East India Company, but on balance it seems very likely.

No one knows if William was present at the Battle of Pulo Aura, near Malacca on 14–15 February 1804, but it formed a delicious story, and it seems likely that he was there. French Rear Admiral Charles-Alexandre de Linois had been sent with his 74-gun flagship *Marengo* and several heavy frigates, in order to inflict maximum damage on armed merchant ships of the British East India Company, because huge fortunes gained by the trade of the EIC were contributing mightily to the British Treasury's contribution towards beating Napoleon. The East India Company ships, in turn, gathered in a single large convoy once a year, and Royal Navy battleships normally arrived to guard them. In this case, the Royal Navy ships had been delayed in the Atlantic and were not going to arrive in time to guard the convoy, so the convoy of sixteen East Indiamen from Canton, China, plus fourteen smaller merchant ships, departed for India on their way back to England. They were loosely commanded by Commodore (honorary title, but with no actual authority) Nathaniel Dance, when they spotted Linois' squadron heading for them. In retrospect, it seems that Dance had fore-knowledge that Linois would be lying in wait for the merchant ships, so he conceived a clever plan for dealing with the French, and somehow persuaded the normally recalcitrant merchant captains to play along. It was obvious that even though Linois' squadron was not large, yet he still had a strong advantage over the British fleet and could potentially capture most or even all of them.

Dance spread the word around his convoy that some of his larger East Indiamen were to fly the Royal Navy's blue ensigns and otherwise pretend to be British Navy battleships, and they were instructed to follow his orders with the kind of precision expected of Royal Navy ships. Dance ordered his ships to open fire at long distance (so that Linois would not be able to discern that the cannons in question were pitifully small), and Linois lost his nerve when he saw those ships tacking with apparent precision. Linois fled back to the French Island of Mauritius, claiming that he could see that the British fleet contained at least eight powerful battleships. Linois soon became the laughing-stock of the Indian Ocean because he had retreated in the face of determined but weak merchant ships, and Napoleon was outraged when he heard of it. When Linois was captured in the Atlantic on his way home, Napoleon refused to include him in any prisoner exchange, so he remained a British prisoner for ten years until Napoleon went into exile temporarily in Elba. If William had taken part in that operation against Linois, he no doubt could have dined out on telling that story for years.

If William had been fortunate enough to secure permanent employment with the Honorable East India Company, he could have been comfortable for the rest of his life. However, the first recorded moment of his life that comes to our attention is when he, most likely motivated by patriotism, volunteered to enlist in the British Navy aboard the receiving ship, the 32-gun frigate *Ceres*, on 5 October 1811, anchored at the Nore (not far from London). He is clearly not the same mulatto William Waters, who registered at age 29 in Philadelphia in 1798 for an American sailor's Protection Certificate. On 23 November, he was placed briefly aboard the elderly 74-gun battleship *Namur*, which had recently been cut down a whole deck from having once been a 90-gun three-decker, and was presently serving as a 70-gun floating dormitory. On 9 December, he was transferred into the crew of the 28-gun frigate *Ganymede* under Captain John Brett Purves. The frigate was sailed to the naval base at Plymouth, *en route* for Gibraltar and Cadiz, Spain (this was a rare moment in which Spain and Great Britain were on the same side in the war against Napoleon).

On 2 January 1812, about nine weeks after he had enlisted, William was promoted to petty officer as a quarter-gunner. Enlisted men, particularly those who had enlisted less than three months earlier, were almost never promoted to petty officer without good reason. The good reason in this case was no doubt his presumed lengthy and exemplary service in ships of the East India Company, perhaps even including participation as a gunner in the Battle of Pulo Aura.

Two months later, on 3 March, the frigate was going through sail-handling drills, and William slipped and fell from the main topsail yard, which would have meant a minimum distance to the quarterdeck of 55 feet (almost 17 metres), enough to kill most people. In the case of William, it broke both his legs (the left with a compound fracture, and the right with a simple break), as well as various unspecified internal injuries. He was whisked below to the tender mercies of the ship's surgeon and the loblolly boys (whose job was to hold him down while the surgeon made his cuts and amputations). The surgeon, Felix Delany, who seems to have been at the top of his profession, decided to cut off William's left leg just below the knee, but to immobilize the broken right leg so that it could recover. Other than administering occasional tots of rum, the surgeon was able to do little to dull the pain. Some five weeks later on 7 April, the frigate delivered William to Haslar Royal Naval Hospital near Portsmouth (the hospital was finally closed in 2009, and is now available to the public with apartments for rent). At the time that it was built in the 1750s, Haslar was the largest brick building in all of Europe. It could accommodate 2000 patients, but in this war typically it held about 400 at any given time. William was fitted for a wooden leg, taught how to use it, and was then discharged into the world on 26 May, fewer than 50 days after he had arrived at the hospital and only eleven weeks after the accident – nowhere near enough time for the damage to have been healed. Sometimes, former seamen with a wooden leg were hired to serve as cooks on warships, but William presumably did not see that as one of his skill-sets. Instead, he had to make do with a skimpy pension of twenty pounds per year, which was clearly nowhere near enough on which to live.

Luckily, he had learned a variety of sailors' songs in his years of sailing on East India Company ships, and so he dressed himself in a seaman's easily recognizable outfit of blue coat, waistcoat, and vertically striped trousers, with an outrageous Napoleon-style hat decorated with three ostrich feathers, over a judge's full-bottom wig, so that he could be instantly identifiable on the streets of his part of London (near the elegant St Giles-in-the-Fields), or in the Great Rooms of taverns and clubs, or outside theatres, such as the Adelphi. Out of all the busking musicians, William made the greatest impression, and many portraits of him in action were made, some original artwork, and some engravings by the likes of the Cruikshank brothers. Some of them reveal that he carried an old hat attached to his arm, into which audience-members were encouraged to contribute money or tips. For a time, he was known as King of the Beggars.

Sailors who played musical instruments were more sought after than others, and it is likely that William had learned to play the fiddle during his service with the East India Company or perhaps even earlier as a boy. Almost all the depictions of him show him playing the fiddle, except for one showing him playing the flageolet (a glorified, more sophisticated version of the penny-whistle). Sometimes he played in small bands with other musicians, but usually he played alone.

Musicologists have pointed out for years that many sailors' songs and all sea chanteys have the familiar call-and-response format well known in the songs of West Africa, and some scholars have made the leap to saying that the sea chantey was therefore invented and born in West Africa. To my mind, it is a question of 'both-and.' In other words, sea chanteys were developed at least as early as the construction of one of the largest medieval warships, Henry V's ship *Grace Dieu*, launched in 1418. A chantey used in operating her had one response line as 'With a rumble-O,' doubtless referring to the rumble noise made by pairs of giant triple blocks in the main halyard, and its other response line as 'With a heave a-low,' referring to numbers of sailors heaving down towards the deck the tail rope of the halyard. Surely, there were not enough Black people living in England in 1418 to have had any influence on the structure of that particular chantey.

Of all the songs that William sang, one was his signature tune, *Polly, will you marry me?* So far, the words and the tune have not been identified, even though he apparently sang that song everywhere that he went. It is most likely that he invented both. Polly, of course, is the diminutive of the names Pauline or Paulette. Some of the most popular sailors' songs of the period include the following: William Boyce's *Come, cheer up, me lads, tis to glory we steer,* and *The Sailors' Christmas Day;* and four songs by Thomas Arne: *Rule Britannia; It was pleasant and delightful on that midsummer's morn; When Sally was a young lass, a pretty little thing, she listed in the Navy for to serve the King;* and *There was a jolly sailor once worked on the foaming sea;* five songs by opera composer Charles Dibdin I: *Tom Bowling; Outward Bound; The East Indiaman; Poll & my partner Joe;* and *Strike the bell, second mate;* and George Frederick Handel's *Drink old England dry;* and *Lord Anson Forever; The Midwatch* with words by Sheridan and tune by Thomas Linley II (Mozart's best friend, who tragically died at age 22 in a boating accident); *The Naval Pace-egging song,* attributed to Linley (with a chorus: *Here's a lass and three jolly lads all in one mind*); Henry Purcell's song, *Britons strike home* was also popular, even though over a century old; William probably sang with gusto the short song, *Come all you bold seamen, wherever you're bound, and always let Anson's proud memory go round*, although many singers, reflecting on the recent death of Nelson, substituted Nelson for Anson. The pirate dirge *My name is Captain Kidd as I sailed, as I sailed*, by Jeremiah Clarke (the same tune was re-used years later for the church hymn, *What wondrous love is this, O my soul, O my soul?*), and *Well done, Jack*, attributed to Maurice Greene; many popular naval folksongs are anonymous, including *Queer bung-your-eye; Spanish Ladies; All things were quite silent; Jack Tar and the press gang; On board of a man of war; On board a Ninety-eight; A topman and an afterguard; Yon Johnnie was a shoemaker; My son John was tall and trim, and he had a leg for every limb; Johnnie Todd he took a notion; From Boston Harbour we set sail; Sam's gone away aboard a man of war; The Anti-Gallican privateer; The Tiger privateer; The female captain; The female rambling sailor; The handsome cabin boy; The rolling sailor; The rambling sailor; The jolly roving tar; The saucy sailor; Don't forget your old shipmates; Lovely on the water; The Maid of Amsterdam; The Morning Glory; Come, my own one; Fare thee well, my dearest Nancy; Adieu, sweet lovely Nancy; Pretty Nancy of Yarmouth; The Gauger* (Customs & Excise officer) and *My Polly on the shore*. William most likely did not sing chanteys because chanteys were normally banned in the Navy and on East Indiamen (chanteys could drown out officers' orders at a crucial moment), and for that reason there were very few chanteys used anywhere before 1815, as they are generally not needed aboard small merchant ships. The army had at least two songs that were fun to sing, so William probably sang them as well. A well-known recruiting song from a century earlier was *A gay fusilier went-a-marching down through Rochester*, attributed to Jeremiah Clarke (the tune was later robbed by the Australians for *Waltzing Matilda*). Another popular army song from the same period was *Over the hills and far away*. At Christmas-time, he likely added to his repertoire the nonsense song *The Derby Ram* [Derby, by the way, is pronounced 'Darby'], which begins "As I was going to Derby all on a Christmas Day," because it includes a verse about the wool from this giant ram being used to produce new clothes for all the Royal Navy sailors based at Portsmouth.

The frigate *Ganymede* was too small to be required to have a chaplain aboard, but most East Indiamen were large enough to require a chaplain under British law, so it is likely that the crew sang hymns on those ships. One hymn tune from the Methodists about 1790 was a major favorite with the sailors. The tune was called *Cranbrook*, written in the style of Charles Dibdin by Thomas Clark, and it was used to accompany words in Common Measure, such as *While shepherds watched their flocks by night*. That same tune was later used for the nineteenth-century Yorkshire dialect song *On Ilkley Moor bar t'hat*. It is possible to imagine William singing hymns to that tune on Sundays, whether in the streets or in taverns. Some observers wondered how appropriate it was for sailors to sing such hymns only a day after singing off-color songs in the evening, but the late Reverend John Wesley had publicly asked, "Why let the devil have all the good tunes?"

Depending on his audience, William undoubtedly sang sailors' songs that would not have been performed in a concert hall or a genteel living-room accompanied on a harpsichord, such as *The Saucy Little Trim-rigged Doxie*, and *While Cruising Round Yarmouth One Day for a Spree*.

While William sang many songs in his efforts to make money, and presumably told tall tales about his life at sea, he also played his fiddle, and sometimes a flageolet (a type of thin, longways flute). He no doubt played popular English Country Dance tunes, such as *Jackey Tarr; The Sailor's Wife Jig; Devil among the Tailors; Flowers of Edinburgh; The College Hornpipe; Lord Howe's Hornpipe* (since Americans were technically fighting for independence against Admiral Lord Howe, they re-named that dance and tune *Fisher's Hornpipe*, and the American name stuck); *The Dressed Ship; The New-Rigged Ship; Well Done, Jack* (with its powerful, ironic naval words); *Lilli Burlero; The Siege of Limerick*; and a handful of dances with tunes by Handel: *Barberini's Tambourine; Elverton Grove; Lord Anson Forever; Prince William; The Rakes of Rochester*; and *Sun Assembly*. While playing the fiddle, he also danced, something that is difficult enough for people with two legs, let alone one peg leg. Nearly all the portraits show him dancing.

It is likely that Waters played one dance from the 1720s with ironic intent, *Elephant's Stairs*, with a lovely tune attributed to Handel. The Royal African Company, for many years the monopoly responsible for transporting enslaved Africans to various places in the Americas, had its principal offices on the south side of the Thames in Southwark, just across from St Paul's Cathedral in London. The symbol of the Royal African Company was an African elephant with a Howdah or castle sitting on top. That part of London is still known as Elephant & Castle (most visibly through the name of a Tube stop and a pub), and Elephant's Stairs is simply the name of the steps leading down to the Thames in that part of Southwark so you can take an oared ferry over to London. In the twenty-first century, that symbolism is mostly lost, even though the steps are still in place, but many people would have understood it in Waters's day. Black members of the audience may also have requested dances whose tunes were written by Black composers, including *Strawberries & Cream* by Charles Ignatius Sancho of London (the first Black man to cast a vote in a Parliamentary election); *The Saint-George* by Joseph Bologne Chevalier de Saint-Georges of Paris; and *Bill of Rights*, by Newport Gardner, an impressive slave who was a school-teacher in Newport, Rhode Island.

William was so recognizable that he began to be parodied in theatres, which in turn encouraged him to perform outside the Adelphi. The long-running stage production there (for 1000 performances) was known as *Tom & Jerry*, written by William Moncrieff. William the sailor himself was parodied and played by a white actor in black-face, who was undoubtedly well paid by William's standards, while William derived no financial return from it at all.

William, according to skimpy records, was married to a woman named Elizabeth (no idea if she were Black or white), and they had both a daughter and a son. It is not clear whether they were married before he enlisted in the Navy, or sometime after. The family is believed to have lived on Dyott Street, not far from the British Library & Museum. However, William's high-energy performances failed to bring in enough money to keep the family out of poverty, and when he fell ill in 1823, he had to be taken in by the St Giles workhouse, once located at the corner of Shorts Gardens and Endell Street. He died there about 21 March 1823, a little under 50 years old, and his widow was permitted to pick up his slim pension.

The same people who had made so much money, making parodies of William's performances (while paying him nothing), wrote and published a song that claimed to be his Last Will & Testament. Some of those parody plays (and possibly even this song), incidentally, even made it as far as New York City, where it is likely that no one had any memory that New York had been William's birthplace.

WILLIAM WATERS'S LAST WILL AND TESTAMENT

Master William Waters-O, a minstrel of the Holy Land,

Well known among my betters-O, and at the Adelphi and the Strand;

Convinced that death will soon me call, this day for my old Poll I've sent,

And in the presence of them all I thus make my Will & Testament.

I do declare with my last breath, and sign it in plain black and white,

That Tom & Jerry's sudden death has poor Black Billy killed outright.

And when that Billy's dead and gone, I hope his friends will not be slack

About his death to make a song, and hang St Giles's Church in black.

Now, I do advise my little son, if he should live to be a man,

To do just as his daddy's done and drink good gin whene'er he can.

To the British Museum I bequeath my smart cocked hat and feathers three,

And hope that fame they will receive as poor Black Billy's legacy.

Next, to the Adelphi I bequeath my Fiddle, which may be worth a groat,

And unto Dusty Bob I leave my jacket for to mend his coat.

Unto Bob Logic, that rum swell, I do present my timber toe,

In hopes that he will hand it well in flooring of the charlies-O.

I do bequeath unto Black Sal one penny for to buy a bun,

Likewise my shirt, so full of holes – a flea thereon he could not run.

My trowsers (tho' not worth a pin) by public auction shall be sold

All for to buy a drop of gin to warm her heart when it is cold.

Thus, poor Black Billy's made his Will; his property was small good-lack,

For till the day death did him kill, his house he carried on his back.

The Adelphi now may say 'Alas!' and to his memory raise a stone;

Their gold will be exchanged for brass since poor Black Billy's gone.

Professor Mary L. Shannon at Roehampton University in the UK researched the William Waters story as thoroughly as can be done, resulting in the book *Billy Waters is Dancing, or, How a Black Sailor Found Fame in Regency Britain*, Yale University Press, 2024, running to 373 pages. The crowning achievement of the book is perhaps reprinting all the nineteen pieces of period art-work showing William making his music and dancing, including even a twentieth-century miniature ceramic statue. Readers will notice that I have interpreted the scant available evidence about William somewhat differently from Professor Shannon.

This entry was paraphrased from Wikipedia, and the few documented facts of Waters' life as set forth in Professor Shannon's book mentioned above, but with additional historical, geographical, naval, and musical details by the author. The author was further informed by having constructed and operated a full-sized copy of the 24-gun British frigate *Rose* (1756–1779), which had a splendid 16-year sail-training career, followed by starring with Russell Crowe in *Master & Commander: The Far Side of the World*; she is now on permanent display at the Maritime Museum of San Diego. The author also had a many-decades-long career as a professional folk-singer, often with five solo concerts per week, specializing in British Isles sailors' songs of the eighteenth century.

THE REVEREND JOSEPH LEONARD, *FREE BLACK*, FL. 1785 (NOVA SCOTIA & SIERRA LEONE) (ANGLICAN; METHODIST)

With the independence of the United States in 1783, numerous Loyalists felt obligated to move out of the United States. Many of them moved to Nova Scotia, which is geographically close to New England, but is decidedly colder than much of the USA. Quite a few Loyalists landed at Digby, near the Annapolis Valley, and among them were many Blacks, who settled at Brindley Town. Joseph Leonard was a Black who landed at Digby and moved to Brindley Town. No one today knows in which American colony he had originally lived. Leonard had been licensed by officials of the Anglican Church to be a lay preacher, service leader, and school teacher, and he was identified as a leader among the Black community. However, Leonard went way beyond the scope of his license. In the absence of any ordained clergy in the area, he performed marriages, baptisms, and funerals, and even celebrated the Eucharist without having been officially ordained as a priest – perhaps a nod to Martin Luther's pronouncement of the "priesthood of all believers."

Before the Revolution, whenever the Church of England proposed sending one or more bishops to America to ordain additional clergy, Congregationalists, Presbyterians, Baptists, and other "free" churches complained and demonstrated vociferously, so in the interest of keeping the peace, no bishops were ever sent (except two retired bishops, who came of their own accord). Actually, the German-speaking Moravian Church sent bishops in Apostolic Succession to America, who could easily have performed the functions required by the English-speaking church, but for some reason they were never asked to do that. The American successor to the Anglican Church, the Episcopal Church after the Revolution arranged to have American clergy consecrated in Britain, the first being Bishop Samuel Seabury from New England in 1784, followed by William White in Pennsylvania in 1787 and Samuel Provoost in New York in 1787, and James Madison in Virginia in 1790. The British sent Bishop Charles Inglis to Nova Scotia in 1788, and Jacob Mountain to Quebec in 1793, where he made an effort to be on good terms with the Roman Catholic bishop there. The Loyalist settlers, even those belonging to the free churches, apparently did not make any kind of fuss in opposition to these two British bishops being placed in Canada on this side of the Atlantic.

Bishop Inglis had not been in Nova Scotia long before he heard about Joseph Leonard. Inglis travelled to Digby and confronted Leonard, whose reaction was that Inglis ought to ordain him on the spot. Inglis naturally refused, and took away all of Leonard's other privileges, but it soon became very obvious that Leonard was the best man to handle all the jobs he had been doing. Inglis was intelligent enough to reinstate Leonard, except for the items that required ordination.

Soon after this, many of the Blacks in Nova Scotia chose to sail to the new British colony specially created in 1787 in Sierra Leone on the west coast of Africa, with its capital known as Freetown, for former American slaves. Once the majority of his flock had decided to move there, Leonard decided to accompany them. He became a Methodist pastor at some point along the way. He wrote a petition opposed to the firing of school teachers over doctrinal differences. No other record survives to say how long Leonard lived in Sierra Leone or what his achievements were there.

This entry was paraphrased from Wikipedia, with historical and religious details added by the author.

WRITER THE REVEREND ABDUL MASIH, *NATIVE RESIDENT OF INDIA*, 1776–1827 (DELHI AND LUCKNOW) (ANGLICAN)

The Apostle Thomas founded a Christian church at Madras (now called Chennai) about AD 50. None of the Four Canonical Gospels had been written yet, so he wrote his own, which survives in translation to the Pali language (the ancient language of Nepal) at the Buddhist Monastery of Himis at the village of Leh in Ladakh, northern India. Even the Pali translation is an older document than most of the earliest surviving fragments of the four Canonical Gospels of the Christian Bible. Thomas is known to have ordained indigenous women as priests (if it was all right for an Apostle to have done that, why do some churches resist the practice today?). Thomas also ordained local Indian men of color, and for many centuries indigenous clergy were numerous in what later become the Church of South India. Gradually, that practice was replaced by white missionaries sent out from Europe.

The Jesuits sent many of those missionaries to India, and they had a serious bias when they reached the Portuguese colony of Goa. The Jesuits built some very fine church buildings there in the seventeenth century, but parishes around the periphery were run by indigenous people. Some of them even travelled to Rome and were ordained, which annoyed the Jesuits. One of the first Goan Indigenous priests was the Reverend Matheus de Castro (1594–1679). Another was the Reverend Antonio Joao de Frias (1664–1721) from the village of Talaulim, where the elegant church of 1682–1695 was St Anne's, or Santana as it is popularly spelled. De Frias worked hard to build the Church of Our Lady of Sorrows on the island of Divar, 1699–1710, obviously influenced by the design of Santana. The Reverend Do Rego was born in Neura, close to Talaulim, and was ordained in Lisbon. When he returned to Goa, he had been given an impressive title and the authority that accompanied it, so he was responsible for constructing Santana, although its architect is anonymous. It was clear that Santana was intended to outdo all the Jesuit churches in Goa.

Against this background of Indigenous Roman Catholic priests, Abdul Masih was an Indigenous missionary in India, who was ordained as first a Lutheran pastor and later an Anglican priest. He was also a religious writer. It is often claimed that he was the most influential Indigenous Christian in shaping nineteenth-century Christian missions in India. He was born in Delhi under the name of Sheikh Salih to a devout

Muslim family. While he was young, his father instructed him in both Persian and Arabic. He moved to Lucknow, where he studied and taught, and was greatly respected as a Muslim scholar.

Masih became friends with an East India Company chaplain, the Reverend Henry Martyn, who introduced him to two other Company chaplains, the Reverend David Brown and the Reverend Daniel Corrie. Masih was apparently hooked by listening to Martyn preaching on the Ten Commandments, and then he studied Martyn's Urdu translation of the New Testament. Then, in 1811, he was baptized in the historic St. John's Church, Calcutta by David Brown, and changed his name to Abdul Masih, which means in Arabic, 'Servant of the Messiah.' After eight years of study, he was ordained by Lutheran missionaries in 1819. In 1825, he was ordained in the historic St. John's Church, Calcutta as an Anglican priest by Bishop Reginald Heber, the second native of India to receive that distinction. Heber was extremely impressed with Masih's sincerity, calm, and appearance. Masih travelled around India, preaching and teaching, and winning converts, some among very high-ranking Muslims. He also wrote commentaries on Matthew's Gospel, the Letter to the Romans, and Hebrews. He knew that Bishop Heber had written a number of well-known hymn texts, so he tried his hand at that as well.

He returned home to look after his ill mother, but then he himself caught an illness that stayed with him for several years. Just before his death in 1827, he asked that the fourth chapter of John be read to him, and then requested that some people sing a hymn he had written:

Beloved Saviour, let not me In thy kind heart forgotten be.
Of all that deck the field or bower, Thou art the sweetest, fairest
  flower.
Youth's morn has fled, old age come on, But sin distracts my soul
  alone.
Beloved Saviour, let not me In thy kind heart forgotten be.

This entry was paraphrased from Wikipedia, with historical details added by the author.

WRITER ZAMBA ZEMBOLA, ONCE ENSLAVED, CA. 1780-CA. 1860 (CONGO, SOUTH CAROLINA, UK)

Zamba Zembola claimed to have been born in the Congo about 1780. Experts have not been able to agree as to whether the book he wrote was genuine or a forgery. A certain Graham White wrote that he knew Zamba from the 1820s to the 1840s. Zamba claimed that his father was a regional king, who did business with slave-traders, one of whom was Captain Winton. Winton provided Zamba with at least part of a Western education, and eventually gave him passage aboard one of his slave ships to America. Zamba was at that time a free man, so he recorded the squalid conditions in which the slaves on the ship were kept. Upon his arrival in South Carolina, Zamba was kidnapped and enslaved, and nothing that he could say or do was of any avail to get himself released.

Eventually, he wrote a narrative entitled *The Life and Adventures of Zamba, an African Negro King; and his experience of Slavery in South Carolina*. Zamba worked as a plantation slave in South Carolina for about forty years, which would have brought him to about age sixty, which was past the age at which he could contribute to the positive cash flow of his owner. The narrative came into the hands of Peter Neilson, a Scottish abolitionist, who arranged to have the work published. Immediately, the prestigious magazine, *The Spectator,* claimed that the book was a forgery, and the *Baptist Magazine* agreed, although the *New Monthly Magazine* called the book, "a genuine and interesting sketch of African domestic manners." Some modern writers have claimed that Neilson must have written the book, rather than being simply its editor, and wondered why Neilson had consistently failed to produce Zamba for questioning. Zamba could easily have not been available to the press because he had died in the meantime, or moved back to the Congo. The question of its authenticity will have to remain clouded, but much of the information that it contains has a ring of truth to it, so reference to it is included in this volume.

This entry was paraphrased from Wikipedia.

ACTOR RICHARD POTTER, *FREE BLACK*, 1783–1835 (MASSACHUSETTS, SCOTLAND, & NEW HAMPSHIRE)

Richard Potter was born in Hopkinton, Massachusetts. His parentage seems to have been mostly unknown, but he did attend Hopkinton schools. He sailed to Europe and joined John Rannie, a Scottish ventriloquist and magician. Rannie came to the United States in 1800. Potter toured with Rannie as one of his assistants. In 1811, Rannie returned to

Writers, Poets, Business People, Actors, and Clergy

Scotland, but he encouraged Potter to continue with what he had taught him. Potter joined African Masonic Lodge No. 459, and took part in the establishing of Prince Hall Masonry.

Potter toured the eastern half of the United States. He was so good at acting, ventriloquism, hypnotism, and magic (supposedly the best in the nation) that he made a lot of money, and yet encountered very few incidents of racial discrimination, except for one episode at Mobile, Alabama. In 1808, he married Sally Harris, who is believed to have been a Penobscot Native American (Harris is otherwise a Scottish surname). They had three children. A few years later, he purchased almost 200 acres in Andover, New Hampshire, where he built a modest house of his own design, called Potter Place. The house was later incorporated into a much larger Victorian mansion, which has been interpreted inaccurately by some that the house he designed was big enough to have been called a mansion. They were buried on the estate.

This entry was paraphrased from Wikipedia.

WRITER MARY PRINCE, *ONCE ENSLAVED*, 1788-AFTER 1833 (BERMUDA, TURKS & CAICOS, UK)

Mary Prince was born in Bermuda in 1788, and she was the first Black woman to publish an autobiographical account of her experience as a slave born in the colony of Bermuda. Mary was born in Devonshire Parish (located just east of the main city of Hamilton) to a sawyer named Prince (enslaved to David Trimmingham). Mary's mother was a house slave to Charles Myners. Mary had three younger brothers and two sisters named Hannah and Dinah. When Myners died in 1788, her mother and all the children were acquired by Captain George Darrell, who planned to use all of them as house slaves. Darrell gave Mary and her mother to his daughter, with the idea that Mary should be the companion servant to his young granddaughter Betsey Williams. However, in 1800 at the age of twelve, Mary was sold to Captain John Ingham of Spanish Point. Mary's two sisters were also sold the same day to other owners.

Ingham and his wife were apparently cruel and often lost their tempers. Mary and other slaves were often severely flogged for minor offenses. Ingham sold Mary in 1803 to a man on Grand Turk Island who distributed hot peppers from Mexico. The Turks & Caicos Islands are just north of what is now the Dominican Republic, and east of the Bahamas

Islands. The Bermudians had used the Turks & Caicos Islands for over a hundred years for the extraction of salt from sea water. The production of salt for export in the Turks & Caicos was an important part of the Bermuda economy, but it was very labor-intensive. Salt-raking had initially been performed by white people because Spanish and French raiders were likely to seize Black people. Black people were considered to be valuable property, and so they should not be left where they could be confiscated by raiders. When the threat of confiscation faded away in time, Black people were sent out to do the raking.

Mary had worked in the salt ponds as a child, with the salt water up to her knees, and there were many times where she was forced to rake in the summertime for seventeen hours a day. Generally, though, salt-raking was reserved for men, whereas the women did the packaging of the salt, which was slightly easier work.

Mary was brought back to Bermuda in 1812, because Robert Darrell had moved there with his daughter. Mary related in her book that she was physically abused by Darrell, and forced to bathe him under threat of further beatings. Mary said that she resisted Darrell twice. Once, when he beat his own daughter (which he apparently did frequently) and Mary tried to intervene, and the other time when she had to defend herself after she had dropped a kitchen utensil on the floor. After that, Darrell hired her out as a laundress.

In 1815, Mary was sold again for a fourth time, this time after she had wet her bed. The new owner was John Adams Wood of Antigua. She worked in his household as a domestic servant, but at this time she began to show signs of arthritis, which left her unable to work much of the time. While Woods was away sailing, Mary earned money for herself by taking in washing, and by selling coffee, yams, and other provisions for ships that called at Antigua. While in Antigua, she joined the Moravian Church. She was baptized in the English Church and accepted for communion, but she was afraid to ask Wood for permission to attend church.

Late in 1826, Mary married Daniel James, a formerly enslaved man who had purchased his freedom by saving up money from his work. He worked as a carpenter and a cooper. Mary claimed that she was flogged more frequently after her marriage because Wood and his wife did not want to have a free Black living under their roof.

In 1828, Wood and his family travelled to England in order to visit their son at his school and bring their daughters back to the Caribbean. Mary requested that they take her with them. Mary and the Wood family found that they disagreed more and more often, so four times they told her that she was free to go, but the piece of paper they offered her also said that no one else should ever hire her. She finally did leave them, and she took refuge with the Moravian Church in Hatton Garden (near Holborn in the City of London).

After a while, she began to work for Thomas Pringle, an abolitionist writer. Wood, when asked, refused to free Mary, and yet refused to sell her to anyone else. Various bills submitted to Parliament on Mary's behalf failed to pass. Pringle therefore hired her to work in his own household. Mary, of course, was still not capable of writing English as well as she would like, so Pringle arranged for Susanna Strickland to write down Mary's account of her life. Pringle served as editor, and the book was published in 1831 as *The History of Mary Prince*. The publication occasioned two libel lawsuits, one of which she won, and the other by Wood she lost.

Here is Mary's description of being sold away at an early age:

> *It was night when I reached my new home. The house was large, and built at the bottom of a very high hill, but I could not see much of it that night. I saw too much of it afterwards. The stones and timber were the best things in it. They were not so hard as the hearts of the owners.*

Here is Mary's description of slavery:

> *I have been a slave myself – I know what slaves feel – I can tell by myself what other slaves feel, and by what they have told me. The man that says slaves be quite happy in slavery – that they don't want to be free – that man is either ignorant or a lying person. I never heard a slave say so. I never heard a Buckra [white]man say so, till I heard tell of it in England.*

It seems that Mary never made it back to Antigua and her husband because of the danger that she could have been badly treated by the Wood family.

This entry was paraphrased from Wikipedia, with geographical additions by the author.

5

Military Heroes and Political Leaders

RUSSIAN GENERAL-IN-CHIEF ABRAM PETROVICH GANNIBAL, *ONCE ENSLAVED*, CA. 1695–1781 (CAMEROON, TURKEY, ESTONIA, RUSSIA)

Very little can be accurately known about the birth and early life of Abram. The best evidence shows that he was born in northern Cameroon, not far from Lake Chad, but some people insist that he was born in Sudan or Ethiopia or Eritrea. He was kidnapped as a child and enslaved to Ottoman Turks, and his father (a local chief) is believed to have been killed in trying to prevent the raid on their village by the Ottomans or their allies. Abram stayed in Turkey about one year, serving in the household of Sultan Ahmed III.

The Russian Ambassador to Turkey, Sava Vladislavich-Raguzinsky, had been asked by Tsar Peter the Great to acquire a few "clever little African slaves" for the royal palace in Moscow. Abram found himself ransomed by bribes to the Sultan's viziers and taken to Russia (during a period of time when the Russians and Turks were not at war with each other). When he arrived in Russia in 1704, he was presented as a gift to Tsar Peter the Great, who had just founded his new capital city of St. Petersburg the previous year. Peter freed him, adopted him, and raised him in the court household as the emperor's godson, which also entailed giving him a first-class education. He was baptized in 1705 at St. Paraskeva Church in Vilnius, Lithuania, with Peter as his godfather; he did not know the actual date of his birthday, so he used the date of his baptism as his annual birthday. He soaked up everything that he was taught, including eventually becoming proficient in up to six languages.

Abram was sent to Metz in northeastern France (just south of the Luxembourg border, and east of Reims) in 1717 to further his education. Metz had once been a German town captured by Louis XIV, so it was often involved in various European wars. In 1718, Abram joined the French Army and two years later enrolled at the French artillery academy at La Fere, east of Amiens and north of Soissons-sur-Marne and northeast of Reims. There, he hoped to study military engineering.

At that time, war broke out between France and Spain, and he was promoted to captain in the War of the Quadruple Alliance. He was wounded in the head and taken prisoner by the Spanish. They released him in 1722, so he returned to his studies in Metz. This was the time in which he was so impressed by the story of the Carthaginian-African commander Hannibal (who had cleverly defeated Roman armies at Saguntum, Spain in 218 BCE, then crossed the Alps with the help of African elephants, and badly defeated the Romans at Trebia, Lake Trasimene, and Cannae) that he added Hannibal's name as his own surname. In Russian, the closest transliteration of Hannibal comes out as Gannibal, so that was his new surname.

Abram visited Paris, where he rubbed shoulders with the likes of such Enlightenment luminaries as the Baron de Montesquieu and Francois-Marie Arouet de Voltaire; Voltaire dubbed Gannibal the "dark star of the Enlightenment." The next year, Gannibal returned to Russia, where he worked as an engineer and a mathematics teacher for one of the Tsar's elite guard units.

After the death of Tsar Peter in 1725, Prince Menshikov took power. Menshikov did not like Gannibal, so he exiled him on some pretext to Siberia in 1727. Gannibal travelled to Kazan, then Tobolsk and Irkutsk, and finally to a place far to the east to Selenginsk near the Mongolian border. In 1730, he was pardoned, mostly because the empire felt that his engineering skills were critical, and he completed his service in Siberia in 1733, during which time he had been in charge of several construction projects, including a fortress, and where he officially became a master engineer. In this period (1731), he married his first wife, a Greek woman, Evdokia Dioper, but she had been ordered to marry him for political reasons, and she had no interest in staying faithful to a man whom she despised. She gave birth to a white child, which proved that she had been unfaithful, so he had her put in prison for the next eleven years. Very soon after, he began living with Christina Regina Sioberg (1705–1781), and she produced her first child in 1735. A year later, he married her, even though he had not yet divorced his first wife. The couple had ten children, including a son named Osip, who was the grandfather of the great Russian poet and playwright Alexander Pushkin. Gannibal's eldest son, Ivan, was a talented naval officer, who founded the city of Kherson in southern Ukraine in 1779, and who attained the rank of General-in-Chief. Meanwhile, Gannibal was granted a divorce in 1753, but once he had paid a modest fine, all the children from his second marriage were retroactively deemed legitimate, and were accepted as stalwart members of the court.

Elizabeth became the new Russian ruler in 1741, and she made sure that Gannibal was a prominent member of her court. She made him a major-general, and appointed him superintendent of Tallinn in what is now Estonia for ten years. She gave him an estate called Mikhailovskoye at Pskov, 200 miles southwest of St. Petersburg and 200 miles southeast of Tallinn. The estate had hundreds of serfs to keep things in order for him. She granted him a coat of arms of his own design, featuring an African elephant (as a tribute to the Carthaginian General Hannibal), surrounded by copious military trophies. In 1756, Gannibal was appointed chief military engineer in the Russian army, and three years later he received the title of General-in-Chief. In 1762, Elizabeth died and was replaced by Catherine the Great, so he took that moment to retire to his estate at Pskov, where he lived for almost thirty years, not allowing himself to become involved in all the various political squabbles and wars in which Russia was fighting, in spite of many offers to come out of retirement.

This entry was paraphrased from Wikipedia, with historical and geographical additions by the author.

CLAN MOTHER MOLLY 'KONWATSI'TSIAIENNI' BRANT JOHNSON, *MOHAWK*, 1736–1796 (OHIO, NEW YORK, & ONTARIO)

Molly (sometimes Mary) Brant was most likely born in the Ohio country as a Christian Mohawk, but she was raised and educated at a mission school at Canajoharie on the south bank of the Mohawk River in New York, in the best European tradition. She learned to read and write

English, and do arithmetic. Her Mohawk name is translated as "Someone lends her a flower." The well-known Joseph Brant was either her brother or half-brother, younger than she by seven years. When Molly was a teenager, her mother married a man named Brant, and so both she and her brother took their stepfather's name.

When she was eighteen, she accompanied her stepfather and a delegation of Mohawk leaders to Philadelphia. They intended discussing what to do about fraudulent land sales that had been foisted on the Mohawk. She must have learned a great deal about politicians in that one visit. She probably knew the Northern Indian Agent, Sir William Johnson, Baronet, in the 1740s and 1750s, but it was not until 1759 that they became romantically linked, when she was twenty-three. She bore him the first of nine children in that year. Her most important jobs, of course, were running the household and bringing up her children, but she was also seen as an extremely useful advisor to Johnson. Her children were: Peter Warren Johnson (named after Royal Navy Commodore Warren, who had assisted Massachusetts Governor William Shirley in the American capture of Louisbourg, Nova Scotia in 1745, the operation that successfully prevented the French from executing their careful plan to conquer permanently all of British North America); Peter was killed as a British soldier in 1777 outside Philadelphia; Elizabeth, who married Dr. Robert Kerr; Magdalene, who married John Ferguson; Margaret, who married Captain George Farley; Mary, who never married, Susanna, who married Lieutenant Henry Lemoine; Ann/Nancy, who married Navy Captain Hugh Early; George; and one other who died at birth.

In 1763, the family moved into elegant Johnson Hall at Johnstown, New York, designed by architect Peter Harrison, who was to design many buildings for the Johnson family and for Molly's brother Joseph. The house was actually built out of wood carved to look like cut stone (and it is still open to the public in the warmer months of the year), but just in case of some kind of trouble on the frontier the house has a pair of stone blockhouses where people could take refuge from any enemies. Johnson Hall soon became a popular meeting place for Mohawk and other Iroquois, and Molly, of course, as a Clan Mother was the hostess in charge of entertaining the guests. She could not help learning about the delicate balance of power on the frontier. Molly and her brother Joseph donated land about seven miles up-river from Canajoharie for an Anglican church that Johnson paid for in 1769, now known as Indian Castle Church. It was designed by Harrison, and it still stands, but the graceful octagonal steeple has been missing for years, and the compass-headed windows are now reduced to simple rectangles; the so-called Palladian window over the altar has completely disappeared, and the doorway was placed on a long side instead of the original short side opposite the altar – the least that the people in charge can do is put those details right. The building now belongs to a non-denominational historical association. Not far away, near Fort Plain, is the somewhat similar Lutheran stone building, Old Palatine Church, built 1770.

All this came to a halt, when Sir William suddenly died in 1774. His heir was his son John from a previous marriage. John, who had no interest in Native American matters, ordered Molly and her children out of the house, so they moved about fifteen miles (24 km) back to the family house at Canajoharie, where she established a trading post. When the American Revolution broke out, Benedict Arnold had correctly predicted that whoever controlled nearby Lake Champlain would control the war, so American rebel forces soon filled much of the area. Molly gave shelter and food to Loyalists, and secretly supplied them with arms and ammunition. Molly found out that their former friend and neighbor General Herkimer was leading a substantial force to Fort Stanwix to relieve the siege of the place by the British, so Molly passed the news along to her brother and to her stepson Sir John Johnson. Joseph arranged an ambush in which many of Herkimer's troops were killed at the Battle of Oriskany, and Herkimer himself died from sepsis after having his leg amputated after the battle. The American survivors knew whom to blame, so they attacked Molly's house at Canajoharie and thoroughly sacked it. Luckily, she had been able to escape with her children to Onondaga, a neutral Iroquois capital, and later Fort Niagara, where Joseph made sure that they were safe. Late in the war, she moved to Carleton Island, where she was told she would be safe, but a short while later the people responsible for drawing up the details of the peace treaty ruled that Carleton Island was to be part of the United States, so she moved again, this time to Cataraqui, which was renamed Kingston, Ontario. No trace of her house there is to be seen, because it was the site of a twentieth-century fuel-storage depot. Molly Brant was truly a major figure in the Revolutionary War and late colonial period for both Canada and the United States, for both Native Americans and white folk, and she deserves to be much better known today.

This entry was paraphrased from Wikipedia, with geographical and historical additions by the author

CONTINENTAL ARMY LIEUTENANT-COLONEL LOUIS-JOSEPH 'ATAYATAGHLONGHTA OR ATIATOHARONGWEN' COOK, *FREE BLACK &* *ABENAKI, ADOPTED BY MOHAWK*, CA. 1737–1814 (NEW YORK, QUEBEC)

Louis-Joseph Cook was born near Saratoga, New York somewhere before 1740, to an African father and an Abenaki mother, so he was given an Algonkian name meaning 'variegated bird'. In 1745, a joint French and Mohawk raid took the family prisoner. The Mohawks adopted him and gave him an Iroquois name that translates to 'he unhangs from the group.' He grew up near a Jesuit mission, where they taught him to read and write. He converted to the Roman Catholic religion, and the priest gave him the name of Louis-Joseph, Cook having been the last name of his father.

With his intellect and ambition, Louis-Joseph soon became an important chief. He was fluent in French, English, and Iroquois. During the French & Indian War, he joined the Quebec Mohawks on the French side against the British near Lake George and Lake Champlain. When the American Revolution broke out, he took up arms against the British again, to fight on the American side in the invasion of Quebec. He retreated with the Americans, and later joined them in fighting in the Oriskany and Saratoga campaigns.

Since most of the other Mohawk fought on the British side, Louis-Joseph began to identify more closely with the Oneida, who were essentially the only northern tribe to fight on the American side. In May 1778, he accompanied the Oneida to Valley Forge, Pennsylvania. General von Steuben's military secretary Etienne du Ponceau was walking in the woods near his quarters when he encountered a tall man in American uniform singing arias from a fashionable French opera. Du Ponceau later commented, 'He would have been a valuable acquisition to the French Royal Opera, where I have never heard a voice of such extraordinary power, and at the same time capable of modulation.'

Of course, Louis-Joseph did not pursue a career in opera, but continued his wartime leadership role on the American side, where his powerful voice was most likely useful in giving orders. On 15 June 1779, Congress finally made it official by commissioning him as a lieutenant-colonel, the only known commission at any rank in the Continental Army, Navy, or Marines given to a man of African descent. Rhode Island assembled an entire regiment of Blacks to fight in the Revolution, and they fought with distinction and bravery, but all their officers were white.

After the Revolution, Louis-Joseph worked with the Oneida in a futile effort to make sure that their land was secure against real estate speculators, who occupied political posts at almost every level. The New York government declared his arrangements null and void, and they seized the land to resell for development. He continued to represent the Oneida in negotiations between 1792 and 1798, but it was all for naught: the Americans forced the Oneida to accept a paltry amount of money for their New York lands, and they were made to move to inhospitable lands in northern Wisconsin. In more recent years, the Oneida have turned their humiliation into income by opening profitable gambling casinos, and some of the income from the casinos has paid for a major portion of the Museum of the American Revolution in Philadelphia, which opened in April 2017; in return, the Museum's captions reveal that one of the major themes of the American Revolution involved powerful US real estate speculators using the war as a smokescreen behind which they were able to rip off huge tracts of land from the Indigenous people. This aspect of the war is known to relatively few people in modern times. In fact, the much larger American Revolution Museum in Yorktown, Virginia, which also opened in April 2017, fails to mention this important aspect of the war at all, in spite of the fact that Virginians numbered among the most numerous and most rapacious of the real estate speculators.

Louis-Joseph settled in a Mohawk community in the St. Lawrence Valley. Despite his advanced age, he fought at the Battle of Lundy's Lane in 1814, where American forces invaded Canada and were defeated. Louis-Joseph fell from his horse and was seriously injured. He died of his injuries and was buried near Buffalo, New York, with full military honors at his funeral.

This entry was paraphrased from Wikipedia, with historical and geographical additions by the author.

THOMAS PETTERS/PETERS, *ONCE ENSLAVED*, 1738–1792, FOUNDER OF SIERRA LEONE (NIGERIA, NEW ORLEANS, NORTH CAROLINA, SOUTH CAROLINA, NEW YORK, PHILADELPHIA, BERMUDA, NOVA SCOTIA, NEW BRUNSWICK, LONDON, SIERRA LEONE)

Thomas was a member of the Yoruba Tribe and the Igbo clan in Nigeria. He was captured by a rival tribe when he was 22 years old in 1760 in the middle of the Seven Years' War, and sold to a French slave trader. The French slave ship *Henri IV* delivered him to New Orleans. He managed to escape three times but was quickly recaptured, which made his captors eager to sell him to a British man outside the colony, so he ended as slave to Scotsman William Campbell in Wilmington, North Carolina on a plantation, where he was trained as a millwright in 1776. Encouraged by the proclamation issued by Virginia's Royal Governor Lord Dunmore in 1775 that offered freedom to any Rebel-owned slaves who joined Loyalist forces (later altered to drop the military requirement), Thomas escaped and eventually reached New York City, where he enlisted in the Black Pioneers Company of the British Regiment of Guides & Pioneers. He was quickly promoted to sergeant in 1779, the highest rank available to Blacks in the entire British Army of the time.

It appears that Thomas had established a relationship with a slave named Sally in South Carolina in 1770–1, and she produced a daughter named Clairy in 1771. When Thomas was well established in New York, he got word to her to join him there, so she and her young daughter ran away, and the couple were officially married in 1779. Their son John was born in 1781, followed by at least five more children. Thomas was involved in various British military operations, including possibly the unsuccessful assault on Charleston, South Carolina in the summer of 1776 under Commodore Sir Peter Parker and Lieutenant-General Sir Henry Clinton, the British capture of Philadelphia in the autumn of 1777 under General Sir William Howe, and probably the successful British capture of Charleston in May 1780 under Lieutenant- General Sir Henry Clinton again. Thomas was wounded at least twice in these operations.

As the British evacuated various American cities in the course of the war, they offered slaves there the chance to have lives of freedom, starting in Halifax, Nova Scotia. These former American Blacks came from Boston, Newport, Perth Amboy, Philadelphia, coastal Virginia,

Wilmington NC, Charleston, and Savannah, and a handful in service in British Florida in the Saint Augustine area. Although the treaty negotiators in Paris had inserted language declaring that all Black slaves in New York must be returned to their American former owners, British officials casually said that the treaty negotiators were unaware of the real situation on the ground, and therefore any Blacks in New York who wanted to do so might safely go to Nova Scotia. About 3000 did so. The ship that the Petters family sailed on was blown off course and spent some time in Bermuda, but eventually the family settled about 12 miles southwest of Annapolis Royal, Nova Scotia at Brindley Town, later renamed Jordantown, and now called Digby, where the ferries land to and from New Brunswick and Maine (the other major Black settlement in Nova Scotia was at Birchtown, close to Shelburne on the south coast).

The British government had promised the Loyalist settlers in Nova Scotia (and from 1784 onwards, New Brunswick) food, supplies, and deeds to land. However, the 3000 Black settlers were well outnumbered by the roughly 26,000 white Loyalists, who were always given priority over the Blacks to the extent that there was practically nothing left for the Blacks, many of whom died of starvation. Thomas was one of the more literate Blacks, so he found himself penning petitions on behalf of many of his fellow sufferers, but when he found that the petitions were being blatantly ignored by petty officials, he decided to raise the money to travel to England and deliver petitions there. The Nova Scotia and New Brunswick governments feared that this would put them in a bad light, and so they did their best to prevent Thomas from making the voyage, but he arrived in London in 1791. With the help of abolitionists Granville Sharp, William Wilberforce, and Thomas Clarkson, and his former commander, General Sir Henry Clinton (who introduced him to some powerful men), it was decided that Clarkson's brother John (a lieutenant in the Royal Navy) would be appointed governor of the new British colony of Sierra Leone with a capital city of Granville Town, and that Thomas would be his assistant with the grand title of Speaker General in recruiting Canadian Blacks as residents of the new colony. Over 400 settlers had been sent there directly from London in 1787 (leaving Britain at the same time as the fleet of convict ships headed for Australia, which caused all sorts of consternation and confusion among the Blacks, some of whom feared that they were instead going to be forced to sail to Australia), but local indigenous people tried to stop the colony by burning Granville

Town to the ground in 1790. The colonists decided to rebuild it under the new name of Freetown.

Of the roughly 4000 Canadian Blacks, about 1200 initially signed up to travel to Sierra Leone, where they arrived in 1792, thus greatly augmenting the 400 earlier settlers. They had sailed the Atlantic aboard four ships and eleven brigs for a total of fifteen vessels. Legend says that Thomas Petters led the new arrivals ashore, singing one or more old Christian hymns. However, when the actual governance of the colony was revealed, the new and former immigrants had no power at all. All power was vested in a committee in London, and John Clarkson was to be their mouthpiece. In spite of his impressive title, Petters had no power, and there was no role for any democratically-elected council from among the Black residents. Petters complained to Governor Clarkson and to anyone else who would listen, all to no avail. Petters was so disappointed after all his strenuous labors that his health was prey to local diseases, and he died from malaria on 25 June 1792. Two years later, John Clarkson quit as governor and was replaced by the Scottish co-founder of London University, Zachary Macaulay (father of the famous historian Thomas Babington Macaulay). Also in 1794, the colony received another major setback when the French Navy attacked and destroyed much of the town.

A number of Krios (descendants of the first Black Canadian settlers) can claim descent from Thomas Petters, although some of his descendants live in Canada. No eye-witness images of Petters are known to have survived, but the Krio Descendant Union commissioned a full-size statue of him to be cast and erected in Freetown in 2011 as one of the most important founders of Sierra Leone. In 2007, the acclaimed BBC television series *Rough Crossings* portrayed Petters and his fellow British and American slaves and former slaves.

This entry was paraphrased from Wikipedia, with historical and geographical additions by the author.

VIRGINIA STATE NAVY 'LIEUTENANT' MARK STARTIN OR STARLINS, CA.1740-CA.1786, *ENSLAVED* (AFRICA & VIRGINIA)

Virginia, which had one of the longest shorelines of any of the British North American colonies, was also the wealthiest of all the mainland North American colonies. Initially, Virginia failed to spend much money on its state navy, which was under the leadership of Commodore James Barron. Many of its earliest armed vessels were small, such as the schooner *Patriot* (about 50 feet long on deck), which was manned by a crew of twenty and carried only ten or twelve swivel-guns plus small-arms, and no carriage-guns. By 1780, Virginia had built an excellent fleet of warships ranging from fourteen to twenty carriage-guns, although by being in the right place at the right time, Benedict Arnold was able to destroy or capture most of that fleet.

Virginia's coast has numerous tricky shoals, so that many skilled pilots were needed for ships to navigate. Even though the Virginia Legislature passed laws stating that enslaved Blacks were prohibited from serving as pilots, white pilots could not handle the amount of business, and therefore many of the qualified pilots turned out to be enslaved Blacks, whose owners were reasonably certain that they could count on the loyalty of the enslaved pilots. When war broke out, Virginia's warships needed permanent assistance from these enslaved Blacks. The schooner *Patriot* had at least two of these pilots in her crew. One of them was Caesar Tarrant (ca. 1740–1797), owned by Carter Tarrant of Hampton; Caesar was married to another slave, Lucy Rogers of Hampton. Caesar was so highly regarded for his service as pilot and helmsman that the Legislature came to an agreement with his owner whereby Caesar was freed in 1789, (and Cesar Tarrant Middle School, with a different spelling of his first name, opened in 1970 in Hampton).

African-born Mark Startin or Starlins was originally one of these pilots on *Patriot*, but there were occasions when he was capable enough to take command of the schooner for extended periods, and was accorded the salutation of "captain." On one occasion, he was on the verge of capturing a more powerful British sloop outright when two additional vessels with a total of more than fifty trained British seamen showed up unexpected, and Mark had to retreat in a hurry. Mark was held in high esteem by Commodore Barron, and although Mark may not actually have received a paper commission as an officer, the responsibilities that he willingly shouldered were normally handled by a commissioned officer with the rank of lieutenant. When the war was over, Mark had to return to his prewar position of being enslaved. The fact that the Legislature never even debated purchasing his freedom suggests that he must have died by about 1786, by which time they had awarded freedom to several other Blacks with lesser accomplishments.

This entry was paraphrased from Wikipedia, with historical, geographical, and maritime details added by the author.

HAITIAN GENERAL FRANCOIS-DOMINIQUE TOUSSAINT 'L'OUVERTURE' BREDA, 1743–1803, *ONCE ENSLAVED*, (HAITI & FRANCE)

The economy of British and French Caribbean Islands was based on growing sugarcane, which they felt required them to get the work done by a brutal form of slavery. The Spanish, Danish, and Dutch islands also grew sugarcane, but generally not as intensively. The smaller islands often changed hands as a result of frequent wars, but their slave systems were usually not as brutal as the two largest islands: Saint-Domingue or Haiti (the western one-third of Hispaniola) for the French, and Jamaica, an island a few miles to the southwest of Haiti for the British.

Slavery of any kind almost asked for the enslaved to revolt, and when that slavery was particularly brutal, the revolts were also brutal, and were usually put down by additional brutality. Padre Jean was a slave in Haiti, and he organized a revolt in 1676 in the area of Port-de-Paix, about forty miles northwest of the former capital at Cap Haitien (previously called Cap Francois), and a short distance south of Ile de la Tortue, often called Tortuga. Padre Jean freed several hundred slaves, and then fled to hide for three years on Tortuga, where he was discovered and assassinated.

The next Revolutionary in Haiti was Francois Mackandal, who is thought to have been born in Senegal or Guinea in the 1720s. He knew some Arabic, because he was apparently a Muslim. He made a study about the plants that grew there to find out which ones were deadly poisonous, and he organized a widespread plot to add these poisons to the food and water supplies so that hundreds of the slave owners and their animals died. Later, Mackandal's network spread additional terror among the slave owners by roaming about the countryside setting buildings on fire and killing the occupants. The French finally captured Mackandal in 1758 after six years of his campaign. He was burned at the stake in the main square of Port-au-Prince.

Only months after Mackandal's death, Nana Mensah Takyi, known popularly as Tacky, launched his rebellion in Jamaica in April 1760. Tacky had been born in the Coromantee region in the center of Ghana to the Fante ethnic group. As a tribal elder, he was used to fighting against the

Ashanti, Nzema, and Ahanta, and selling the resulting prisoners of war to a middle-man, who sold them to the British as slaves. He should not have been surprised, then, when he himself was taken prisoner and sold to the British. Tacky spent several years planning his rebellion, setting up a secret network among other Coromantee slaves, and intending to take over the entire island of Jamaica and establish a Black republic there. He started the uprising in St. Mary's Parish, which occupies the section of the island along the north coast, just north of the modern capital, Kingston. Voodoo shamans coated the rebels with a powder that they said would prevent their being killed, but they were killed anyway. The top Coromantee slave in Kingston was a female Fante called Akuba, who wore a royal robe and crown as she sat under a canopy. British authorities arrested her and ordered her deported, but somehow she managed to get ashore in Jamaica again. This time, she was executed. Slaves in the western end of the island were led by Apongo (who had the English name of Wager). The British relied largely on militia units of trained Black soldiers. Tacky was caught and killed fairly soon, but Apongo took longer before he was sentenced to die in a cruel death. Another leader rose up, called Simon, but he was quickly killed. Late in 1761, Governor Moore declared the rebellion at an end.

The focus shifted to Haiti next: Dutty Boukman had been born in Senegal about 1767, and was sold first to a plantation in Jamaica, but they sold him to a plantation in Haiti. He seems to have been a Muslim with at least some knowledge of Arabic. Around the middle of August 1791, Boukman led the last of a series of meetings at Bois Caiman to organize a slave revolt. Among his co-conspirators were Jean-Francois Papillon (d. early nineteenth century), Georges Biassou (1741–1801), and Jeannot Bullet (d. 1791). Boukman was at first successful, with 1800 plantations destroyed and 1000 slaveholders killed, but French troops killed him in early November. Jeannot took over the movement, but he was so arbitrarily cruel to anyone he did not like that he was arrested and executed in late November 1791 on the orders of Biassou and Papillon. Papillon (born in Africa, died in Spain 1805) freely admitted that he didn't think it was possible to free all the slaves, but he hoped that with new Black masters they could run the plantations more benignly without white interference. After the French mobs executed their Royal Family in January 1793, Spain felt free to try to take over Haiti (which had been French only since 1697, and Papillon and Biassou for a time headed up 'Black auxiliary troops' to assist Spain to do this. In July 1794, an unexpected massacre took place at Fort Dauphin (later renamed Fort Liberte, about 25 miles or 40 kilometres east of Cap Haitien on the north coast), and the Spanish decided to wash their hands of the Black auxiliaries. Papillon was sent to Cuba, where the governor was worried that he might foment a slave rebellion there, so he was sent to Cadiz, Spain in 1796, where he died in custody in 1805. Biassou was smarter, because he left Haiti and moved to Spanish St. Augustine, Florida in 1795, where he was put in charge of Black militia troops there. He died in 1801.

Head and shoulders above all the foregoing Haitian revolutionaries was Francois-Dominique Toussaint "L'Ouverture" Breda, given that nickname because he seemed to make openings in the enemy's line. He was born enslaved at Cap Francois, Haiti in May 1743 to two slaves, but was freed in the early 1770s. At about the time he was freed, he met and married in a Catholic ceremony his wife Cecile (who was at first a slave until he paid to have her freed), and they had two sons and one daughter. He attempted to run a coffee plantation with several slaves of his own, but it was a financial failure, so Cecile left him for a wealthy white planter. He began a relationship with Suzanne, whom he made his second wife in 1782; although she remained a slave for about a decade; they had at least two sons. He had a good Catholic education, and is believed to have been familiar with the writings of Epictetus, Macchiavelli, and Abbe' Guillaume-Thomas Raynal, the contemporary anti-slavery writer. For some reason, he himself was unable to write well until late in his life.

When the French Revolution began, Toussaint was a Royalist, partly because the French Revolutionaries showed no interest in helping improve the lives of Blacks. In 1793, Toussaint fought with the Spanish against the French, but as soon as the French republican government abolished slavery in February 1794, he switched to fighting with the French against the Spanish (who had hoped to take back Haiti and make it a Spanish colony). In the meantime, the British had landed a force in Haiti in the hope of picking up the colony while it was in turmoil, so Toussaint felt obliged to defend against the British as well as the Spanish. The British, incidentally, fared no better than French or Spanish troops in tropical Haiti, for they lost a reported 20,000 to 60,000 dead before May 1798, mostly due to disease. By 1796, Toussaint had been responsible for driving out the foreigners, and consolidating power under the French Governor Laveaux, who in turn made Toussaint his Lieutenant-Governor. When it seemed that the new French government was considering reimposing slavery in Haiti, Toussaint wrote to them in firm opposition.

Toussaint was by this time possibly the richest man in Haiti, owning many plantations and hundreds of slaves, which seems to the modern reader a distinct contradiction, but it was not seen that way in his day.

Toussaint was fully aware that it was vital to the future of Haiti for substantial income to be derived from the plantations, which had been profitably growing such crops as sugar, coffee, and indigo. Although the French planters had been brutal to their slaves, they had also had the foresight to invest in proper irrigation for their plantations, with the result that Haitian fields yielded two-thirds more crops for a given area of land than their Jamaican equivalents, where the planters were just as brutal to the slaves. Toussaint worked out a system by which the plantation workers would receive one-quarter of the proceeds from the plantation, and the rest of the income would be invested by the state in building roads, bridges, schools, city buildings, and irrigation systems. It probably would have worked if everyone involved had been completely honest and committed to the system.

In April 1798, Toussaint made a treaty with General Maitland and the remaining British that they would leave the island by the end of August, which they did, in return for Toussaint's promise not to foment unrest in any British Caribbean colonies. Toussaint also appointed a former white planter, Joseph Bunel (married to a Black Haitian wife) as his diplomat in the United States, where southern states were worried about the possibility of Haitian-style unrest among Blacks in their states. President Adams was a great fan of the Haitian Revolution, although both Washington and Jefferson were horrified by what it could mean for southern US plantations. Both the British and the Americans urged Toussaint to declare independence from France, but he saw no reason to upset the status quo – big mistake! Napoleon was anything but status quo. Toussaint is now widely known as the Father of Independent Haiti. He gradually established control over the entire country. Although he had not been formally taught anything about military theory or governance, he had an uncanny knack of picking the right path most of the time.

With considerable aid from Alexander Hamilton (himself born on a Caribbean Island) starting in February 1799, Toussaint wrote and set up a proper constitution for Haiti in 1801 that established him as Governor-General for Life, which did not sit well with Napoleon. In 1802, he was invited to a conference with French General Jean-Baptiste Brunet, but it was really a ruse for arresting him. He was deported to France, where he was locked up at the Chateau de Joux, high in the mountains near the

Swiss border. He died there in 1803, arguably the most affable of all the Haitian revolutionaries. As he was boarding the frigate that was to transport him to France, Toussaint warned, "In overthrowing me, you have cut down in Haiti only the trunk of the Tree of Liberty. It will spring up again from the roots, for they are numerous and they are deep."

This entry was paraphrased from Wikipedia, with geographical and historical details by the author.

LOYALIST COLONEL JOSEPH THAYENDANEGEA BRANT, *MOHAWK*, 1743–1807 (NEW YORK, OHIO, ONTARIO)

Joseph Brant was born in what is now Ohio by the banks of the Cuyahoga River in 1743. His father died soon after, and his mother returned to New York with the boy and his sister Mary/Molly. They lived in her ancestral village of Canajoharie on the bank of the Mohawk River, where the mother remarried. Many of their neighbors were German-speaking settlers from the Palatinate, and relations between them were friendly. A good friend of the Brants was Sir William Johnson, the British agent for dealing with the northern Indians. Joseph, as a young teen, watched the ebb and flow of what is called in America the French and Indian War, in which Mohawks lost a great many men dead fighting for the British while many of the other Iroquois tribes had remained neutral. At about age fifteen, Brant started taking part on the British side, but at first only as a scout. He was part of Johnson's capture of Fort Niagara in 1759, and Jeffery Amherst's capture of Montreal in 1760, which sealed the end of French Canadian "New France." The British awarded Brant a silver medal for his service. At about this time, Brant's sister Molly became Johnson's common-law wife (after his two previous Native American wives had died). Molly bore him eight children.

In 1761, Johnson arranged for Brant to attend the Rev. Eleazar Wheelock's "Moor's Indian Charity School" in Connecticut, where he learned to speak, read, and write English, do arithmetic and learn other subjects, including Latin and Greek (and he already knew French). In 1763, Johnson arranged for Brant to attend King's College (now known as Columbia University) in New York City, but then Pontiac's War broke out, which made it difficult for Native Americans to attend white colleges. So instead, he studied for a few months at the school run by the

Rev. Cornelius Bennet at Canajoharie. However, in early 1764, he joined a force of Mohawk and Oneida who fought on the side of the British against the Algonquian-speaking Lenape in Ohio, burning three large towns and killing their cattle, but no actual humans. In July 1765, Brant married Margaret or Peggy, an English girl from Virginia who had been captured very young by Lenape Native Americans, but raised as the adopted daughter of Christian Mohawk Chief Issac (*sic*). They had two children, Isaac and Christine, before Peggy died of tuberculosis early in 1771. Brant then married a second wife, Margaret's sister Susanna, but she died in late 1777 while staying at Fort Niagara. In 1780, Brant married Catharine, daughter of a Mohawk woman and Irishman George Croghan, who worked for Johnson as his deputy. Brant and Catharine had seven children, Joseph, Jacob, John, Margaret, Catherine, Mary, and Elizabeth. Brant spent much of his time as an interpreter, and in translating parts of the Prayerbook and the Gospel of Mark into Mohawk, but at the same time he was designated by the Mohawk as their warrior chief. Sir William Johnson died in 1774. His son John ordered his stepmother, Brant's sister Molly, to leave the elegant house, Johnson Hall, with her eight children. Sir John Johnson had no interest in working with the Mohawk or any other Native Americans, so that job devolved upon a cousin, Guy Johnson, who was somewhat incompetent (Guy also had a house designed by Harrison in 1766, now much enlarged).

When the American Revolution broke out, Brant joined Guy in moving to Canada for safety, but that was unpleasant because the British governor there, General Sir Guy Carleton, personally disliked Johnson and had contempt for Brant. Guy Johnson took Brant with him to London in late 1775 in order to give testimony as to how things stood on the ground in America. While they were in public, they agreed that Brant should always wear his Mohawk clothes and regalia for effect, although he was perfectly comfortable wearing British clothing, They spent quite a bit of time with George Germain, the colonial secretary, trying to persuade him to address past Mohawk land grievances in exchange for Mohawks fighting on the British side in the war that appeared to be about to begin. Brant was treated as a celebrity, and was interviewed by James Boswell for publication. Brant was accepted into Freemasonry, and was handed his ritual apron in person by George III at a formal reception at St. James' Palace.

When Brant returned to New York, General Sir William Howe was preparing to capture New York City, Brant is said to have distinguished himself with bravery at Jamaica Pass in the Battle of Long Island, where he became lifelong friend of General Hugh Earl Percy, later Duke of Northumberland, his only lasting friendship with a white man. After he had travelled in disguise back to his family home, he campaigned among the warriors of the Iroquois Confederacy to enlist their efforts on the British side, but most Native Americans had no interest in anything but remaining neutral. The was a war between white men, and the Iroquois had no part to play in it, they said. Brant pointed out that if the Americans won, the Indians would lose most or all their lands, but if the British won, they had already set aside lands, mostly in Canada, for the Iroquois. The Oneida and Tuscarora, said they were inclined to fight on the American side, if at all, and it turned out that even they lost their lands after US independence. Louis-Joseph Cook, a Mohawk leader who supported the Americans, became a lifelong enemy of the slightly younger Brant.

The best that Brant could do was to recruit a regiment called Brant's volunteers, which contained just a handful of Mohawk and Tuscarora amid a much larger number of white Loyalists. It was a measure of Brant's charisma that these white men were happy to fight under a Native American without even getting paid. Benedict Arnold, who had been convinced that Lake Champlain would be the key to victory, initially captured a number of British warships on the lake. The 14-gun schooner *Royal Savage* had been named as a tribute to Brant, but Arnold maintained the name as a tribute to Oneida leader Han Yerry 'Tewahangarahken' Doxtader (ca. 1724-ca. 1800), who had led his Oneida to fight for the Americans.

Shortly before the important Battle of Saratoga in the fall of 1777, Molly Brant passed along a message to her brother that American General Nicholas Herkimer (a former friend and neighbor of Brant) was marching with 800 men to relieve Fort Stanwix (at Rome, about 55 miles west of Canajoharie, and open to the public), so Brant laid an ambush. About 250–350 Americans died versus only 50 Loyalists at the Battle of Oriskany. Herkimer had to have his leg amputated after the battle, but he died from infection. The Oneida accompanying the Americans destroyed Canajoharie, making sure to burn Molly Brant's house. Brant had been told by Burgoyne that his warriors were not welcome to fight in the coming Battle of Saratoga, so Brant and his entourage spent the winter at Fort Niagara, while Burgoyne surrendered his entire army at Saratoga, the pivotal battle of the entire war.

In 1778, Brant and his Volunteers conducted an active guerilla war on the frontier, raiding rebel settlements along the Mohawk Valley, stealing cattle, burning houses, and killing resisters in New York and Pennsylvania. In May, he attacked Cobleskill, and in September it was German Flatts (where he limited the killing to two people). He was not involved in the battle at Wyoming in July, even though his fame was such that people liked to attach his name to any action in the area, the more brutal, the better. After Continental soldiers destroyed Brant's home village of Onaquaga while it was undefended, the American commander described it as "the finest Indian town I ever saw." After that, Brant temporarily joined forces with Walter Butler. Brant found Butler arrogant, patronizing, and disagreeable, but he was obliged to accompany him to Cherry Valley, where Brant had several friends. The Seneca in Butler's party butchered everyone there, which sickened Brant. A Continental Army Lt. Colonel was the highest-ranking American captured at Cherry Valley, and the Seneca stripped him and tied him to a stake, preparatory to torturing him, but Brant freed him.

Early in 1779, Brant rode to Montreal to meet with Governor Frederick Haldimand, the Swiss-born military commander of Quebec. Haldimand wrote that Brant was easily the most civilized of all the Iroquois chiefs, and not at all a "savage." Brant's destructive rampages through the country-sides of New York and Pennsylvania were not without careful purpose: these were the areas from which the Continental Army could derive its food, so General George Washington urgently ordered General John Sullivan to burn all the Iroquois villages and farms that they could find. Brant had only his 100 Volunteers with which to oppose Sullivan's army of several thousand, so he lost the only battle they fought at Newtown. About 5000 Seneca, Cayuga, Mohawk, and Onondaga were made homeless and hungry, and they tried to take refuge at Fort Niagara, where many died of exposure.

In 1780, Brant resumed small-scale attacks on the homes and crops of rebel settlers along the Mohawk River. In 1781, he was sent west to Fort Detroit to help defend against George Rogers Clark's expedition from Virginia. He completely defeated Clark's force, but he was wounded in the leg and had to remain in the fort over the winter. One of his greatest challenges was to keep the Iroquois from falling away from their allegiance to the British, especially after they heard that the British had surrendered at Yorktown in October 1781. Then in 1782, he received orders from Haldimand, ordering a cessation of hostilities, which annoyed him greatly. What was worse, the Iroquois were not mentioned in the Treaty of Paris, which was ratified in the spring of 1783. The British negotiators at the peace conference had unilaterally decided that it was up to the Iroquois to make their own deal with Congress.

When as was expected, Congress made a giant land-grab of Native American lands, including the lands of tribes who had fought on the American side, Brant secured from Haldimand the right of the Mohawk to settle in the Grand River Valley in Ontario. Using designs that he had secured before the war from Johnson's friend, the architect Peter Harrison, he built St. Paul's Church, and a fine house for himself at Brantford. Later, he built himself a handsome house in Burlington to a Harrison design, which has been inaccurately reconstructed after it was unwittingly destroyed by mistake early in the twentieth century. Brant lived comfortably at Brantford, farming crops, cattle, sheep, and hogs. At one point he owned as many as forty Black slaves. Brant also owned a third house built for him at Cataraqui (later renamed Kingston) near his sister Molly's house. No images of that house survive, and the site was obliterated before archaeologists could document its footprint (it measured 40 by 30 feet, and was a story and a half high over a high basement, probably with a mansard roof; the front elevation likely had a central breakfront with pediment on top). Brantford to Kingston is about 225 miles or 300 km, whereas Burlington to Kingston is 212 miles or 341 km.

Late in 1785, Brant sailed to London to ask George III for support in defending the confederated Indians from being attacked by the Americans. Brant and his sister Molly were granted generous pensions. The British agreed to compensate fully the Mohawk for their losses (Loyalists, by contrast, were compensated for only a fraction of their losses). The British declined to become involved in the American attacks on the Indians. While in London, Brant attended balls, dined with the Prince of Wales, and finished his work on the Mohawk language Anglican Prayerbook. He met Home Secretary Lord Sydney, later calling him a "stupid blockhead," who made no effort to understand the Iroquois. Then he undertook a diplomatic visit to Paris. He arrived in Quebec City in June 1786.

Late in 1786, Brant helped to reinstate the Western Confederacy (Shawnee, Lenape, Miami, Wyandot, Ojibwa, Ottawa, and Potawatomi), and he attempted to draw a boundary along the Ohio River between the Indian lands and the USA. In 1790, American forces bent on attacking the Western Confederacy were badly defeated, and again in 1791. The western Indians asked Brant and the Iroquois to fight on their side. Brant refused, but did ask the new governor of Quebec, Lord Dorchester, for British help. Dorchester turned him down. In the meantime, the US asked Brant to mediate. He suggested that the US cease further white settlement west of the Ohio River, and that the US should deal with the Indians as a confederacy and not deal with individual tribes.

In 1792, the US invited Brant to Philadelphia. There, he met President Washington and his cabinet for the first time. The US offered Brant a large pension and substantial land for the Mohawk in upstate New York to lure him back, but he declined. Brant made a speech to the Western Confederacy, telling them that they could not defeat the US indefinitely, but they refused to listen, and they were badly defeated at the Battle of Fallen Timbers in 1794.

At home, Brant often found himself on the wrong side of General John Graves Simcoe, the governor of Upper Canada (Ontario). Brant attempted to sell land he owned along the Grand River, and invest the proceeds in a trust fund for the Mohawk so that they could remain financially and politically independent of the British. Simcoe made a rule that Brant could sell lands only to the Crown. Brant simply disregarded Simcoe's rule, and Simcoe refused to issue land deeds to the new owners.

In 1797, Brant travelled again to Philadelphia to meet US officials and British diplomat Robert Liston. Brant was invited to address Congress, so he told them that he would "never again take up the tomahawk against the United States. He also met French diplomat Pierre-August Adet, and offered to have the Mohawk lead a revolution in Canada against the British. On his return to Canada, he was badly treated by the British leadership in regard to land sales, but eventually they backed down at least temporarily. Brant also influenced Native American leaders in the United States when he recommended that they unite in establishing a separate political entity.

Brant died in 1807 at age 64 at his house in Burlington, still involved in intractable land disputes. His last words were, "Have pity on the poor Indians. If you have any influence with the great, endeavour to use it for their good." Brant has sometimes been criticized for not being Indian enough, but he had been brought up as a neighbor of German and Scots-Irish settlers, and he knew that there was no turning the clock back. Therefore, he sought always to secure the best possible future for Native Americans by making sensible accommodations with the settlers. Brant's colorful and productive life is inextricably intertwined with the main themes of history from both the United States and Canada, as well as Native Americans.

This entry was paraphrased from Wikipedia, with historical, geographical, and architectural details added by the author.

BLUE JACKET/WEYAPIERSENWAH, *SHAWNEE WARRIOR CHIEF*, CA. 1743–1810 (OHIO, ILLINOIS, INDIANA)

Blue Jacket's early life is rather a mystery, as he does not appear in the historical record until 1773, when he was approximately thirty-three years old. At that time, he was living in a Shawnee village along the banks of the Scioto River, which is a tributary of the Ohio River. He is known to have participated in Lord Dunmore's War in 1774, and he allied with the British in the American Revolution because he thought (correctly) that the British would uphold Shawnee rights better than the Americans.

When the American Revolution was ended, Ohio was almost overrun by would-be settlers and real estate speculators, and Indian land rights were very low on the list of American priorities. President George Washington wrote to Governor Arthur St. Clair of the North West Territories (the Native Americans recognized neither the political subdivision of the North West Territories nor the authority of St. Clair) to ask him if he thought the Native Americans were more inclined to war or to peace. He replied that they wanted war. Washington and his Secretary of War, General Henry Knox, ordered General Josiah Harmar in late October 1790 to assemble an army at Fort Washington (now called Cincinnati) and attack the Native Americans. One of the leaders of the Native Americans was Blue Jacket, and he badly defeated Harmar. In November 1791, Blue Jacket led the confederated Native Americans to fight General St. Clair, and badly defeated him at the Battle of the Wabash, the worst defeat ever suffered by United States forces at the hands of the Indians.

Americans were so alarmed by this defeat that they assembled a professional army commanded by General Anthony Wayne. On 20 August, the two armies clashed at the Battle of Fallen Timbers, just south of modern Toledo, Ohio. This time, Blue Jacket's army was badly defeated, and he was forced to sign the Treaty of Greenville in August 1795, letting the US have most of modern Ohio. In 1805, Blue Jacket was backed into a corner and forced to sign the Treaty of Fort Industry, which let the US have even more of Ohio. Blue Jacket's last years saw the rise of Tecumseh, who made a noble effort to reclaim Shawnee lands in Ohio. Blue Jacket died in 1810.

In 1877, a book was published that asserted that Blue Jacket was actually a white boy who had been kidnapped and adopted by Shawnees in the 1770s, named Marmaduke van Swearingen. This story soon had legs and was used as the basis of many period novels. A century later, some forensic experts felt obliged to look into it, and they reported back in 2006 that DNA from Blue Jacket showed no match at all with the DNA of the Van Swearingen family.

This entry was paraphrased from Wikipedia, with historical and geographical details added by the author.

ROYAL NAVY CAPTAIN JOHN 'JACK PUNCH' PERKINS, *FREE BLACK*, CA. 1746–1812 (JAMAICA) RN

John Perkins is believed to have been born to a mixed-race couple in or near Kingston, Jamaica about 1746. He crewed on and later commanded merchant vessels, and served as a coastal pilot for Royal Navy ships navigating the tricky shoals and reefs around Caribbean islands. The first time his name appears in records is as a pilot for the Royal Navy 50-gun ship *Antelope* in 1775, the flagship of the commander-in-chief of the Jamaica station. It was written of him: "His knowledge of the different ports, &c in the West Indies was, perhaps, seldom equalled, and never surpassed."

Presumably with the official rank of ensign, he was appointed to command the 10-gun schooner *Punch* (from which he received his nickname). Over the next two years, Perkins captured 315 enemy American vessels, which averages to about three per week. The Jamaican Legislature backed up that claim, which must have made Perkins quite wealthy from prize money. The Navy promoted him to lieutenant in 1779. His successes continued (more than 400 ships by this time, both American and French, warships and merchant ships). The *Naval Chronicle* reported: "He annoyed the enemy more than any other office. By his repeated feats of gallantry, and the immense number of prizes he took."

He was next given command of the 12-gun American-built schooner *Endeavour*. He continued to capture or destroy numerous enemy vessels. Jamaica Governor Archibald Campbell wrote a letter of recommendation: "By the gallant exertions of this officer, some hundred vessels were taken, burnt, or destroyed, and above three thousand men added to the list of prisoners of war in favour of Great Britain; in short, the character and conduct of Captain Perkins were not less admired by his superior officers in Jamaica, than respected by those of the enemy."

At various times, Admiral Sir Peter Parker and other admirals employed Perkins in secret missions against the French in Haiti. In 1782, Perkins captured a much larger vessel with several important French officers aboard. Admiral George Brydges Rodney was commander of the Jamaica station; he promoted Perkins to the rank of commander in 1782, and added two additional guns to the schooner that Perkins commanded. In those days, a commander was entitled to command any ship of 18 guns or fewer (by the 1790s, this had been increased to 26 guns or fewer). Unfortunately, for reasons most likely to do with race, the promotion was dis-allowed by the Admiralty, and Rodney was ordered to take the additional guns away again. Lieutenants were not permitted to command any vessel of more than 12 guns. Nothing Rodney could write to London did any good. By the end of the war in 1783, Perkins was on half-pay as a lieutenant without a ship. He had been the highest-ranking Black in the Royal Navy during the American Revolution.

The Caribbean, of course, was always a good place for commerce, so Perkins presumably had little trouble finding employment sailing merchant ships all over the Caribbean. The British had imposed new trading regulations in the meantime, and American ships were no longer welcome to call at British Caribbean islands, even though they had used to be the only ships bringing food supplies to the islands. The British were unable to supply much food to their islands, and the new settlers in Canada were not really in a position to help, either. The solution was for British Caribbean ships to sail to the United States and buy food there, which was permitted under the regulations. We may imagine that Perkins, with his wealth of sailing experience, was a captain employed in that trade to Pennsylvania, New York, and New England, but probably not to the southern states, where a Black captain was possibly liable to being kidnapped.

Only a few years after the end of America's war for independence, a new war had broken out against Revolutionary France, and Perkins made sure that the Royal Navy knew that he was anxious to serve. He also enlisted the Jamaica Legislature's help in getting his former promotion reinstated, and if possible, promoted all the way up to captain. However, the British mostly needed him, it seems, in a clandestine operation, under

Admiral Philip Affleck, to supply weapons to the slaves in Haiti. Captain Thomas McNamara Russell of the 32-gun frigate *Diana* was conducting relief operations in Haiti, and he heard that a British officer was about to be guillotined at Jeremie after he had been arrested for supplying arms to rebellious slaves. Russell requested that the officer be released, and the French initially agreed, but later refused. Russell sailed his ship along the coast until he met the 12-gun Royal Navy schooner *Ferret* under Lieutenant Nowell. They sent Nowell's first lieutenant Godby ashore to recover Perkins, while the French authorities could clearly see the two warships ready for action. Godby successfully negotiated with the French authorities, and Perkins returned to Jamaica.

In September 1793, Perkins (still reduced to being a lowly lieutenant) commanded the small 4-gun schooner *Spitfire* in Commodore John Ford's squadron, requested by French Royalists to attack certain parts of Haiti. One of the vessels they captured was the French Navy 12-gun schooner *La Convention Nationale*, which they renamed ironically *Marie Antoinette*, and gave command of her to Perkins. Ford described Perkins as "an Officer of Zeal, Vigilance, and Activity." The schooner remained with the newly-promoted Admiral Ford when they briefly captured the major city of Port-au-Prince, and made prizes of all 45 vessels in the harbor. In 1797, Admiral Sir Hyde Parker issued a new re-promotion for Perkins as commander, so he was transferred to command a new brig, the 14-gun *Drake*. Only months after he had departed from the schooner *Marie Antoinette*, her crew mutinied because of bad treatment by her new commander, and they sailed her to Martinique to return her to her former owners.

The brig *Drake* was part of a small squadron under Commodore Hugh Pigot, including the 32-gun frigates *Hermione* and *Quebec*, and the 12-gun cutter *Penelope*, and they managed to cut out eight enemy warships at Port-de-Paix in the northwest of Haiti on 20 April 1797. On 28 October 1798, *Drake* captured by herself the French privateer *La Favorite*, producing substantial additional prize money for Perkins (for a single-ship capture, Perkins was entitled to one quarter of the total value of the captured ship). On 24 November 1799 off Cape Tiburon, *Drake* worked with the 32-gun frigate *Solebay* to capture four French corvettes, *L'Egyptienne* (18 guns). *L'Eole* (16 guns), *Le Levrier* (12 guns), and *Le Vengeur* (8-guns).

On 6 September 1800, Perkins finally received his coveted promotion to captain, with which he commanded the 32-gun frigate *Meleager*, but early the next year he moved over to command a much smaller ship, the 22-gun *Arab*. In March 1801, in company with the 18-gun British privateer *Experiment*, *Arab* attacked a pair of warships that turned out to be Danish, and therefore not at that time officially enemy vessels (actually, Nelson fought in his famous Battle of Copenhagen the following month in April 1801, so Perkins was off only by a few days). The Danes managed to escape. In April 1801, Perkins captured from the French the two formerly Dutch Islands of Sint Eustatius and Saba, and he landed a detachment of the Royal East Kent Regiment to take possession. Perkins made prisoners of the French garrisons, and captured forty-seven fort cannons plus 338 barrels of gunpowder; the cannons and powder were of course left in place so that the islands could be defended. Sint Eustatius, while under Dutch rule during the American Revolution, had once been an extremely profitable island, due to inter-island trade (which was not always legal).

In 1802, Perkins was transferred to command the brand-new 32-gun frigate *Tartar*. In 1802 and 1803, *Tartar* was part of Commodore John Loring's squadron, which captured five French warships, *La Decouverte, La Chlorinde, La Surveillante, La Vertue,* and *Le Cerf.* The first two were taken into British service. It turned out that when she surrendered, *La Surveillante* had on board Marshal Jean-Baptiste Donatien de Vimeur Comte de Rochambeau. Rochambeau, the son of the hero of the Franco-American victory at Yorktown, Virginia in 1781, had been the brutal commander of all French forces in Haiti until he had surrendered to the rebels shortly before his encounter with the Royal Navy. He had been fortunate that the rebels had not sent him to the guillotine, so enflamed were they about his brutality.

On 25 July 1804, while sailing in company with the 74-gun battleship *Vanguard* under Commodore James Walker and other ships, *Tartar* spotted the French 74-gun battleship *Le Duquesne*, which was accompanied by two 16-gun brigs, and immediately Perkins sailed towards the French ships. Being easily the fastest ship of her squadron, *Tartar* found herself all alone in combat with the much more powerful French battleship. Fortunately, Perkins was clever enough to maneuver his ship so that she was always facing one end of the battleship with his broadside, while the battleship was unable to bring many of her extremely heavy guns to bear on the frigate. While *Tartar* kept the French ships from escaping, the battleships in the rest of the British fleet finally caught up, and so the French were forced to surrender. The crewmembers of all the British ships present shared equally in the lucrative prize money.

In January 1804, half a year before the event described above, one of the commanders of the slave rebellion in Haiti, Jean-Jacques Dessalines, officially declared independence from France. Admiral Sir John Thomas Duckworth and Field Marshal Sir George Nugent, Baronet, Governor of Jamaica, jointly decided to send Perkins and *Tartar* to Haiti to observe what was happening in that country. One may assume that in all his years of sailing among the Caribbean islands in wartime and peacetime, Perkins had managed to pick up a certain amount of French, whether proper French or the patois that was often used in the islands. Perkins was accompanied by Edward Corbet, a government official appointed by Nugent. Perkins wrote in one of his reports to Duckworth, "I assure you that it is horrid to view the streets in different places stained with the blood of these unfortunate people, whose bodies are now left exposed to view by the river and sea side. In hauling the seine, the evening we came to our anchor, several bodies got entangled in it. In fact, such scenes of cruelty and devastation have been committed as is impossible to imagine or my pen to describe."

Later in 1804, Perkins felt obliged to resign his commission for health reasons (asthma). Some say that he finally visited England in 1805, although there seems to be no evidence for this. He retired to Mount Dorothy, a small plantation that he owned in Saint Andrew Parish next to Kingston, which he worked with the aid of twenty-six enslaved people. Undoubtedly, although he may have inherited the plantation, he had developed the property thanks to all the prize money he had amassed over the years. He died in 1812 in Jamaica, highly regarded by all the officers and men who had served with him in the Navy. Perkins is not known to have been married.

This entry was paraphrased from Wikipedia, with historical, geographical, and naval details added by the author.

AMERICAN JUDGE WENTWORTH CHESWELL, *FREE BLACK*, 1746–1817 (NEW HAMPSHIRE)

Wentworth Cheswell (most likely pronounced as if written "Chezzle") was born an only child in Newmarket, New Hampshire, a mill-town on a wide estuary about 8 miles west of Portsmouth. His father, Hopestill

Cheswell, was the free Black son of a biracial family, and his mother was Katherine Keniston Cheswell, a Caucasian. His father was a widely respected house-wright, who built houses from Portsmouth to Boston, and therefore had money enough to enroll young Wentworth (named after two Royal governors of the New Hampshire colony, Benning and John) at a prestigious boarding school (then for boys only), Governor Dummer Academy, founded in 1763 in Byfield, Massachusetts, near Newbury (in 2005 renamed the Governor's Academy; the school is now coeducational). There he studied Latin, Greek, reading, writing, arithmetic, swimming, and horsemanship.

After he returned home to Newmarket, he began purchasing land to establish a farm, while at the same time setting himself up as a schoolmaster. He owned his own pew in the Congregationalist Meeting House. At age 21, he married 17-year-old Mary Davis of Durham (a Caucasian), and she bore him thirteen children, four sons and nine daughters: Paul (1768), Thomas (1770), Samuel (1772), Sarah (1774), Mary (1775), Elizabeth (1778), Nancy (1780), Mehitable (1782), William (1785), daughter #6 (1785), Martha (1788), daughter #8 (1792), and Abigail (1792).

In 1768, Wentworth was elected town constable, the first time that any Black person was elected to public office in North America. He continued being elected to various public offices for most of the rest of his life. Cheswell assisted in 1774–5 in spreading various alarms about British plans to steal New Hampshire's official supply of gunpowder, and in carrying orders from Portsmouth to Newmarket. Nearly all the residents of Newmarket, including Cheswell, were in favor of the American cause, and they said so by signing the Association Test in April 1776. Cheswell volunteered to enlist as a mounted private under John Langdon in Langdon's Company of Light Horse Volunteers. He was a year too late to have been one of the New Hampshire troops who drove the British away from Lake Champlain with New England troops from New Hampshire, Massachusetts, Rhode Island, Connecticut, and New York, under the leadership of Benedict Arnold. However, he rode about 250 miles with his Company close to Lake Champlain, when they joined the Continental Army under General Horatio Gates in defeating the British under General John Burgoyne at the two Battles of Saratoga in September and October 1777. Benedict Arnold had a prominent role in securing those victories. These were the pivotal battles of the entire war, because they showed the world that the Americans had staying-power and could defeat the British. As a result, the French and the Spanish were encouraged to join the conflict, thus eventually closing the door to any chance of a British victory. Cheswell's enlistment ended at the end of October 1777. One of the problems of running the Continental Army was that many of the men enlisted for relatively short times, because their families were dependent on them for support. The pay given out for military service was usually in much depreciated paper money, which would not buy much support for the needs of families.

After the war, Cheswell opened a shop next to his schoolhouse to supply additional income. He also served his town as a selectman (member of the town council), auditor, assessor, scrivener and other roles. He was interested in artifacts dug up in the soil around the town, and wrote a journal about his finds, that some people have described as containing the seeds of modern archaeological theory. In 1801, he was one of a committee that assembled to found the town's first library. He himself had a particularly fine private library of books and manuscripts, which were to be loaned at various times to interested scholars.

In 1805, Cheswell was elected a Justice of the Peace (judge) for Rockingham County, the first African-American judge in American history. Much of his job was executing deeds, wills, and other legal documents, but he also presided in court trials. He served in that capacity until he caught typhus fever, that caused his death in 1817.

This entry was paraphrased from Wikipedia, with historical and geographical details added by the author.

DOUBLE-AGENT JAMES ARMISTEAD LAFAYETTE, *ONCE ENSLAVED*, 1748/60–1830/32 (VIRGINIA)

James learned as a boy to read and write (although probably not at the Bray School in Williamsburg). At an early age, he worked on the tobacco plantation of Colonel John Armistead in New Kent County, Virginia (a few miles west of Williamsburg). Armistead's son William took on James as his manservant. William was strongly committed to the independence movement, so he quickly figured out how to have James help him move the cause of independence forward.

Virginia's last Royal Governor, John Murray Earl of Dunmore, issued a proclamation in 1775 that any enslaved people working on Virginia plantations could gain their freedom simply by registering with him, and many Virginia Blacks did so. Dunmore understood that all these Blacks could easily be recaptured if they lived on land, so he rented dozens of ships as dormitories for the former slaves. Tragically for the Blacks, many of them caught and spread smallpox among the residents of the ships.

After Dunmore had departed from Virginia, the system remained in force for any British military force in Virginia. Benedict Arnold arrived in Virginia at the end of 1780 with almost 2000 men, and he made the small city of Portsmouth as his base (the Patriots had burned the much larger city of Norfolk, just across the Elizabeth River, to the ground on New Year's Eve 1775-6. The reason was that the shallow waters around that port could protect Arnold's base from attack by American and French forces. Arnold's orders called for him to capture the Virginia Legislature with absolutely no bloodshed. In January 1781 and later in May he almost captured them in Richmond, and then a few weeks later Arnold's cavalry under Colonel Banastre Tarleton narrowly failed to capture them at their new home in Charlottesville. James, at the request of General the Marquis de Lafayette, attached himself to Arnold's camp as a literate escaped slave, who could be relied upon to spy on the activities of American forces.

Arnold reported to General Sir Henry Clinton in New York that he had come close to achieving his goal three times, but now Virginia would have to be subdued in a 1782 military campaign to be led by General the Earl of Cornwallis. Arnold strongly urged Clinton that Cornwallis be ordered to make his winter quarters in Portsmouth because it was entirely safe from attack by American and French forces. However, Cornwallis was very disappointed with Portsmouth, as it offered little opportunity for night-life, whereas Yorktown only a few miles east of Williamsburg offered a comfortable existence. As soon as James learned of Cornwallis' proposed move to Yorktown, he urgently passed the information along to Lafayette, who was able to persuade American and French forces to descend on unprotected Yorktown in strength. The capture of Yorktown by the allies on 19 October 1781 was the final, if unexpected, nail in the coffin of British rule in the United States, so James' vital part in it should not be overlooked. Otherwise, James worked for the British as a trusted courier, and found that he could overhear important information about British plans; it was almost as if as a Black he was simply not noticed to be in the room with the British officers – wearing a virtual invisibility cloak!

As the war was winding down, Virginia enacted legislation in 1782 to free any Virginia slave who had fought in the Continental Army, but although James had worked for the Continental Army, he had not ever carried a gun, and so he did not qualify. James wrote several petitions to

Congress for manumission, but Congress ignored them. James drafted a petition to the Virginia Legislature, endorsed by William Armistead, and by Lafayette. A special bill to grant James his freedom passed both houses of the Legislature and was signed into law in January 1787; the Legislature later compensated Armistead for his loss of such a valuable slave.

James, who had never employed the last name of Armistead, was so overjoyed by Lafayette's help in securing his freedom that he began calling himself James Armistead Lafayette. James, with his second wife, acquired a prosperous 40-acre farm in New Kent County, where they brought up their children. James himself became a slave-owner there. In 1818, he applied for a Virginia pension based on his Revolutionary War service. He was awarded a lump sum, plus $40 a year.

In 1824, Lafayette made a triumphal tour of the United States, which by that time numbered 24 states. When Lafayette reached Richmond, he saw James in the crowd, descended from his carriage, and publicly embraced his old friend.

This entry was paraphrased from Wikipedia, with geographical and historical details added by the author.

LOYALIST 'COLONEL' TITUS 'TYE' CORNELIUS/ CORLIES, *ESCAPED SLAVE*, 1753–1780 (NEW JERSEY)

Titus Cornelius or Corlies was born in 1753 into slavery in Colt's Neck, Shrewsbury, Monmouth County, New Jersey, and originally owned by a Quaker famer, John Corlies. Titus was one of four slaves owned by Corlies. Most Quakers about 1758 had come around to the idea that they should educate their slaves and set them free at age 21, but Corlies would not hear of it. Instead, he whipped his slaves upon any pretext. In 1775, a delegation from the Shrewsbury Friends Meeting remonstrated with Corlies to no effect. In 1778, the Society of Friends revoked Corlies' membership because of his attitude towards slaves.

Later in 1775, Titus escaped and is believed to have headed south. Corlies ran the following advertisement in the newspaper:

"Run away from the subscriber, living in Shrewsbury, in the county of Monmouth, New Jersey, a *Negroe* man, named *Titus*, but may probably change his name; he is about 21 years of age, not very black, near 6 feet high; had on a grey homespun coat, brown breeches, blue and white stockings, and took with him a wallet, drawn up at one end with a string,

in which was a quantity of clothes. Whoever takes said Negroe, and se-
cures him in any gaol, or brings him to me, shall be entitled to the above
reward of *Three Pounds*, proc. And all reasonable charges paid by John
Corlis."

By coincidence, Titus escaped only one day after Virginia Governor
John Murray Earl of Dunmore had issued a proclamation offering freedom to any [Virginia] slaves who would leave their masters and join the
British Army. He later rephrased that to the effect that slaves need not
join the army, but simply register with him, and Dunmore soon had to
house thousands of run-away slaves, men, women, and children aboard
rented ships in Norfolk Harbor. He could not house them on land because the planters could easily send an army to retrieve them. It is alleged
that Titus joined Dunmore's Ethiopian Regiment.

Like Rhode Island's later Black Regiment, all the officers of the
Ethiopian Regiment were white. Nevertheless, Titus exhibited such leadership ability that he became the leader of a related militia group known
as the Black Brigade, which actually included Blacks and whites in its
ranks. Titus, who accepted the nickname of Tye, was back in New Jersey
at least by 1778, and his militia unit was based at the forested area known
as "Refugeetown" on the coastline at Sandy Hook, near New York Harbor.
He led his unit into battle at Monmouth in June. The battle was incon-
clusive, but "Captain" Tye (as he was then called) took prisoner Captain
Elisha Shepard of the Monmouth Militia and took him to New York City,
where he was imprisoned at the Sugar House.

Tye's knowledge of Monmouth County and his bold leadership
soon made him a well-respected and feared Loyalist guerilla commander.
The British paid him and his men, consisting of Blacks and whites, to
destabilize the region, in retaliation for Rebel hangings of Loyalists and
confiscation of Loyalist property. Royal Governor William Franklin, son
of Benjamin Franklin oversaw the program. In a series of daring raids,
Tye and his men captured many prominent Rebels, and took their farm
animals, forage, and silverware to supply hard-pressed British forces elsewhere. By late 1779, Tye's men, known as the Black Brigade, operated
closely with a detachment of the Queen's Rangers, a white Loyalist group
that was loosely under the command of the famous Major John Graves
Simcoe.

The Black Brigade directed much of its energy to assisting slaves
to escape to the British lines, from which they were sent to Nova Scotia
and freedom. Because members of the Black Brigade knew the homes of

Patriots from their time serving as slaves, the Patriots feared the raids of the Black Brigade more than they feared the regular British Army. At this time, members of the Black Brigade started calling Tye "Colonel Tye," even though he did not have any formal rank bestowed upon him by any governmental agency.

German Lutheran pastor, the Rev. Henry Muhlenberg wrote: "The worst is to be feared from the irregular troops whom the so-called Tories have assembled from various nationalities – for example, a regiment of Catholics; a regiment of Negroes, who are fitted for and inclined towards barbarities, are lacking in human feeling, and are familiar with every corner of the country." Sometimes rumors can be just as powerful weapons as facts. Rumors suggested that the Black Brigade planned massacres of whites in Elizabeth and Somerset County. Brigadier-General David Forman of the New Jersey [Patriot] militia organized the Association for retaliation to protect themselves against raids by the Black Brigade and other Loyalist units. Forman and others begged [Patriot] Governor William Livingston to help combat Tye's raids. Livingston responded by invoking martial law, but that in turn encouraged many more slaves to run away to the British New York. Livingston (who said he was otherwise in favor of ending slavery in New Jersey) then encouraged slave-holders to move their slaves to remoter parts of New Jersey.

In retaliation for Joseph Murray's vigilante executions of Loyalists in Monmouth County, the Black Brigade killed Murray while attacking his home. In a raid on Patriot militia commander Barnes Smock's home, the Black Brigade destroyed an artillery unit. In late June 1780, Tye's men captured a number of Patriot militia leaders from around the state. In September 1780. Tye led a small joint group of the Black Brigade and the Queen's Rangers to the home of Captain Joshua Huddy, who had made a name for himself by executing Loyalists whom he captured. Tye managed to capture Huddy, but in a surprise counter-attack, some Patriots freed Huddy. Tye was wounded in the wrist by a musket ball. The wound rapidly went septic, and Tye died two days later from the infection.

'Colonel' Stephen Blucke, who commanded another Black Loyalist group, the Black Company of Pioneers, also took over Tye's unit, continuing to operate after the British surrender at Yorktown in October 1781. Most of the former members of the Black Brigade, however, sought refuge in Nova Scotia, where Blucke also went at the end of the war. Before the war ended, however, some vengeful Tories captured Huddy in the spring of 1782 and hanged him on the beach at Navesink, New Jersey, partly in retaliation for his having killed so many Loyalists out of hand, and partly because his musket ball had killed Colonel Tye. The British, incidentally, were quite happy to use his courtesy title of colonel, even though they had not actually given him that rank.

This entry was paraphrased from Wikipedia, with historical and geographical details added by the author.

HAITIAN GOVERNOR-GENERAL/EMPEROR JEAN-JACQUES DUCLOS DESSALINES, *ONCE ENSLAVED*, 1758–1806 (HAITI)

Jean-Jacques Duclos was born into slavery on the Cormier Plantation in northern Haiti. The names of his parents are not recorded. He worked in the sugarcane fields until he was about 30, when he was purchased by Monsieur Dessalines, a free man of color. He worked for this new owner until he gained his freedom about three years later, having taken the new owner's last name as his own. He had two brothers, Louis and Joseph, who also adopted Dessalines as their last name.

When the Haitian Revolution began in 1791 in the north, Jean-Jacques threw in his lot with the thousand s of others trying to end slavery. Jean-Jacques took his cue from Toussaint Breda, who was initially allied with Spanish forces against the French. However, when the French declared an end to slavery in 1794 (thanks to the French Revolution), the two men switched over to fighting with the French to drive the Spanish out.

However, when Napoleon Bonaparte took over the government of France, he wanted to restore slavery in Haiti, because that is the only way he could see for Haiti to generate the giant profits it had once provided for France, which was always in dire need of more money. In 1802, General Charles Leclerc arrived at the head of a large army, so once again Toussaint and Dessalines found themselves fighting the French. Dessalines defeated them in a major battle at Crete-a-Pierrot. When Toussaint was betrayed (and there is some annoying evidence that Dessalines was in on the betrayal) and kidnapped to a prison in France, Dessalines became the leader of the Revolution in 1803. He led his army to a great victory over the invaders at the Battle of Vertieres on 18 November over Leclerc's successor, Rochambeau (who was ignominiously captured a second time, this time by Black Royal Navy Captain John Perkins). On 29 November,

Dessalines declared Haiti to be an independent nation, and on 1 January 1804 it was proclaimed as the Independent Republic of Haiti. Dessalines, it should be said, was entirely illiterate, and apparently never made the slightest effort to learn to read or write, but fortunately he had trustworthy men around him who could do his reading and writing for him. Dessalines was appointed the Governor-General. He named the country Haiti after the indigenous people's (the Taino or Arawak) name for the land.

Dessalines soon ordered the massacre of all French remaining in Haiti, as well as some mulattos, and up to 5000 people were butchered in 1804 (including children and the elderly), although he made some exceptions (such as his former master Dessalines, to whom he gave a job in his household). Dessalines himself married an older woman, Marie-Claire Heureuse Felicitee Bonheur, and she eventually died at age 100. Between them, they had a total of sixteen children, some from previous liaisons, and some from adoption. The nation had not been independent as a republic but a short time, when Dessalines decided to make it an empire instead, with himself as emperor, with the right to name his successor. He was crowned Emperor Jacques I at Cap Haitien formerly Cap Francois) on 6 October 1804.

Haiti was the first country in the New World to abolish slavery. Understanding the value of a strong economy, Dessalines tried unsuccessfully to keep the sugar industry and plantations going without resorting to slavery. Therefore, he did the closest thing to bringing back slavery: he insisted that all people of a certain age should work either as soldiers to defend the nation, or as laborers on the plantations in order to produce exports to help support the nation. Of course, all people working as soldiers or laborers would be paid, although not a great amount. He also insisted on tightly regulating foreign trade.

Various members of his administration, including Alexandre Petion and Henri Christophe, were not impressed at the direction the country was taking, so they launched a conspiracy to overthrow the emperor. He was assassinated on 17 October 1806 at Pont-Rouge, just north of Port-au-Prince. His body was dismembered and mutilated. His murder left a power vacuum, and it was temporarily filled by Petion claiming the southern half of the country and Christophe claiming the northern half.

This entry was paraphrased from Wikipedia, with historical and geographical details added by the author.

MERCHANT SHIP CAPTAIN PAUL CUFFEE/KOFI, *FREE BLACK/WAMPANOAG INDIAN*, 1759–1817 (MASSACHUSETTS)

Paul Cuffee (sometimes spelled Cuffe) was born on Cuttyhunk Island (near Martha's Vineyard, Massachusetts) in January 1759 to formerly enslaved Black Kofi Slocum and Wampanoag Indian Ruth Moses, who had been married in Dartmouth in 1747. Cuttyhunk (an Indigenous name) at the time was mostly uninhabited, but reserved for summertime sheep herding. In 1766, the family (by then ten children) moved to near-by Dartmouth, Massachusetts, just west of New Bedford on the mainland. The father died in 1772 when Paul was 13. Many of the children decided to use a version of their father's first name as their family name (since Slocum had been the name of his father's slave-owner). Paul's mother died in 1787.

Starting in 1773, Paul set sail on whaling ships, happy at the chance to learn navigation skills. In 1776, after the start of the Revolution, the whaling ship he was on was captured by the British, so Paul and the rest of the crew had to spend three months imprisoned in New York City before their release. Paul returned to his family in the part of Dartmouth that was then called Westport (next to Little Compton, Rhode Island). Paul started sailing an open boat to bring goods for sale to Martha's Vineyard and Nantucket, but on some of these voyages he was intercepted by coastal pirates. Finally, without the pirates bothering him anymore, he began to turn a profit on these voyages.

In 1780, when Paul was twenty-one, he and his older brother John refused to pay taxes to the state because free Blacks did not have the right to vote. He was, of course, correct, but the petition to the Bristol County Court was denied. However, the Massachusetts General Court (the legislature) as a result voted to offer voting rights to all free male citizens of the state, regardless of race, arguably the first time this had been done in America.

Paul began a partnership in 1783 with a brother-in-law to construct ships and operate them along the East Coast. They built ever larger ships in Westport for the next 25 years. In February 1783, Paul married Alice Abel Pequit, a widow who was also a Wampanoag. By 1800, he had built the three-masted barque *Hero* measuring 162 tons. He built his largest ship *Alpha* in 1806 measuring 268 tons, meaning it was about 95 feet long on deck. In 1807, he built the 109-ton brig *Traveller*, which was his favorite. When he sailed *Traveller* to Liverpool, the London *Times* said that this was most likely the first vessel to arrive in Europe that was "entirely owned and navigated by Negroes." Until 1807, when the British government ended the slave trade, Liverpool had been one of the centers of the British slave trade. The Liverpool waterfront crowds, especially the resident Blacks, were even more excited when three additional ships owned by Paul and entirely manned by Blacks sailed into the port. At this point, Paul was arguably the wealthiest Black or Native American in the United States.

The slaves whom the British had freed when they occupied American cities in the Revolution – Boston, Newport, New York, Perth Amboy, Philadelphia, Norfolk, Wilmington, Charleston, Savannah, and St. Augustine – had been assembled in Nova Scotia, where they could see no useful future. They petitioned the British government to purchase a colony for them to settle in West Africa. The British were able to buy Sierra Leone, and the first settlers (many of them the poor from the slums of London) arrived at the capital city of Freetown in 1787. Over the next few years, a few thousand Blacks from Nova Scotia were sent there at their request, although the local government announced that they expected all the new settlers to pay a substantial quit-rent tax, which greatly worried the new settlers that they were exchanging one kind of slavery for another.

More than a few free Blacks in the United States considered that their interests might be served by moving to Africa. That annoyed the British, who pointed out that Sierra Leone was reserved for British Blacks, not residents of the United States, which is one of the reasons that President Monroe eventually snatched a next-door piece of land to Sierra Leone in 1822. He called it Liberia, the Land of Liberty, and he thoughtfully named its capital city after himself: Monrovia.

Paul, as a devout Quaker, was interested in Sierra Leone, particularly as a place to evangelize, and he was encouraged by his Quaker friends in Philadelphia. In the last week of 1810, Paul sailed from Philadelphia, arriving at Freetown on 1 March 1811. He found that the colonial authorities were not welcoming to Americans, and charged enormous customs duties on any goods he wanted to sell there. The authorities also insisted that all men from age sixteen on had to join the militia, which involved, among other things, swearing allegiance to King George III. Many inhabitants refused to do that, in case they might find themselves drafted into military service. Paul helped the local Blacks to establish a mutual-aid group dedicated to improving prosperity and industry in the colony. They called it the Friendly Society of Sierra Leone. He then visited Liverpool to see what could be done to improve the lot of the residents of Sierra Leone. Residents of Liverpool were very impressed that his ship was owned by Black people, and that the captain and all the crew were Black. He returned to Freetown, and helped the leaders come to a plan to establish saw mills, grist mills, a rice-processing factory, and a salt works.

Just at that moment, relations between the United States and Great Britain took a turn for the worse. The United States had placed an embargo against British goods, which also included goods from Canada, the British Caribbean colonies – and Sierra Leone. In fact, when he returned to Newport, the US Customs seized his ship and its cargo, and Paul had to go all the way to the White House to complain to President Madison. This was probably the first time that a Black man had been received as a guest at the White House. Madison then understood that Paul had not intended to circumvent the embargo, so his ship and goods were returned to him. Madison also understood that Paul was his best chance to understand more clearly how United States policies impacted both Black Americans and Blacks resident in the new colony of Sierra Leone, and so he questioned him extensively.

It was only a few more months before war broke out between the United States and Great Britain, the so-called War of 1812. Although US propaganda blamed the war on the British Navy taking crewmembers off American ships (which they actually did in a few instances), real estate speculators in Congress, hoping to conquer territory in the provinces of Quebec and Ontario (where there was money to be made from the lucrative beaver fur trade), were the real driving force behind starting the war. US troops had not been able to conquer and hold a single square foot of Canada by the end of the war in late 1814. As a Quaker, Paul was of course a pacifist and entirely opposed to war. He was also in despair that the war would prevent him from improving the lot of the people of Sierra Leone.

As the war dragged on, it became more difficult to make money out of his ships, which had to pay for their construction costs. By the end of the war, he found that his biggest ship, *Hero,* had been declared unfit to go to sea and had to be scrapped in Chile, but she was after all about fifteen years old, the magic age at which oak ships have to be rebuilt or scrapped.

A few days before the end of 1815, Paul sailed out of Westport with eighteen free Black adults and twenty children, all planning to be new settlers in Sierra Leone. In addition, the ship carried axes, hoes, a plow, a wagon, and the parts to build a sawmill. Paul and his immigrants were not greeted as warmly as before. Governor MacCarthy was having a difficult time keeping the population in order, so the last thing he needed was additional settlers. After a while, the new settlers were accepted, even though the goods that he had imported sold at far below market prices. Paul still believed that once regular trade could be established between Sierra Leone and Europe and America all the new colony's problems would be solved.

Paul, even though he was not doing as well financially as before, paid half the cost of building the new Friends' Meeting House at Westport. He never returned to Sierra Leone because his health failed, and he died at Westport on 7 September 1817.

The African Colonization Society attracted many Blacks who wished to return to Africa. However, in a trend that alarmed Paul, racists and Southern slaveholders actively supported it, because they saw it as a way of ridding America of potentially troublesome agitators who might otherwise disrupt their way of life. At the same time, Haiti seemed to have an appeal for many American Blacks. The second elected president of Haiti, Jean-Pierre Boyer, thought that American Blacks could be helpful in developing his country. He also thought that the presence of many former US Blacks in Haiti would encourage the United States to grant diplomatic recognition for his country, something which the Southern states would not permit. Haiti finally received recognition in 1861 when the Southern states withdrew from the United States.

This entry was paraphrased from Wikipedia, with geographical and historical details added by the author.

HAITIAN GENERAL BENOIT-JOSEPH ANDRE RIGAUD, *ONCE ENSLAVED*, 1761–1811 (HAITI & FRANCE)

Andre' Rigaud was born at Les Cayes in the south of Haiti in 1761, His father was Andre' Rigaud, a wealthy French sugar planter, and his mother was a slave, Rosy Bossy Depa. The father recognized the mulatto boy as his son and freed him. He sent him to Bordeaux in France, where he was trained as a goldsmith. The lad was known to wear a brown wig with straight hair so as to resemble as closely as possible a white man.

As an adult, he returned to Haiti in the early 1790s, and became active in politics. He championed the interests of free people of color (most of whom lived in the south of Haiti), and professed to uphold the ideals of Revolutionary France and the Declaration of the Rights of Man and the Citizen. He believed in the civil equality of all free people. France sent three civil commissioners to deal with the colony, and Rigaud was detailed by one of them, Etienne Polverel, to govern the south, as they abolished slavery in 1793–4. Rigaud was made a general in the French Revolutionary Army in Haiti, as was Toussaint, who was senior to him.

Rigaud worked with Toussaint to re-establish the plantation economy, although with paid labor rather than slaves. Unlike Toussaint, Rigaud believed in some sort of race-based caste system, in which men with lighter skins were superior in rank to those with darker skins. In June 1799, Toussaint's army invaded Rigaud's land in the south in what came to be known as the War of Knives, and Rigaud was defeated.

Rigaud then boarded a ship to return to France, but he sailed during the Quasi-War between the United States and Revolutionary France, so the French schooner *La Diane* on which he sailed was captured by the 12-gun USS *Experiment* on 1 October 1800. The Americans took Rigaud as a prisoner-of-war to the British Caribbean Island of St. Kitts, where he was released a few months later and completed his journey to France.

Rigaud returned to Haiti as part of General Charles Leclerc's expedition, ordered by Napoleon to reassert French control over the island and restart slavery again so that hard-pressed France could have some money coming in from Haiti. Leclerc was Napoleon's brother-in-law, so he had genuine authority behind him. However, although Leclerc was able to trick Toussaint into being captured and sent as a prisoner to France, Toussaint's deputy, Jean-Jacques Dessalines was able to defeat the French Army, which had lost over half its men to tropical diseases. Leclerc and Rigaud left Haiti in 1803, and Rigaud found himself locked up in the same fortress as Toussaint, although it is not recorded if they met and talked there before Toussaint's death in 1803.

Rigaud returned to Haiti again in late 1810. He managed to get established as president of the southern half of Haiti, having pushed his former ally Alexandre Petion out of the way, while Henri Christophe held power in the north. However, Rigaud died in September 1811, and soon after that, Petion established his own power in the south.

This entry was paraphrased from Wikipedia, with historical and geographical details added by the author.

FRENCH GENERAL THOMAS-ALEXANDRE DUMAS
DAVY DE LA PAILLETERIE, *ONCE ENSLAVED*, 1762–
1806 (HAITI & FRANCE)

Thomas-Alexandre Dumas was born near Jeremie in Haiti in 1762, the son of the Marquis Alexandre-Antoine Davy de la Pailleterie and Marie-Cessette Dumas, a slave of African descent. His father initially sold him as a slave in 1775, but purchased him back a few months later as part of a bizarre scheme to pay for their passage to France. Then, he took him to France in 1776, freed him, and had him educated. The father treated the rest of his family very differently: he sold Thomas' mother and her three other children. His father paved the way to have Thomas enter the French military. He enlisted in the French Army in 1786 as a 24-year-old private, so as not to trouble his father, but his father died only two weeks after his enlistment in the Queen's Dragoons.

His first few years in the dragoons were spent at Laon, Picardy, near what later became the Belgian border. In 1789, at the beginning of the French Revolution, his unit was sent to Villers-Cotterets in response to a wave of violence there. He then became engaged to the innkeeper's daughter, Marie-Louise Labouret. By July 1791, his unit served as riot police under the Marquis de Lafayette. Some of the other military police killed a few dozen people who had been calling for the King's removal, but as Dumas pointed out two years later, he believed that his intervention saved the lives of 2000 people. He was promoted to corporal in 1792 and served along the Belgian border.

In October 1792, he was commissioned as lieutenant-colonel in a special legion that was not an official part of the French Army, the American Legion, also called the Black Legion and the Saint-Georges Legion, because the great Black composer Joseph Bologne Chevalier de Saint-Georges was its commanding officer. Then he married Marie-Louise Elisabeth Labouret the following April, French General Dumouriez attempted to take over the government by coup d'etat, but Dumas and Saint-Georges opposed him, and protected the historic northeastern city of Lille from the coup supporters. However, in 1793 Saint-Georges was falsely accused of stealing money, so the Legion had to be disbanded.

In 1793, Dumas was promoted to Brigadier General, and above, in charge of the French Army in the Pyrenees from his base at Bayonne on the coast of the Bay of Biscay. By age 31 he was promoted to General-in-Chief, commanding 53,000 troops of the French Army of the Alps. In

1794, he won a victory, opening the high Alpine passes for the Second Italian campaign against the Austrian Empire. Equipping his solders' boots with ice crampons, he was able to scale ice cliffs and capture Mont Cenis, taking almost 2000 prisoners.

In 1794, Dumas was briefly assigned to command the Ecole de Mars military school, near Paris, and then he was ordered to be the military governor of the Vendee near Nantes on the West Coast of France. There he concentrated in improving military discipline, and particularly on eliminating abuses of the local population by the soldiers. In 1795, Dumas fought in the Army of the Rhine in Germany, but he was wounded in the French attack on Dusseldorf. Dumas participated in the siege of Mantua, Italy in 1796–7. The Austrian soldiers nicknamed Dumas as the Black Devil in 1797, whereas the French (including Napoleon) called him the Horatius Cocles of the Tyrol, making a reference to the hero who had saved Rome by defeating enemy troops over the Eisack River. Shortly after that, he had a nasty argument with Napoleon, which temporarily sidelined his career.

Dumas was part of the French attempt to conquer Egypt and the Eastern Mediterranean in 1798–1801. For that, he was a commander of the French cavalry, but on the march from Alexandria to Cairo he had a major argument with Napoleon, his commanding officer. Afterwards, Napoleon is said to have announced that he had no need of Dumas, and could easily replace him with a mere brigadier. He fought in the Battle of the Pyramids. Dumas discovered a collection of treasure in the basement of the house he was staying in, so he turned it over to Napoleon. The entire expedition was defeated by British Admiral Nelson's naval victory at the Battle of Aboukir Bay, so Dumas left Egypt to return home. However, the ship ran aground near Naples in March 1799, and he was imprisoned until early 1801.

Dumas returned to France, and a year later he and his wife Marie-Louise, who had previously given birth to two daughters, had a son, Alexandre Dumas (1802–1870), who eventually became one of France's most beloved writers, and his most famous military characters were inspired by his father.

When he was recovered from the illnesses he had picked up in the prison, he expected to be hired to command an army, but in spite of many messages to Napoleon, no commission was forthcoming. In fact, he could not even secure a pension for all the good work he had previously done as a soldier, to say nothing of the back-pay he was owed. He died of stomach cancer in February 1806. His widow, his surviving daughter, and his son were thrown into deep poverty. Alexandre was not even able to obtain an education because they had no money. Marie-Louise, who never received a widow's pension, blamed the fiasco on Napoleon's implacable hatred. Over a century later in 1912, following a long fund-raising campaign headed up by writer Anatole France and actress Sarah Bernhardt, a statue of General Dumas was erected in Paris. However, in 1941 Nazi German military authorities, probably motivated by racism, had the statue destroyed. That statue has unfortunately not yet been replaced.

This entry was paraphrased from Wikipedia, with historical and geographical additions by the author.

BRIGADIER GENERAL AUGUSTE CLAIRVAUX/ CLERVAUX, *ONCE ENSLAVED*, CA. 1763–1804 (HAITI AND FRANCE)

Auguste Clairvaux, a mulatto, was born in Haiti about 1763. His white father took him to France to be educated. He joined the French Army and was promoted eventually to Brigadier General by 1800. He was sent to Haiti, and quickly found that he was more in sympathy with the Haitian rebels than he was with the French, who were seeking to re-impose slavery on the territory. On 10 October 1802, he joined the Black rebels and was appointed to command a large group of them. Alexandre Petion saw what he had done, and decided to do likewise. Only two years later, Clairvaux died. At the moment, no further information is available about Clairvaux.

This entry was paraphrased from Wikipedia.

UNITED STATES BRIGADIER GENERAL PUSHMATAHA, *CHOCTAW PARAMOUNT CHIEF*, CA. 1764–1824

Pushmataha (like many Indigenous Americans, he is believed to have had only a single name) was born about 1764 to two members of the Choctaw tribe near the future site of Macon, Mississippi, near the Alabama border. The names of his parents are unknown, and it is thought that the parents may have been killed in a raid by a neighboring tribe. He was therefore a likely orphan, but Native Americans generally adopted orphans and treated them well. When he was thirteen, he took part in a war against the Creek, and then he participated in wars against the Osage and Caddo tribes west of the Mississippi in his twenties. By the first decade of the 1800s, he had fought in a number of different conflicts and had established a widespread reputation as a warrior. Many of these conflicts were as a result of other tribes trying to take over the Choctaw traditional deer-hunting lands, and also competition among tribes for the lucrative fur market for trade with white people. In this period, his military experience extended into the lands that eventually became the states of Arkansas and Oklahoma.

By 1800, Pushmataha was widely seen as not only a military leader but also a spiritual leader. About 1800, he was chosen as the Mingo or regional chief of the Six Towns district, the most southerly of three districts of the Choctaw, primarily in Mississippi. He was described as possessing sharp logic, humorous wit, and lyrical and eloquent speaking style, all of which earned him renown in councils. He took on a central role in diplomacy, first meeting with representatives of the United States government in 1802 at Fort Confederation. He negotiated the Treaty of Mount Dexter with the United States in November 1805, and even met with President Thomas Jefferson while he was still in office.

The War of 1812 was otherwise a minor sideshow in the Napoleonic War, but its coming was foreshadowed. British warships from time to time took a small number of sailors off American merchant ships and impressed them into the Royal Navy, and that was the official United States reason for the war. The real reason was that real estate speculators in Congress saw a perfect opportunity to invade Canada and seize much of Ontario (where enormous profits could be made from the lucrative trade in beaver fur, as John Jacob Astor demonstrated) while the British were tied down fighting Napoleon. A secondary reason was that Shawnee tribesmen under the leadership of Tecumseh, who hoped to build a separate nation inside the borders of the United States, were trying to secure British backing for their cause. In 1811, Pushmataha was quoted as saying, *These white Americans . . . give us fair exchange, their cloth, their guns, their tools, implements, and other things which the Choctaw need but do not make . . . They doctored our sick; they clothed our suffering; they fed our hungry . . . So in marked contrast with the experience of the Shawnee, it will be seen that the whites and Indians in this section are living on friendly and mutually beneficial terms.*

In the middle of 1813, Pushmataha raised a company of 500 Choc-taw warriors. In late December 1813, he helped to defeat an army of Creek at the Battle of Holy Ground, also called Kantachi. With larger numbers of Choctaw, Pushmataha joined General Andrew Jackson's army arrayed against the Creek, whom they defeated at the Battle of Horseshoe Bend. Nobody in North America knew it yet, but the United States and Great Britain had already signed a peace treaty in Europe ending the war, when British General Sir Edward Pakenham was killed in his assault on New Orleans in early 1815. Fighting against Pakenham were General Andrew Jackson and Brigadier General Pushmataha. One of the most important British aims in capturing New Orleans was trading rights. When the Spanish had owned New Orleans, the British had a treaty right to sail ships up the Mississippi and Missouri Rivers to trade with the interior, and the British were hoping to force the Americans to grant a similar right again in perpetuity. Since Pakenham lost the battle (and lost his life), the British lost all hope of reacquiring that right.

After he had returned from the War of 1812, Pushmataha was elected Paramount Chief of the Choctaw. He used his position to import agricultural technology, including cotton gins, and improved military disciplines. He used much of his military pension to fund an educational system for the Choctaw.

Pushmataha, after standing toe-to-toe with Jackson in 1820 land treaty negotiations, led a delegation of powerful Choctaw to Washington DC in 1824, where he met with President James Monroe and Secretary of War John C. Calhoun in order to secure their guarantees against fur-ther erosion of Choctaw lands by white squatters and others. While in Washington, he sat for a portrait in his US Army uniform, painted by Charles Bird King (which was destroyed by fire in 1865, but various cop-ies survive). He also met with Lafayette, who was visiting Washington at the time. Shortly after that, he fell ill with a viral respiratory infection and died on Christmas Eve. He was buried with full military honors in the Congressional Cemetery. He had five children.

This entry was paraphrased from Wikipedia, with geographical notes by the author.

FRENCH COLONEL LOUIS DELGRES II, *FREE MULATTO*, 1766–1802 (MARTINIQUE, TOBAGO, FRANCE, GUADELOUPE, DOMINICA, ST LUCIA, ST VINCENT)

Louis Delgres II was born a mulatto in August 1766 at Saint-Pierre, Martinique. His father, Louis Delgres I, was a white official in charge of the French king's land and rental income for the Caribbean Island of Tobago (which was at that time in the possession of the French), and his mother was a Black or mulatto slave in Martinque named Elisabeth Morin Guiby. Young Louis lived with his parents in Martinique, and later in Tobago. A document from when he was 33 years old described him as an excellent military officer who was very good at reading, writing, and mathematical calculations. It is possible that he was educated partially in France.

Delgres started his military career in November 1783, just after the end of the American Revolution. He was made a sergeant in the militia in Martinique. The turmoil in Haiti and elsewhere pushed him to decide on his own personal course. He became known as someone opposed to slavery, and he found that this helped his career in the regular army. In September 1791, Louis exiled himself to the next-door Island of Dominica, out of his disgust that power in Martinique was in the hands of the Royalists. In October 1792, he participated in the elections for deputies from the Windward Islands to the National Convention in Paris.

Louis rejoined the ranks of republicans in December 1792 when he came aboard the frigate *La Felicite'*, commanded by Captain Lacrosse. He was elected a lieutenant. When he landed in Martinique, he became part of the army under the orders of Rochambeau (the much less talented son of the victor at Yorktown in 1781), and was promoted to captain. However, in 1794, he was captured by the British who were on their way to capture the Island of Guadeloupe. They took him to England, but he was soon exchanged and returned to France, and then back to the Caribbean. In January 1795, he was reconfirmed as a lieutenant in Guadeloupe, and in March he was sent with the force that reconquered the Island of St. Lucia from the British. He distinguished himself in this campaign, but was seriously wounded. Two months later, he was mostly recovered, so he was promoted again to captain, and was sent on the expedition to capture the Island of St. Vincent from the British. His job there was to fight against the Maroons (a semi-independent force of Blacks and Indigenous men, but he was captured and sent back to England as a prisoner. Over a year later, he was freed on a prisoner exchange.

Louis was sent to Rouen, and then to the Ile d'Aix off the port of Rochefort on the Biscay coast of France. In 1799, he was ordered to accompany some Revolutionary government officials to Guadeloupe, but he refused because he had not been paid for a long time. Finally, Victor Hugues advanced him a substantial sum, so he set sail in November.

In Guadeloupe, he became military advisor to various Revolutionary officials, but when those officials had been denounced and driven into exile, he identified himself with the rebels, and was promoted to Colonel. In January 1802, Louis ordered several white officials fired for corresponding with the exiles, and later he had them arrested. However, in May 1802, General Richepance arrived with an army under orders from Napoleon to re-establish slavery in the French colonies. The local military leaders split into two camps. Some were in favor of working with Richepance, but Delgres and his associates decided that the French slogan of Liberty, Fraternity, and Equality demanded that they oppose the invaders. In May 1802, Delgres had become the chief officer of the resistance at Guadeloupe, based on the more mountainous southwestern half of the butterfly-shaped Island of Guadeloupe known as Basse-Terre. They first attached themselves to a fort at Basse-Terre. They escaped secretly on foot in the middle of the night to the volcano at Matouba, near Saint-Claude. Seeing that their cause was lost, Delgres and his 300 men blew themselves up at the Habitation Danglemont at Matouba, about three miles northeast of the coastal town of Basse Terre, leaving behind the slogan, "Live Free or Die." The Danglemont Plantation house is now mostly in ruins, but it is held in reverence by local officials.

This entry was paraphrased from Wikipedia, with geographical noted added by the author.

FRENCH BRIGADIER JOSEPH SERRANT, *FREE MULATTO*, 1767–1827 (MARTINIQUE, DOMINICA, SWITZERLAND, VENICE, BELARUS, LITHUANIA, POLAND, GERMANY, THE UK, AND FRANCE)

Joseph Serrant was born as a mulatto at Saint-Pierre in Martinique on 10 January 1767. His father was Antoine Serrant, a white planter, and his mother was a Black slave named Elisabeth. He was immediately freed. At age 15, Joseph enlisted as a volunteer in the Regiment de Bouille, and was promoted to corporal for the Dominica campaign (Dominica being the mountainous Island just north of Martinique and south of Guadeloupe, that often belonged to the British). After five years of service, he was discharged, and set himself up in Saint-Pierre as a shoemaker.

At the beginning of the French Revolution, he entered service with the National Guard, and began to hang out at the Dominica Club, where he spent a lot of time with Louis Delgres II. The two men launched a petition drive regarding the status of free men of color, with the result that they were forced into exile in Dominica. While they were there, they embarked on the frigate *La Felicite'*, commanded by Captain Lacrosse. The ship took them to St. Lucia, where they served as various grades of lieutenant. In December, the frigate took them to Pointe-a-Pitre, Guadeloupe. Captain Lacrosse announced the formation of the Republic, the Declaration of the Rights of Man, and the end of slavery. Of course, not everyone believed in the new order.

Serrant was promoted to captain of infantry in the 109th regiment, under the orders of General Rochambeau (the lackluster son of the general who defeated Cornwallis at the Battle of Yorktown in 1781). In this case, he was ordered to Martinique to defend against a British invasion, but he was captured by the British in February 1794 and sent to prison at Plymouth. In May 1795, he was exchanged, at which point he joined the 106th infantry regiment. The soldiers were ordered to restore order at Ouilly-le-Basset in Normandy, where they had to put down a rebellion.

In August 1796, Serrant was placed in the 87th. Napoleon was always interested in extending his control to all bits of land within range, and Switzerland caught his eye. The 87th was ordered under Colonel Armand Philippon to capture chunks of Switzerland, including Grissons and Valais, and the Italian Piedmont. He was wounded at the Battle of Murazzo in October 1799, but soon recovered and was made colonel in charge early in 1804. Then, he switched to the 5th regiment of infantry, where he participated in the capture of Venice (which had for centuries been an exceptionally prosperous independent city-state with colonies all along the Dalmatian Coast of what later became Yugoslavia, and a major military and cultural power in the entire Mediterranean). Serrant was in charge of capturing various parts of the Dalmatian Coast, including Curzola. He received another promotion, and was awarded the Knight's Cross of the Legion of Honor.

After the Battle of Debilibriche, he was wounded and taken prisoner at the Battle of Gospich in Croatia. Serrant was exchanged and named colonel of the Third Regiment of Croatian Chasseurs. In 1811, Serrant was made commander of the Eighth Regiment of Light Infantry in the army of Prince Eugene de Beauharnais for the invasion of Russia. During the Battle of Ostrovno in Belarus on 25–26 July, he was wounded while protecting Murat's cavalry, so he was awarded a higher grade of the Legion of Honor and promoted to Brigadier General in 1812. He was wounded again at the Battle of Maloyaroslavets, not far west of Moscow. Then he had to take his regiment safely back to Europe, where he was taken prisoner at Vilnius, Lithuania in December 1812. He was able to escape, and travelled all by himself across Poland in order to rejoin the Prince Eugene de Beauharnais at Magdeburg, half way between Hannover and Berlin in Germany.

When he got back to France in April 1813, Serrant was placed on convalescent leave until January 1814, when he was sent down to Savoy near Genoa. There he attacked Annecy, the Gorge des Usses, and Saint-Julien from January to March 1814. The following November, he was rewarded by being created a Chevalier de Saint-Louis. In May 1815, he was sent to Lyon, but by August he was placed on the inactive list. He was officially retired in February 1825. On 7 November 1827, Serrant died at Clermont-Ferrand. No one seems to know if he was ever married or had children. Although he had slavery in his parentage, he was described as being able to pass for white.

This entry was paraphrased from Wikipedia, with historical and geographical notes by the author.

HAITIAN KING HENRI CHRISTOPHE, *ONCE ENSLAVED*, 1767–1820 (GRENADA, HAITI)

Henri Christophe was born on 6 October 1767 of Bambara ethnicity from West Africa. He is believed to have been born on the Island of Grenada, but some accounts state that he was born on the Island of St. Kitts. His mother was a slave, but his father was a free man. As a boy, he moved to Haiti. When he was twelve, it is claimed that he served as drummer boy in the Chasseurs Volontaires de Saint-Domingue, a regiment composed mostly of mixed-race men, but with a few Blacks. The name Volontaires is confusing: the actual Blacks were not volunteering themselves as much as their owners were volunteering the Blacks. This regiment fought at the unsuccessful joint American-French assault on the British at Savannah, Georgia in 1779, and it is claimed that Christophe was at least slightly wounded in that battle, where it is thought that he may have been a drummer-boy.

It is claimed that Christophe worked at a number of trades as an adult, including a stone-mason, a stable-hand, and a sailor, but one story has more of a ring of truth: he worked in, and eventually was manager of the Couronne Hotel at Cap Francois. He was awarded his freedom about age twenty-one. He brought his sister Marie there; she married and had children. When the slave uprising began in 1791, he joined the revolutionaries as an officer, and was quickly promoted to colonel. He fought at the side of Toussaint in the north, and fought in numerous battles. By 1802, Toussaint had promoted him to general.

When the French sought to reverse the Haitian Revolution by sending thousands of French soldiers under the Vicomte de Rochambeau (the feckless son of the victor at Yorktown in 1781), they kidnapped Toussaint and imprisoned him in a fortress prison near the Swiss border. Jean-Jacques Dessalines became the leader of the struggle, and Christophe fought beside him. The French withdrew the last of their surviving troops from Haiti in late 1803, but a French army was occupying Spanish-speaking Santo Domingo. The French commander ordered all Black children below the age of fourteen (both boys and girls) to be rounded up and sold into slavery. Dessalines ordered Christophe to slit the throats of his opposition, and to burn many villages and structures. Dessalines horrified many of his closest allies by his brutality, both against the French and against other Haitians, so that more than a few of them plotted against him. Among these were General Nicolas Geffrard, who was in charge of mopping-up operations in the south, the navy minister Etienne Elie Gerin, and General Alexandre Petion. When they approached Christophe to ask him to join them, he neglected to tell Dessalines. They assassinated Dessalines on 17 October 1806.

Christophe retreated to the northern section of Haiti and quickly realized that Haiti could best be governed as two separate countries. He had himself proclaimed president of the north in 1807, while his former colleague Petion (backed by General Boyer) became president of the southern republic. In April 1811, Christophe proclaimed that the northern state was actually a kingdom, and he had Archbishop Jean-Baptiste Joseph Brelle crown him at the domed cathedral at Milot. Brelle had previously crowned Dessalines as emperor in the cathedral at Port-au-Prince. He designated his son Jacques-Victor Henry as his official successor.

Christophe built the massive Citadelle Laferriere not far from Milot in the north, as well as six chateaux and eight palaces. The Sans Souci Palace is now an impressive ruin, and a useful tourist attraction. The southern half of the country, ruled by Petion, made an effort to leave the amount they worked as decisions of the plantation workers, but the northern half was subjected to high taxes, so the workers were forced to work almost as hard as they had under slavery, which in turn left the northern kingdom financially solvent. Christophe made arrangements with the British, whereby northern Haiti agreed not to threaten the British Caribbean colonies, and the British Navy would warn Haiti about any potential attacks by the French. In 1807, the British outlawed the slave trade, a move that was welcomed in Haiti. Because of increased ocean-borne trade with Britain, northern Haiti prospered mightily. By contrast, the United States, which might have been thought to be a natural ally of Haiti, relaxed its trade restrictions only about 1810, just before they had to be tightened up again for the War of 1812.

Trouble returned in April 1814. Napoleon was forced to abdicate, and he moved to the Island of Elba off the coast of Italy. The French throne was claimed by Louis XVIII. France was effectively bankrupt, so she looked for a ready source of cash. Haiti seemed to be a reliable source of cash, if only slavery could be re-imposed there. The Treaty of Paris, which was ratified on 30 May, left Spanish-speaking Santo Domingo in the hands of France. France was further granted an additional five years of the slave trade in order gain back losses incurred by the abolition of slavery. France then intended to send a large military force to Santo Domingo in order to swarm across the border into Haiti. Haiti then made efforts to publicize to the world what was being done, and to form a closer relationship with Great Britain. As a result, the French invasion never occurred.

However, Napoleon escaped from Elba and attempted to take over the government of France at the end of February 1815. Therefore, much of Europe was thrown into chaos until Napoleon was recaptured at the Battle of Waterloo on 18 June. This time, the treaty that ended the fighting left Haiti in a much more robust situation. France, by contrast, was left with fewer resources, partly as a result of how readily Frenchmen had flocked to Napoleon's standard, rather than the standard of Louis XVIII.

Christophe established a remarkably fair legal system, which was known as the Code Henry. He also backed a national education system. In spite of that, he was not popular in his kingdom, and those who ran the other half of Haiti in the south looked longingly at the kingdom's large wealth. Christophe spent much of his life living inside the protective walls of the Citadelle Laferriere. However, in 1820, when he was only fifty-three, Christophe loaded his pistol with a silver ball and shot himself in the temple. His son, who was supposed to become the next king, was assassinated only ten days later.

This entry was paraphrased from Wikipedia, with geographical and historical notes added by the author.

TECUMSEH, *SHAWNEE WARRIOR CHIEF*, CA. 1768–1813 (UNITED STATES, CANADA)

Tecumseh was a Shawnee Warrior Chief who was born the fifth of eight children about 1768 near the modern town of Chillicothe, Ohio (about 50 miles south of Columbus). Tecumseh's father Puckeshinwau was killed in the Battle of Point Pleasant against expanding American colonists in 1774 (Virginians had acquired the Kentucky area from the Iroquois, but the Shawnee maintained that the Iroquois were not the rightful owners of that land), so his older brother Cheeseekau mentored him until he too was killed fighting the Americans in 1792. Tecumseh joined Blue Jacket's struggle against further American settlement on Native American lands, but that ended with the defeat at the Battle of Fallen Timbers in 1794. The Shawnee lost most of Ohio at the follow-up Treaty of Greenville in 1795.

Tecumseh's younger brother, Tenskwatawa (also given as Lala-wethika), founded a religious movement that called upon Native Americans to reject European influences and return to a more traditional tribal lifestyle. As a result, he was known as the Prophet. In 1808, Tenskwatawa and Tecumseh jointly founded Prophetstown (its English name) in modern Indiana, where the Tippecanoe River meets the Wabash River, just northeast of modern Lafayette. The site is now known as Battle Ground. While Tecumseh was on a trip to the south to recruit allies, William Henry Harrison defeated Tenskwatawa at the Battle of Tippecanoe in 1811, and made sure that there was nothing left of Prophetstown although Tenskwatawa himself survived until 1836). William Henry Harrison (then territorial governor of Indiana) persuaded a number of Native American chiefs, but by no means all, to sign the Treaty of Fort Wayne in 1810, turning over huge amounts of good, productive land to the United States. Tecumseh ordered Harrison and President Madison to cancel it, but they refused.

Tecumseh saw the War of 1812 developing, so in 1811 he wrote the following:

> *Where today are the Pequot? Where are the Narragansett, the Mohican, the Pocanet, and other powerful tribes of our people? They have vanished before the avarice and oppression of the white man, as snow before the summer sun . . . Sleep not longer, O Choctaws and Chickasaws . . . Will not the bones of our dead be plowed up, and their graves be turned into plowed fields?*

Remembering that the War of 1812 was mostly caused by Members of Congress hungry for Canadian real estate for them to develop (in large part due to the lucrative trade in beaver fur, as John Jacob Astor demonstrated), Tecumseh saw that his interests and those of the British were aligned, so he helped the British to capture Detroit in August 1812. In 1813, he led an unsuccessful military campaign against the United States in Ohio and Indiana. However, American naval forces under Oliver Hazard Perry surprisingly were able to defeat the powerful British fleet and take control of Lake Erie in 1813. Tecumseh saw British Major General Sir Isaac Brock as being the man to win along the northern frontier, which he did for a while, but Brock was killed at a battle in the Fort Niagara area, and after him the British had no good commanders in Canada. Tecumseh, without British help, assaulted Fort Wayne and Fort Harrison, but without success. A legend asserts that Brock had awarded Tecumseh with the temporary local rank of Brigadier, but that now appears to be no more than a legend.

In 1813, Tecumseh and his men joined British General Henry Procter to attack Fort Meigs. Procter did not deploy his men adequately, so Procter felt forced to halt the siege. After the battle, Native Americans began butchering their prisoners, but Tecumseh rushed forward and stopped the slaughter. Afterwards, Procter decided to retreat well into Canada from his base at Amherstburg, but Tecumseh begged him not to do so. As a result, Procter promised to make a stand at Chatham along the Thames River. Tecumseh arrived at Chatham, only to find that Procter had retreated still further to Moraviantown. At Moraviantown, Procter commanded the left side of his forces and Tecumseh was in charge of the right. The forces on the left collapsed almost immediately, so the Americans concentrated all their force against the right. Tecumseh was killed. His body was buried on the battlefield in an unmarked grave on 5 October 1813.

The Treaty of Ghent in 1814 called for the United States to restore Native American lands to their full extent in 1811, but the United States had no intention of following through on that promise, and there was no punishment mechanism to enforce it. William Henry Harrison described Tecumseh as "one of those uncommon geniuses, which spring up occasionally to produce revolutions and overturn the established order of things." Tecumseh is definitely a hero to Native Americans, and he was someone who played a major role in Canada's defense in the War of 1812, and he also played a major role in United States history.

This entry was paraphrased from Wikipedia, with historical and geographical notes by the author.

HAITIAN PRESIDENT ALEXANDRE SABES PETION, *FREE MULATTO*, 1770–1818 (HAITI, FRANCE)

Alexandre Petion (where the T is pronounced as if it were SS) was born in Port-au-Prince, Haiti in April 1770. His father was a wealthy Frenchman, and his mother was a free mulatto woman, which suggests that his skin would have been quite light in color, although portraits of him show him to have been quite dark with typical African features.

At age eighteen, he was sent to France to study at the French Military Academy in Paris. A few years later, the Haitian Revolution was under way, so he returned to the land of his birth. At first, he was involved in repelling the British forces who had invaded the northern part of the country. The British had gone on record, despite considerable objection at home, that they favored a restoration of the status quo from before the struggle, namely that the white slave-holders would continue to operate their plantations with slave labor. Petion allied himself with Rigaud and Boyer against Toussaint, but Toussaint won that struggle. When Toussaint and Dessalines captured the town of Jacmel in the south, Petion and others went into exile in France in March 1800.

In February 1802, French General Charles Leclerc and 32,000 French troops arrived in the hope of asserting control over the situation, and Petion, Rigaud, and Boyer came along with them. After the French had seized Toussaint and imprisoned him on the Swiss border, and the Haitian resistance gathered strength, Petion threw his support to Dessalines, and together they defeated Leclerc in the Battle of Vertieres on 18 November 1803 in the north near Cap Haitien. Dessalines declared independence on 1 January 1804. Later that year, Dessalines declared himself Jacques I, Emperor of Haiti. After the assassination of Dessalines in October 1806, Petion stood up for democracy, but Henri Christophe wanted more autocratic power. They compromised by Petion being elected President of the southern Republic of Haiti while Christophe was president of the northern State of Haiti, a position that he soon modified to King of Haiti. Christophe insisted that Haiti had to generate enough income to be able to stay afloat in the sea of independent nations, which meant that every able-bodied person had to donate a certain number of hours of working for the country. Petion, by contrast, felt that it was more important to establish democracy in its purest form, which turned out to generate almost no income for the country.

In June 1816, Petion made himself president-for-life, and two years later he suspended the legislature. He seized the large plantations from their rich owners and redistributed the land to the peasants, who nicknamed him Papa Bon-Coeur (good-hearted father). The economic result of this move was nothing short of disastrous, making the survival of the state questionable. He gave sanctuary to Simon Bolivar in 1815 and provided him with soldiers and military supplies, which helped win independence for all the countries that were carved out of Colombia and its surrounding territory. Petion named Boyer as his successor. Boyer took control in 1818 when Petion died of yellow fever. Two years later. King Henri Christophe died, and Boyer reunited the nation as one entity.

This entry was paraphrased from Wikipedia, with historical and geographical notes added by the author.

HAITIAN 2ND PRESIDENT JEAN-PIERRE BOYER, *FREE MULATTO*, 1776–1850 (HAITI, FRANCE)

Jean-Pierre Boyer was born at Port-au-Prince on 15 February 1776, the same year in which the United States declared independence. His father was a white French tailor, and his mother was a freed slave from Congo. His father sent him to France for his education. During the French Revolution, he fought as a colonel. He returned to Haiti, and in the early years of the Haitian Revolution he found himself on the opposite side from Toussaint. He allied himself with Andre Rigaud in an effort to keep control of the southern part of Haiti.

Boyer and Alexandre Petion returned to France as exiles, but they came back to Haiti in 1802, accompanying the French troops led by General Charles Leclerc. However, it soon became obvious that the real purpose of the French invasion was to reimpose slavery and place restrictions on free people of color. At that point, Boyer joined the patriots under Petion and Dessalines, and together they took the country to independence. After Petion had risen to power in the southern half of the country, he chose Boyer, who had an aristocratic bearing, as his successor. It is said that Boyer was under the influence of a beautiful and extremely clever woman, Marie-Madeleine "Joute" Lachenais (1778–1843), who had been for a time Petion's girlfriend, and then she guided Boyer; it seems that after a time she became Boyer's wife, and she certainly bore him a daughter, after having borne Petion two daughters. It is said that she was the most powerful woman ever in the history of Haiti.

Henri Christophe made himself King of the northern half of Haiti, while Petion was the President of the southern half of Haiti. Christophe did not win many friends, because he could clearly see that Haiti desperately needed to have substantial income in order to keep its head above water in a dangerous world, so he worked out a system in which every citizen had to work a percentage of his time for the State. Petion, by contrast, thought that if he seized all the big plantations of his part of Haiti and parcelled them out among would-be subsistence farmers, that would be the most democratic solution. Unfortunately, that did not work, as the farmers were too lazy. Instead, when Boyer became President, he felt that the most important thing he could do was obtain France's recognition of Haitian independence, which could be obtained only by agreeing to pay France a large indemnity.

After the death of Christophe and his son in 1820, Boyer made a successful effort to rejoin the two parts of Haiti as one. By coincidence, in November 1821, Jose Nunez de Caceros, the President of the Spanish two-thirds of the island, declared independence from Spain. For a while, Caceros proposed uniting the country with the newly independent constituents of Colombia, but Boyer felt that such a situation would be an open invitation to France and Spain to mount a joint assault on both parts of the island. Therefore, in February 1822, Boyer took a force of 50,000 soldiers to the Spanish section of the island, and took over control of the country. The union of the two countries fell apart in 1844, just after Boyer had gone into exile in Jamaica.

At the same time, Greece declared its independence from the Ottoman Empire in 1822, and Haiti was the first nation in the world to offer Greece recognition. Boyer answered the Greek request for financial assistance by saying that Haiti was too far into its own debt to be able to contribute, but he hoped Haiti would be able to contribute in the future. He filled the letter with all sorts of allusions to the great heroes of ancient Greek history, showing that he was very familiar with their history.

In 1824, it was becoming obvious that United States Blacks were still being poorly treated at home, and some of them were anxious to emigrate to [British] Sierra Leone, or to Liberia, which had recently been purchased by President James Monroe (hence the name of its capital city, Monrovia). Boyer and his associates thought that Haiti would be an ideal place for the American Blacks to come. However, Boyer's treasury was essentially empty, and he was unable to pay the substantial costs of relocating so many Blacks. In spite of that disadvantage, about 6000 American Blacks paid their own way, but most of them were disappointed and returned to the United States within a short space of time.

Boyer's Haiti was still obligated to pay France the huge indemnity for recognizing Haitian independence, so he attempted to place production quotas for all the Haitian small farms. This was, to say the least, not popular. To add insult to injury, a massive earthquake occurred in the north. The rural population revolted, so Boyer left the country in 1843 for Jamaica, making sure to bring Marie-Madeleine with him, but she died in the act of moving. Boyer then sought refuge in France. He died in Paris in 1850.

This entry was paraphrased from Wikipedia, with historical and geographical notes by the author.

ROYAL NAVY SENIOR CHIEF PETTY OFFICER 'WILLIAM BROWN,' *FREE BLACK*, 1776–1835 (GRENADA & UK) RN

'William Brown' (an assumed name) was born on the British-Caribbean Island of Grenada in 1776, and learned first to be a shipwright, and later a sailor. No record of his birth exists, because Brown is a name he adopted (based on his skin color) so he could not be traced. At school, he learned to read and write in both English and French. When he finished school between age 10 and 11, he got a job in a shipyard on the nearby island of Carriacou, building inter-island schooners (people still construct sea-going vessels on the beach at Carriacou, by eye and not using paper plans), but at age 14 he decided that he wanted instead to learn to sail such schooners. He joined the crew of a schooner. By age 18, he was already commanding a schooner, sailing on most voyages up the island chain as far north as Antigua or perhaps St Kitts, and by age 20 he was even part-owner of a square-topsail schooner.

In 1796, Brown left home in a hurry in order to avoid a family dispute with his father. At Barbados, he enlisted in the British Navy, and when the frigate on which he was sailing reached English Harbour, Antigua, he was placed in the 650-member crew of the giant 74-gun battleship *Orion*. Most enlisted Blacks in the Navy, of course, had little opportunity for advancement. Being of slight build, and thus not useful for hauling heavy cannons, Brown was assigned to work high in the rigging, which suited him perfectly. The top of the main topgallant mast was almost 200 feet above the water. Sometimes a petty officer would order the topmen aloft and would time them with his pocket-watch for placing a hand on the carved ball at the top of the topgallant mast. Brown excelled in that exercise.

A Black man enlisting in the Navy in those days had little chance of promotion, so by the time that Napoleon was defeated nineteen years later, few people would have been surprised if Brown had not received any promotions. Yet, by that date in 1815, Brown had been promoted to the top enlisted man in the entire Navy. Normally, an enlisted man was not permitted to talk to the captain, but Brown knew various important Caribbean facts of which British officers were clueless, so he would talk to a junior officer, who always passed the information to the captain.

The first such event was about ship construction. Nearly all European and North American ships were constructed of oak, which typically lasts only 15 years before it rots. Ship-building oak does not grow well in Spain, even though cork-oak, which is not suitable for ship-building, grows well there. The Spanish, however, owned the Island of Cuba in the Caribbean, where Cuban mahogany grows, and they built their navy's warships out of mahogany, both at Havana and with timber imported to Spanish shipyards. This mahogany is very different from Central American mahogany; it is so heavy that a piece of it will sink in water, and a ship built out of it will last 120 years or more, but unfortunately the species has been extinct for a long time, thanks to over-harvesting.

Brown knew (but the British officers did not know) that the downside of mahogany ships was that this wood was highly flammable. When Brown's fleet of 15 battleships was attacked in February 1797 at the Battle of Cape St. Vincent off the coast of Spain by a Spanish fleet of 25 mostly larger ships, Brown passed this information to Captain James Saumarez, who passed it along to his admiral, Sir John Jervis (pronounced 'Jarvis') aboard his 102-gun flagship *Victory* (the same *Victory* that is still on display to the public in Portsmouth, Hampshire). At Brown's suggestion, the admiral ordered his ships to fire extra paper and cloth wadding in their cannons at close range at the Spanish ships, with the result that a number of the Spanish ships left the battle heading for home at top speed with clouds of smoke pouring out. The British won the Battle of Cape St. Vincent on 14 February 1797 and captured four giant Spanish battleships of 112 guns apiece. Thank you, William Brown. An amazing eye-witness oil painting of this battle by Robert Cleveley can be seen at the National Maritime Museum at Greenwich, UK, although it does not show Brown's ship *Orion*.

Brown was of course paid the standard pay for an enlisted man of his rank in the Navy, and every time that his ship or fleet captured enemy ships, a complicated formula resulted in all the sailors (and officers) receiving an appropriate share of the "prize money." Acting on the friendly advice of the Purser, Brown took out an account at Coutts Bank in the Strand, London, and most of his pay and prize money were deposited there for safe-keeping. Similarly, a captain, an admiral, or a colonial governor could award a generous purse to any member of the crew who had been particularly useful in accomplishing an important objective, and Brown presumably came in for his share of those awards during the course of the war.

The 1750s were the era of professional geneticists, such as Robert Bakewell, who engineered improved English farm animal breeds – the Dishley Longhorn cattle with its extremely meaty carcass, the Leicester Longwool sheep, the Shire horse (of which the Clydesdale is the best known), and the English white pig, today the most numerous pig on earth. Some as yet anonymous Virginia gentlemen wished to engineer a new American breed of tree to produce superior ship-building timber, so in 1762–3 (Britain had temporarily conquered Cuba, so English-speaking people had a small window of time in which they could come in person to purchase items in Cuba) these Virginians took Cuban mahogany seedlings and crossed them probably with temperate relatives like the Kentucky Coffee Tree and the Chinaberry Tree. By the time the grove of trees was mature enough to harvest the wood a century and a half later, the whole enterprise had been forgotten. Therefore, a grove of giant mahogany trees 150 feet tall stands today in Louisa County to the west of Richmond, causing experts to wonder how trees that cannot survive north of Zone Ten can be growing so healthily in Zone Seven!

Admiral Horatio Nelson with 14 British battleships attacked the French fleet of 13 mostly larger battleships at the Battle of Aboukir Bay at the mouth of the River Nile in Egypt on 1 August 1798, and captured or destroyed all but one of the French ships. Brown and *Orion* participated in this lopsided battle. Captain Saumarez was badly wounded and had to spend months in hospital. He was replaced by Captain Sir Edward Codrington, who owned substantial property in the Caribbean, and he warmed to Brown's advice.

Three years later, Captain Saumarez had been promoted to Admiral Sir James Saumarez in charge of the tiny fleet of five British ships guarding the British base at Gibraltar. Gibraltar was a headland on the coast of Spain projecting into the entrance of the Mediterranean. It had been captured by the British in 1704, and it was useful in stopping ships from entering or leaving the Mediterranean. A joint French-Spanish fleet of nine battleships, much more powerful than the defending British fleet of five ships, came with the intention of capturing Gibraltar, and two of the Spanish ships were 112-gun giants that had been built out of flammable Cuban mahogany in Havana. Saumarez did not panic, because he remembered Brown's advice, and he ordered his ships to fire extra wadding into those two Spanish giants at close range. The two ships were soon blazing fiercely, and suffered enormous explosions when the flames reached the gunpowder magazines. Over 3000 Spaniards died. The joint enemy fleet (commanded by the same French Admiral Charles-Alexandre de Linois who would flee from a British fleet of merchant ships at the Battle of Pulo Aura in February 1804 – see the story of William Waters above) then panicked and sailed away as fast as they could, and Gibraltar remained British after the Battle of Algeciras on 12 July 1801. Even though Brown and *Orion* were not physically present for this battle, thank you, William Brown.

Napoleon conquered Italy in 1800. This was important because all the world's gunpowder was made of one-third sulfur, and Italy contained the three volcanoes (Etna, Stromboli, and Vesuvius) that supplied all the sulfur used by all the European countries and the Americas for making gunpowder. Napoleon confidently thought that the British would therefore quickly run out of gunpowder and ask for peace, because they could not fight without gunpowder. However, Napoleon had reckoned without Brown. Brown told his captain that two British Islands close to Grenada (St. Vincent and St. Lucia) contained stinky walk-in volcanoes with all the sulfur that the British needed. Napoleon's plot was foiled. Thank you, William Brown.

In 1803, the British learned that the French intended to make a maximum effort to capture all the British islands in the Caribbean, using warships from their naval base at Fort-de-France, Martinique. The British were at that moment powerless to stop the French. Brown spoke to his captain. He told him that 600-foot-tall Diamond Rock ('le Rocher du Diamant') stands with almost vertical sides about one mile southwest of Martinique. Brown had climbed that rock for a lark while a teenager. He said it was possible to land sailors on the rock and have them haul up heavy cannons; an 18-pounder cannon weighed 4700 lbs (2140 kg). A sea-level cannon has a range of three miles (5 km), hence the three-mile territorial limit still in force around the world today. However, a cannon at 600 feet/183 metres high has a range of 10–12 miles/up to 20 km. Those cannons on the top of Diamond Rock could prevent French warships from entering or leaving their base at Martinique. While Brown's ship *Orion* was undergoing her 15-year rebuild, the Navy authorized the capture operation of Diamond Rock by the 74-gun ship *Centaur*, commanded by Commodore Sir Samuel Hood, and Brown was sent to that ship to advise. The rock was captured on 7 January 1804, and a battery of heavy cannons on top was ready for firing on 1 March. The rock was even commissioned HMS *Diamond Rock* as a ship in the Royal Navy! Hood, who had commanded one of the ships at the Battle of Algeciras under Admiral Saumarez, is believed to have offered Brown a commission as lieutenant, but he could not guarantee that the racist Admiralty might not countermand the promotion, so Brown thanked him profusely but cheerfully remained a senior enlisted man. For the rest of the war, the French never made any headway in capturing the British islands. Thank you, William Brown.

Orion, with Brown back aboard, took part in Nelson's glorious victory over the combined French and Spanish fleets off the coast of Spain on 21 October 1805, known as the Battle of Trafalgar. The British with

27 battleships captured 21 of 33 French and Spanish mostly larger battle-ships, and destroyed one additional ship. *Orion* managed to capture one French battleship during the battle. Alas, Admiral Nelson aboard his flag-ship *Victory* was killed by a sharp-shooter, perched high in the rigging of the French battleship *Le Redoutable*. The bodies of most people killed in sea battles were dropped over the side with cannonballs attached to them during a funeral service. However, Nelson was a national hero, so his body had to be sailed all the way back to England for a public funeral service at St Paul's Cathedral in London some two months after the battle. Since dead bodies are subject to decay, Nelson's body was fitted into a barrel of rum (some say it was French brandy), which is why some people have referred to rum as 'Nelson's Blood.' Nelson's flagship *Victory* was eventually preserved in a drydock at Portsmouth for the public to visit.

The French were on the verge of capturing Denmark again, so in or-der to keep the French from acquiring for free the warships of the Danish Navy, Admiral Gambier commanded his British fleet to capture the Dan-ish Navy. The British captured all 18 Danish battleships and destroyed three more under construction in the shipyard. Brown aboard *Orion* (commanded by Captain Sir Archibald Collingwood Dickson) took part in that victory. This was the second Battle of Copenhagen (16 August 1807), the first one having been won by Nelson on 2 April 1801, in which 12 Danish battleships had been captured and three were destroyed.

After these important achievements, Brown was promoted to senior enlisted man in the entire Navy – not bad for a Black man from a remote island! *Orion* spent the rest of her career keeping watch on French naval bases on the west coast of France, to make sure that no French naval ships ventured forth, and organizing sabotage expeditions on the French shore. After several years of punching into the giant waves of the Bay of Biscay, *Orion* was hopelessly falling apart and was leaking badly, so she was ordered to be scrapped. Brown and the entire crew were transferred to a newly-built 104-gun three-decker ship, *Queen Charlotte*, the Navy's biggest ship in 1813, crewed by 820–1000 men.

When Brown had been in the Navy for 19 years, the Napoleonic War came to an end in 1815. About two weeks before the end of the war, Brown was not keeping his guard up as well as usual. An officer came aft to talk to the captain: "Sir, I have some very bad news to report about William Brown. This enlisted man with such an exemplary record has now turned out, after 19 years of Naval service, to be a woman in disguise!" Captain Robert Jackson thought about it a moment, and then replied: "William Brown is the finest Captain-of-the-Foretop with whom I have ever had the privilege of serving. AS YOU WERE!"

Because the Navy had no interest in continuing to pay the 820–1000 sailors in the crew when there was no longer a war, *Queen Charlotte* had to be demobilized immediately. The London newspapers, including *The Times*, trumpeted the story that the Navy's top enlisted man was not only Black, but also a woman, presenting that as being extremely funny. A copy of one of those newspapers soon reached Grenada. The reason that Brown had left Grenada in such a hurry in 1796 was that his father had said that he was sick and tired of her masquerading as a man; that she was a woman, and that very day she was to marry a friend of his who had just paid him for her. After one rocky night with this strange man, Brown saw that her "husband" had passed out from drinking too much rum, and that's when he/she left. The "husband" knew that under British law all a wife's possessions belonged to her husband in those days, so when he read the story in the *Times* that Brown was now well-to-do, he brought suit through his London lawyer for all Brown's pay and prize money.

Brown went to Captain Jackson in London and asked him what should she do now? Jackson then asked Brown if she had ever signed any paper to prove that she was married. When Brown said no, Jackson volunteered to talk to the judge, and the judge gladly threw the case out of court.

While the various European navies were involved in beating each other up during the Napoleonic Wars, few people noticed that North African pirates from Algiers were busy gobbling up British, European, and American merchant ships that had entered the Mediterranean. The officers and crews were sold all over North Africa as valuable Christian slaves. Admiral Edward Pellew, later Lord Exmouth, was ordered to take a naval task force, that also included some Dutch warships, to Algiers with *Queen Charlotte* as his flagship, commanded by Captain Robert Gordon, and force the Arabs to return the thousands of slaves. Obviously, a flagship of 1000 men ought to have experienced men who had worked together, so even though he was no longer the captain, Robert Jackson volunteered to get the old crew back. More than 80% came back. Because Brown had the reputation of having been the glue that had held the crew together, Jackson went to Brown and said, "I have put you on the crew muster-list, but of course I could not put down the *London* William Brown from *Grenada*, who is known to be a woman, so you are the *Liverpool* William Brown from *Jamaica*, at your old rank, of course."

Therefore, Brown had the opportunity to serve an additional two years in the Royal Navy. The fleet arrived at Algiers with guns blazing on 27 August 1816. After the Mediterranean operation was eventually and successfully concluded, there is no information about where Brown was or what she did. We also have no idea what her original name was. We do know the year of her death in London, 1835. There is even an engraved portrait of Brown wearing the uniform of Chief Petty Officer.

Most people who know anything about the Napoleonic War are aware that the cruel French tyrant Napoleon Bonaparte was eventually defeated by Admiral Horatio Lord Nelson at sea at the Battle of Trafalgar in October 1805 and by General Arthur the Duke of Wellington on land at the Battle of Waterloo in June 1815. It can be argued that those worthy gentlemen could never have accomplished what they did without William Brown smoothing the way first, even if Nelson, Wellington and Napoleon probably never heard of Brown. No doubt, such prominent writers as Thomas Jefferson and Jane Austen had heard about Brown, but anything they may have written about Brown has been lost. The Black Plaque Project has placed a plaque in honor of William Brown on the wall of the Master Shipwright's Palace on Watergate Street at the historic Deptford Royal Naval Dockyard, Deptford, London, a building familiar to Brown.

Oh, in case you were wondering, women could buy widely available herbs that suppress or eliminate monthly periods. The women who supplied those herbs in the marketplaces of most towns (including Saint George's, Grenada) were sometimes called witches. These herbs are still available today, but it is probably best not to ask a gynecologist for a prescription!

I have written a much more detailed version of this story, about four times as long, which would therefore not be suitable for including in this book, but it would be useful for helping to make a movie. The William Brown story would be ideal for making a documentary-like film or a biopic, so reader, please help me see that such an outcome happens. Movie producers are notoriously difficult to contact. Thank you.

This entry has been paraphrased from Wikipedia (which contains several inaccuracies). The author consulted the Black Plaque Project staff for their information about Brown. The author was further informed by having studied for many decades British Naval history of the eighteenth and early nineteenth century, and by having raised the money for, constructed and sailed the full-sized copy of the 24-gun British frigate *Rose*

(1756–1779). The modern ship had an impressive sixteen-year sail-training career before starring with Russell Crowe in *Master & Commander: The Far Side of the World,* and now she is on permanent display at the Maritime Museum of San Diego under her movie name of *Surprise.*

Addenda to Colonial Black & Indigenous Cultural Leaders

PRINCE DEMAH, *born enslaved*, painter, ca. 1745-1778 (Marlborough and Boston, Massachusetts, London)

Prince Demah was born to an enslaved woman known as Daphney/Daphne. He and his mother were both baptized in 1745 at Trinity Church, Boston. In November 1769, when he was about 24 years old, he had already demonstrated considerable talent for drawing and painting, so at the urging of his mother (the enslaved cook in the Barnes household), he was purchased by Boston merchant Henry Barnes, who took him with him on a trip to London in 1770. In February 1771, Barnes wrote in his diary that the noted London painter Robert Edge Pine (1730-1788) had accepted Demah for lessons "purely for his genius." Those lessons lasted for the better part of a year. Pine may have received as much as he imparted, because a few years later Pine moved to Philadelphia, where he recorded the appearance of important Americans from the Revolution. Not only did Pine frequently paint left-wing British agitators, but there is some argument (not enough evidence to make him eligible for an entry in this book) that he was himself of mixed race.

Unlike colonial Boston enslaved portrait painter Scipio Moorhead (see above), from whom no surviving portraits have yet been identified, and unlike Baltimore enslaved portrait painter Joshua Johnson/Johnston (see above), some of whose portraits have been identified, but none from the colonial period, three of Prince Demah's many colonial portraits survive in museum collections. His 1773 portrait of William Duguid, a Scottish textile seller based in Boston, can be seen at the Metropolitan Museum of Art in New York, and his portraits of Henry and Christian/

Christianne Barnes of Marlborough, Massachusetts can be seen at the Hingham Historical Society.

According to an advertisement that appeared regularly in the *Boston News-Letter* in 1773, Prince was anonymously plying his trade as a portrait-painter at the shop of Mr. McLean, the watch-maker, near the Town House (the Town House is the impressive brick building designed by Peter Harrison in the 1740s from the burned-out ruin of its predecessor, and known today as the Old State House).

The Barnes family were Loyalists and felt increasing discomfort at the Revolutionary War beginning to swirl around them, so in 1775 they moved to England. Presumably, they did not bother to free the painter, so he enlisted in 1777 in the Massachusetts militia, where he was declared a free man. He showed the tension that had existed between him and the Barnes family by dropping their last name from his name. He died of an un-named illness that he most likely picked up from one of his fellow militiamen.

This entry is paraphrased from Wikipedia.

SACAGAWEA/SACAJAWEA CHARBONNEAU, *once apparently enslaved,* Shoshone exploration expedition guide and interpreter, 1788-1812 (or possibly as late as 1870 or 1884), Idaho, North Dakota, South Dakota, Wyoming, Montana, Idaho, Oregon, Washington, and Missouri.

Sacagawea (sometimes spelled Sacajawea) was born in 1788 near where Salmon, Idaho now stands, into the Shoshone tribe. At age 12, she was kidnapped by members of the Hidatsa tribe who killed many members of her tribe, but an alternate version of the story is that she was born Hidatsa and kidnapped by Shoshone. About age 13 in 1801, she was sold to French-Canadian trapper Toussaint Charbonneau, who made her one of his polygamous wives.

In late 1804, the thirty-three men (plus Newfoundland dog Seaman) of the Meriwether Lewis and William Clark Corps of Discovery arrived at a Mandan village in North Dakota, and decided to build Fort Mandan near the village. They talked to several trappers (mostly French-Canadians), and from them they hired Toussaint Charbonneau, who they thought knew several Indigenous languages, along with his wife, who spoke Shoshone. Sacagawea, the wife in question, was pregnant at that time with her first child, and the couple moved into the fort. In February 1805, she gave birth to a boy, whom the expedition members nicknamed Pomp or Pompey, but the parents called him Jean-Baptiste.

In April, the expedition ascended the narrowing Missouri River against the current, towing the boats from the bank, and one of the boats capsized. Sacagawea apparently volunteered to jump into the chilly water and recover some of the lost items from the boat. In August, the expedition encountered some Shoshone, whose chief Cameahwait was related (either brother or cousin – the same word in Shoshone) to Sacagawea, so she represented the expedition in negotiations to hire some horses and some guides to the western lands. She also danced with great gusto at her joy of meeting the Shoshone. When the expedition later began to run out of food, Sacagawea showed the men how to identify and cook Camas roots to help them recover their strength.

In November, they encountered an Indigenous man wearing a fabulous robe made of sea-otter skins from the West Coast, and Lewis and Clark said they wanted to bring the robe back as a present for President Thomas Jefferson, but they had nothing to trade for it. Sacagawea took off her valuable beaded wampum belt and gave it to them to trade for the robe.

Finally, the expedition reached the Pacific Ocean, and they took a vote (including the enslaved members) as to the best location to build a fort for the coming winter; they called it Fort Clatsop. A large dead whale was washed up on the beach just south of the fort, and Sacagawea insisted on going along to examine it.

On the return trip east in 1806, Sacagawea told them that she was familiar with this land, and the best way through the mountains was modern Gibbons Pass, and later she guided them through the Bozeman Pass, more southerly than Clark had intended, but a much better route (later selected by the Northern Pacific Railway for crossing the Continental Divide). Other than guiding and translating, Sacagawea accomplished a further benefit for the expedition, because the various Indigenous along the way immediately understood that the expedition's intentions were entirely peaceful, because they otherwise would not have brought with them a woman and her baby.

William Clark, who was the younger brother of Revolutionary War hero George Rogers Clark, offered Charbonneau to move in with him in Saint Louis, Missouri, and Charbonneau did so with his family in 1809. Clark formally adopted Jean-Baptiste as his son, and he put him through the local boarding school, after which the boy had a colorful and far-ranging life. Clark also adopted Lizette, the baby girl born to Sacagawea in 1812, but it seems that the daughter caught a disease and died soon after.

At this point, the Sacagawea story becomes rather murky. One group of adherents swear that she died of "putrid fever" in 1812, whereas another claims that she lived until 1884, and still another says that she died in 1870. The evidence for death in 1812 seems to be the most valid.

This entry is paraphrased from Wikipedia, with further information derived from comments made on National Public Radio by North Dakota scholar Clay Jenkinson.

COASTAL PILOTS

Two entries in this book concern Black coastal pilots. Mark Startin/Starlins (ca. 1740-ca. 1786 fought on the American side in the Revolutionary War in the Virginia State Navy, and the service that he rendered should have brought him a commission as lieutenant in that navy, but at the end of the war he was returned to the enslaved position he had held before the war. He is believed to have died before the Virginia Legislature could pass legislation that would have awarded him his freedom.

The other was Captain John "Jack Punch" Perkins, a Black man who started his career as a lowly pilot around Jamaica and other islands and shoals of the Caribbean, and he ended as a widely-respected full captain in the Royal Navy.

Two other Black pilots made big names for themselves on the British side in the Revolutionary War. Joseph Harris (ca. 1740-1776) of Hampton Roads, Virginia (mostly Hampton, Norfolk, and Portsmouth), consistently accomplished such amazing feats against powerful opposition that he would undoubtedly have been invited to take a commission as lieutenant in the Royal Navy, if he had not picked up a disease and died. James "Jemmy" Darrell of Bermuda was frequently cited by Royal Navy officers for going beyond the call of duty to guide Navy ships among the dangerous shoals and reefs around Bermuda, although he was not offered a commission in the Navy. Harris information came from several pages in Andrew Lawler, *A Perfect Frenzy*, New York, Atlantic Monthly Press, 2025. Darrell information came from the research of naval historian Judy Pearson, as revealed in correspondence with the author.

Index

Abels, Michael, 109
Abenaki, 133
Abolitionists, 23, 29, 33, 75, 79, 95,
    96, 106, 124, 126, 136
Accountants, 69–72
Active, 105
Actors, 111–120, 124–125
Adams, John, 142
Adet, Pierre-August, 148
Affleck, Philip, 152
Afonso I (King), 2
African Colonization Society, 166
African Episcopal Church, 98
African Masonic Lodge, 94, 125
African Methodist Episcopal Church,
    83, 97, 98, 106
African Presbyterian Church, 98
African Union Society, 39
Africans, attitudes towards
    Europeans, 73
Aiguillon, Emmanuel-Armand de
    Vignerot du Plessis de Richelieu,
    duc d,' 42
Akuba, 140
Albert James. *see* Gronniosaw,
    Ukawsaw
Aleijadinho. *see* Lisboa, António
    Francisco
Allen, Richard, 82, 84, 97–98, 106
Alvares, Afonso, 2
American Colonization Society, 55
American Revolution, 12–13, 19, 22,
    80, 93, 103, 132, 133, 134–135,
    144–147. *see also* Revolutionary
    War

"An Evening Thought: Salvation by
    Christ, with Penitential Cries"
    (Hammon), 61
Angelo, Domenico, 41
Anglicans, 61, 72, 82, 120–121,
    122–123
Angola, 2, 5, 27
Antelope, 150
Antigua, 126, 127, 185
Apongo, 140
Arab, 153
Architects
    Harrison, Peter, ix, 10–12, 14, 27,
        47, 51, 83, 97, 131, 144, 147
    Jacome, Manuel Ferreira, 49
    Lisboa, António Francisco, 49–51
    Nicholson, Francis, 8, 9
    Rocha, Jose Joachim da, 49
    Silva, Valentim de Fonseca e, 49
    Wilbraham, Elizabeth, 8, 51
Arne, Thomas, 115
Arnold, Benedict, 20, 86, 132, 138,
    145, 155, 157
Asbury, Francis, 82, 83, 84, 98, 123
Ash, Gilbert, 57
Atayataghlonghta. *see* Cook,
    Louis-Joseph
Atiatoharongwen. *see* Cook,
    Louis-Joseph
Austen, Jane, 191
Austin, William, 41
Austria, 33, 70, 169
Ave Maris stella (Rivera, Juan Matias
    de), 26

Babbitt, Elizabeth, 87
Back-to-Africa Movement, 38–39
Bahamas, viii, 14, 22, 35, 81, 96
Bakewell, Robert, 186
Banks, Joseph, 79
Banner, Peter, 37
Baptists, 17, 37, 74, 80, 81–82, 121
Barbados, 5, 9, 23, 46, 59, 65, 69, 70,
    77, 185
Barbados (Williams), 28
Barber, Francis, 75–77
Baron de Montesquieu, 129
Barron, James, 138
bassoon, 25
Batchelors Delight, 7–8
Battle of New Orleans, 90
Beauharnais, Eugene de, 176
Beazley, John, 105
Behn, Aphra, 71
Belarus, 176
Belle, Diddo Elizabeth. *see* Davinier,
    Dido Elizabeth Belle
Belle, Marie, 100
Bennet, Cornelius, 143, 144
Bentzon, Peter, 56–57
Berkeley, George, 9, 35
Bermuda, 7, 9, 25, 125–126
Biassou, Georges, 140–141
Bickerstaffe, Isaac, 41
Biddle, Nicholas, 79
*Billy Waters is Dancing, or, How a
    Black Sailor Found Fame in
    Regency Britain* (Shannon), 120
Bisset, George, 16
Black Brigade, 159–160
Black Company of Pioneers, 160
Black congregations, 74, 81, 82–83,
    98, 99
Black Harry. *see* Hosier, Harry
Black Jacks (Bolster), 6
Black Legion (Saint-Georges Legion),
    168
Black men
    education of, 7–17
    as property owners, 16
    service in American Army, 90–91
    service in British Army, 135

service in Continental Army, 20,
    86, 89, 133, 155–156
service in Continental Navy, x–xi,
    6, 20, 22
service in merchant navy, 105–106,
    163–166
service in Royal Navy, x–xi, 45, 65,
    75–76, 78–79, 93, 103, 184–192
statues of, 170
voting privileges, 18
Black migration, 38–39, 74–75, 93,
    99–100, 106, 111, 120, 121,
    135–137, 164, 184
Black regiments, 6, 133–134, 159,
    159–160, 176–177
Black Tudors (Kaufmann), 2
Blacks, business owners
    Forten, James, 105–106
    Toussaint, Pierre, 106–107
    Zobre, Elisabeth Samson Creutz,
        62–64
Blacks, conversion to Christianity, 60,
    70, 72, 74, 78, 81, 93, 95, 100,
    109–110, 126, 128–129, 133
Blacks, enslaved
    Hammon, Briton, 64–65
    Hammon, Jupiter, 61–62
    Moorhead, Scipio, 51–52
    Roberts, James, 89–92
    Sa'id, Omar ibn, 108–109
    Startin, Mark, 137–139
Blacks, formerly enslaved
    Allen, Richard, 97–98
    Barber, Francis, 75–77
    Breda, Francois-Dominique
        Toussaint, 139–143
    Christophe, Henri, 176–179
    Clairvaux (Clervaux), Auguste, 170
    Commeraw, Thomas W., 55–56
    Cornelius (Corlies), Titus, 158–161
    Davinier, Dido Elizabeth Belle,
        100–102
    Dessalines, Jean-Jacques Duclos,
        161–162
    Diallo, Ayuba Suleiman, 58–59
    Dumas, Thomas-Alexandre,
        168–170
    Equiano, Olaudah, 77–80

Furro, Broteer, 65–67
Gannibal, Abram Petrovich, 128–130
Gardner, Newport, ix, 15–16, 34–40
George, David, 74–75
Gines, Micaela, 24–25
Gines, Teodora, 24–25
Gloucester, John, 83
Gronniosaw, Ukawsaw, 59–61
Hosier, Harry, 84–85
Jea, John, 109–110
Johnson, Joshua, 54–55
Jones, Absalom, 82–84, 98
King, Boston, 99–100
Lafayette, James Armistead, 156–158
Pamphlet, Gowan (Gavin) Vobe, 80–82
Paquet, Charles, 52–54
Peters, Phillis Wheatley, 88–89
Petters (Peters), Thomas, 135–137
Prince, Mary, 125–127
Quamino, John, 11
Rigaud, Benoit-Joseph Andre, 166–167
Sancho, Charles Ignatius, 29–31
Sessarakoo, William Ansah, 69–72
Soubise, Julius Othello, 40–41
Stuart, John, 95–96
Tarrant, Caesar, 138
Toussaint, Pierre, 106–107
Wedderburn (Wetherburn), Robert, 102–105
Yama, Bristol, 11
Zembola, Zamba, 123–124
Blacks, free. *see also* Blacks, enslaved; Blacks, formerly enslaved
Bentzon, Peter, 56–57
Bridgetower, George Augustus Polgreen, 46–47
"Brown, William," 184–192
Cheswell, Wentworth, 154–156
Cook, Joseph-Louis, 133–134
Cuffee (Kofi), Paul, 163–166
Emidy, Joseph Antonio, 45–46
Forten, James, 105–106
Haynes, Lemuel, 86–87

Kweku (Quaque, Quaicoe), Philip, 72–73
Leonard, Joseph, 120–121
Lisboa, António Francisco, 49–51
Marrant, John, 92–94
Meude-Monpas, Josse Jean-Olivier, 42
Nunes-Garcia, Jose Mauricio, 43–45
Perkins, John, 150–154, 161
Potter, Richard, 124–125
Saint-Georges, Joseph Bologne, chevalier de, 31–34
Sancho, Charles Ignatius, 29–31
Williams, Francis, 26–28
Zobre, Elisabeth Samson Creutz, 62–64
Blacks, judges, 154–156
Blacks, living in France, 18, 31–33, 42, 129, 166, 168–169, 170, 173, 174, 175–176, 181, 182–183, 189
Blacks, living in Great Britain, 29, 33, 46–47, 60–61, 65, 70–71, 75–77, 100–105, 110, 111–112
Blacks, memoirs, 59, 60–61, 65, 67, 71, 75, 78, 79–80, 91, 94, 95–96, 99–100, 109, 110, 124, 127
Blacks, merchant captains, 105–106, 163–166
Blacks, military and political leaders
Biassou, Georges, 140–141
Boyer, Jean-Pierre, 182–184
Breda, Francois-Dominique Toussaint, 139–143
"Brown, William," 184–192
Christophe, Henri, 176
Clairvaux (Clervaux), Auguste, 170
Cook, Joseph-Louis, 133–134
Cornelius (Corlies), Titus, 158–161
Cuffee (Kofi), Paul, 163–166
Delgres, Louis, II, 173–174
Dessalines, Jean-Jacques Duclos, 161–162
Dumas, Thomas-Alexandre, 168–170
Gannibal, Abram Petrovich, 128–130
Perkins, John, 150-4, 161

(*Blacks, military and political leaders
    continued*)
  Petion, Alexandre Sabes, 181–182
  Petters (Peters), Thomas, 135–137
  Rigaud, Benoit-Joseph Andre,
      166–167
  Serrant, Joseph, 174–176
  Startin, Mark, 137–139
Blacks, music composers
  Gardner, Newport, ix, 15–16,
      34–40
  Gines, Micaela, 24–25
  Gines, Teodora, 24–25
  Lienas, Juan de, 25
  Nunes-Garcia, Jose Mauricio,
      43–45
  Rivera, Juan Matias De, 26
  Saint-Georges, Joseph Bologne,
      chevalier de, 31–34, 168
  Salvador, Jose de Almeida e Faria,
      43
  Sancho, Charles Ignatius, 29–31
  Williams, Francis, 26–28
Blacks, painters, 49, 51–52, 54–55
Blacks, poets, 61–62, 88–89
Blacks, portraits, 29, 33, 59, 71, 76,
    100, 104, 191
Blacks, reverends
  Allen, Richard, 97–98
  George, David, 74–75
  Haynes, Lemuel, 86–87
  Jones, Absalom, 82–84
  King, Boston, 99–100
  Kweku (Quaque, Quaicoe), 72–73
  Leonard, Joseph, 120–121
  Marrant, John, 92–94
  Nunes-Garcia, Jose Mauricio,
      43–45
  Pamphlet, Gowan (Gavin) Vobe,
      80–82
Blacks, spies, 156–158
Blacks, statues, 137
Blackstone, William, 47
Blair, James, 15
Blake, William, 95
Blucke, Stephen, 94, 160
Blue Jacket, 149–150
Blue Salt, 74

Bluett, Thomas, 58, 59
Bolivar, Simon, 182
Bologne, Joseph. *see* Saint-Georges,
    Joseph Bologne, chevalier de,
Bolster, W. Jeffrey, 6
Book of Negroes, 99
Boston, Prince, 19
Boswell, Alexander, 18
Boswell, James, 75, 76, 144
Boucaux, Jean, 18
Boukman, Dutty, 140
Boyce, William, 115
Boyer, Jean-Pierre, 166, 181, 182–184
Boyle, Robert, viii, 8
Bradford, William, 87
Brafferton Endowment, viii, 8
Brant, Joseph Thayendanegea, 131,
    143–149
Brant, Molly Johnson, 130–132, 143
Bray, Thomas, viii, 13–14, 35, 96
Bray Endowment, 35
Bray School (Newport, Rhode Island),
    viii–ix, x, 15–16, 35, 38, 96
Bray School (Williamsburg, Virginia),
    viii–ix, 13–15, 81, 96
Bray Schools, viii–x, 13–16, 96
Brazil, 23, 43–45, 49, 51
Breda, Francois-Dominique
    Toussaint, 139–143, 161, 177,
    181, 183
Brelle, Jean- Baptiste Joseph, 177–178
Bridges, Charles, 15
Bridges, Robert, 106
Bridgetower, George Augustus
    Polgreen, 46–47
Bristol Yama, 11
British, freeing slaves, 22, 93, 111,
    135–136, 164
British Africans, 95
British East India Company, 71, 102,
    112
Brock, Isaac, 180
Broteer, Furro, 65–67
Brothertown movement, 68, 85
Brown, David, 123
Brown, Mather, 33
Brown, Moses, 17, 19, 20
"Brown, William," 184–192

Brown University, ix–x, 11, 15, 17, 35
Brunet, Jean-Baptiste, 142
Bull, Frederick, 88
Bullet, Jeannot, 140
Bunel, Joseph, 142
Burgoyne, John, 155
Burke, Edmund, 96
Burnham, Benjamin, 57
Butler, Walter, 145

Caceros, Jose Nunez de, 183
Cajigal de la Vega, Francisco, 64
Calhoun, John C., 172
Calvin, Hezekiah, 85
Calvinism, 93
Cameroon, 128
Campbell, Archibald, 150
Canada, 9, 12, 51, 90, 111, 121, 134, 137, 144–145, 148, 151, 165, 171. *see also* New Brunswick; Nova Scotia; Ontario; Quebec
Canatae Domino (Rivera, Juan Matias de), 26
Cannon, George, 104
Cantelo, Hezekiah, 22
Cape Coast Castle, 69, 71, 72, 95
Carcass, 79
Carleton, Guy, 144
Carlile, Richard, 104
Carpenters, 53, 54, 92, 93, 99, 126
Castro, Matheus de, 122
Castro, Severiana Rosa de, 44
Catawba, 93
Cathedral, Mexico City, 25
Cathedral musicians, 24–25
Cathedral of Santiago (Cuba), 24
Catherine II, Empress of Russia, 131
Catherine the Great, 131
Cayuga, 146
Cello, 24, 45
Centaur, 188
Ceres, 113
Chapin, Eliphalet, 57
Charleston, South Carolina, ix, 12, 13, 22, 57, 92, 92–93, 99, 108, 109, 111, 135, 164
Charleston slaves, 22
Charming Sally, 78

Chelselden, William, 27
Cherokee, 8, 13, 91, 92–93
Chesapeake Bay, 7
Cheswell, Wentworth, 154–156
Chickamauga, 13
Chickasaw, 91, 180
Children, education of, viii, 8, 14, 16, 27, 35, 38, 68, 72, 155
Choctaw, 13, 90, 91–92, 170–172, 180
Cholera, 107
Christophe, Henri, 162, 167, 176–179, 182, 183
Church of Bom Jesus de Matosinhos at Congonas (Brazil), 51
Church of England, 2, 72, 93, 121
Church of Our Lady of Carmel at Sabara (Brazil), 50
Church of Our Lady of Sorrows (India), 122
Church of Santo Antonio at Tiradentes (Brazil), 51
Church of Sao Francisco de Assis at Ouro Preto (Brazil), 51
Church of Sao Francisco de Assis at Sao Joao (Brazil), 51
Church of South India (India), 122
Citadelle Laferriere, 178, 179
Clair, Arthur St., 149
Clairvaux (Clervaux), Auguste, 170
Clark, George Rogers, 146
Clark, Thomas, 117
Clarkson, John, 136, 137
Clarkson, Thomas, 33, 136
Clervaux, Auguste. *see* Clairvaux (Clervaux), Auguste
Cleveley, Robert, 186
Clinton, Henry, 135, 136, 157
Codrington, Christopher, 9
Codrington College (Barbados), 9, 23
Coffee, 63, 141, 142
Coke, Thomas, 82, 84
College of Charleston, 12
College of New Jersey (Princeton University), 11, 73
College of Rhode Island (Brown University), 11
College of William & Mary, 7–8, 14
Colombia, 29, 182, 183

Colonial Williamsburg, vii–x, 14
Colored Union Church, 36, 37
Columbia University, 11, 143
Come, cheer up, me lads, tis to glory we steer (Boyce), 115
Commeraw, Thomas W., 55–56
Commuck, Joseph, 47–48
Commuck, Thomas, 48
Conductors, 32
Congo, 2, 123–124
Congregationalists, 9, 12, 37, 67, 85, 86–87, 121
Connecticut, 21, 67, 68, 85, 86–87, 144, 155
Continental Army, 20, 86, 89, 133, 145–146, 155–156
Continental Congress, 19
Continental Marines, 133
Continental Navy, x–xi, 6, 20, 22, 79, 133
Convent of Our Lady of the Incarnation (Mexico City), 25
Cook, James, 79
Cook, Louis-Joseph, 133–134, 145
Cooke, Nicholas, 20
Copley, John Singleton, 52
Corbet, Edward, 154
Cornelius (Corlies), Titus, 94, 158–161
Cornplanter (John O'Bail/Abeel III), 48
Cornplanter (Joseph Commuck), 48
Cornwallis, Charles, 81, 157
Coromantee, 139–140
Corrente, John, 69, 70
Corrie, Daniel, 84, 123
Cosway, Maria, 95, 96
Cosway, Richard, 95, 96
Creek, 13, 74, 91, 93, 171, 172
Crewe, Francis, 30
Crichton, David Bruce, 70
Crolius, Johan Willem, 56
Crooked Shanks (Gardner), 36
Crowe, Russell, x, 120, 192
Cruikshank, George, 104, 114
Cuba, 2, 21, 23, 24, 60, 64–65, 92, 141, 185, 186–187
Cuban folk songs, 24–25

Cuffee, Paul, 163–166
Cugoano, Quobna Ottobah. *see* Stuart, John
Cullen, Susannah, 80

Dance, Nathaniel, 112–113
Dances, 13, 15, 16, 22, 30, 31, 33–34, 36, 42, 48, 117, 118, 120
Darly, Mary, 41
Darly, Matthew, 41
Dartmouth College, 12, 68
David Bruce Crichton, 70
Davinier, Dido Elizabeth Belle, 100–102
Dawson, William, 15
Decatur, Stephen, 105
Delany, Felix, 114
Delaware, 82, 84, 97
Delgres, Louis, II, 173–174, 175
Delhi, India, 122–123
Demane, Henry, 95
Denmark, 23, 189
Desrosiers, Marian, 16
Dessalines, Jean-Jacques Duclos, 154, 161–162, 167, 177, 178, 181–182, 183
Destrehan Plantation House, 53–54
Diallo, Ayuba Suleiman, 58–59
Diamond Rock, 188
Diana, 152
Dibdin, Charles, 115, 117
Dickson, Archibald Collingwood, 189
Diplomats, 69–72
Disease, 7, 22, 26, 38, 39, 98, 111, 141, 167
Dodd, William, 29
Domine ad adjuvandum me festina (Rivera, Juan Matias de), 26
Dominica, 173, 174–175
Dominican Republic, 24, 125
Dominicans, 23
Doxtader, Han Yerry 'Tewahangarahken,' 145
Drake, 152
Duché, Jacob, 82
Duckworth, John Thomas, 154
Dugdale, William, 104
Dumas, Thomas-Alexandre, 168–170

Dutch colonies, 62–63, 153
Dutch Guiana. *see* Suriname
Dutch Reformed Church, 12, 60, 109

Earl, Ralph, 55
Earl, Ralph Eleaser Whiteside, 55
Egypt, 169, 187
Eleazar Wheelock, 12
Elephant & Castle, 3, 69, 118
Elfe, Thomas, 57
Elizabeth (ship), 4
Elizabeth, Empress of Russia, 130
Emidy, Joseph Antonio, 45–46
Endeavour, 150
Engineers, 129–130
England, 1–3, 18, 22, 46–47, 60, 61,
    72, 75–76, 79–80, 100–101, 110,
    126–127
English Country Dances, 13, 15, 22,
    28, 30, 33–34, 36, 41, 42, 45, 48,
    117
Enslaved Blacks. *see* Blacks, enslaved;
    Blacks, formerly enslaved;
    Blacks, free
Episcopal Church, 10, 11, 13, 83
Episcopalians, 37, 81, 82
Equiano, Olaudah, 77–80
Estonia, 130
Ethiopian Regiment, 159
"Evening Thought: Salvation by
    Christ, with Penitential Cries,
    An" (Hammon), 61
Experiment, 153, 167

Faria, Salvador Jose de Almeida e, 43
Farrand, Daniel, 87
Fencing, 32, 33, 41
Ferret, 152
Fiddle, 115, 117, 119
Finch-Hatton, George, 101
First African Baptist Church, 74
First Baptist Church, Williamsburg,
    Virginia, 81
First Congregationalist Church, 19, 37
Flageolet, 115, 117
Flagg, Josiah, 35
Florida, 21, 92, 100, 136, 141
Flute, 45, 117

Folksongs, naval, 114–118
Ford, John, 152
Forepaugh, William, 54
Forten, James, 105–106
Fowler, David, 85
Fox, Charles James, 29, 33
France, 17–18, 20, 23, 31–33, 70, 90,
    129, 161, 166–169, 173–174, 178,
    182–183, 184
Franklin, Benjamin, 11, 159
Franklin, William, 159
Free African Society, 82
Freeman, Elizabeth, 21
Frelinghuysen, Theodorus Jacobus, 60
French and Indian War, 133, 143
French Army, 20, 129, 167, 168–169,
    170, 177, 181–183
French Country Dances, 31, 33–34,
    42, 44
French horn, 92
French Navy, 112–113, 152–153,
    187–189
French Revolution, 33, 42, 107, 141,
    151–152, 161, 168, 175, 182
Frias, Antonio Joao de, 122
Funeral Symphony (Nunes-Garcia), 43
Furro, Broteer, 65–67

Gainsborough, Thomas, 29
Gannibal, Abram Petrovich, 128–130
Ganymede, 113, 116
Gardner, Newport, ix, 15–16, 34–40,
    118
Garrick, David, 29, 41
Gates, Horatio, 155
Gaudeamus (Rivera, Juan Matias de),
    26
Geffrard, Nicolas, 177
General Washington (ship), xi
George, David, 74–75
George I, 9
George II, 10, 70
George III, 12, 68, 88, 95, 96, 144, 164
George IV, 33, 46
Georgetown, Guyana, 62
Georgia, 10, 59, 74, 78, 82, 92, 177
Gerin, Etienne Elie, 177
Germain, George, 144

Germany, 46, 56, 63, 169, 176
Ghana, 11, 34, 39, 41, 59, 65, 69–70, 71–72, 75, 95, 139
Giardini, Felice, 29
Gibson, Edmund, 15
Giddens, Rhiannon, 109
Gines, Micaela, 24–25
Gines, Teodora, 24–25
Giroust, Francois, 42
Gloucester, John, 83
Goa, 122
Gordon, Robert, 189
Gordon Riots, 30
Gossec, Francois-Joseph, 32
Grace Dieu, 115
Greece, 184
Greenwood, John, 62
Grenada, 95, 176, 184, 188, 190, 191
Gronniosaw, Ukawsaw, 59–61
Guadeloupe, 31, 173–174, 175
Guerrero, Francisco, 25
Guiby, Elisabeth Morin, 173
Guyana, 62

Hairdressers, 107
Haiti, 33, 139–143, 152–154, 161–162, 166–167, 176–179
Haitian rebellions, 139, 140, 154
Haitian Revolution, 23, 33, 142, 161–162, 177, 181, 182–183
Haldimand, Frederick, 146, 147
Halifax, Nova Scotia, 14, 22, 99, 111, 135. *see also* Nova Scotia
Hamilton, Alexander, 142
Hammon, Briton, 64–65
Hammon, Jupiter, 61–62, 89
Hampden-Sydney College, 13
Hancock, John, 89
Handel, George Frederick, 35, 115, 117
Hannibal, 129
Harmar, Josiah, 149
Harrison, Peter, ix, 10–12, 14, 27, 47, 51, 83, 97, 131, 144, 147
Harrison, William Henry, 179–181
Harvard College (Harvard University), 7, 9

Hastings, Selina, Countess of Huntingdon, 60, 79, 88, 93
Hawkins, John, 77
Hawks, John, 13
Hawksmoor, Nicholas, 9
Haynes, Lemuel, 86–87
Heber, Reginald, 160
Henri IV (ship), 135
Henry (sub-Saharan Roman Catholic Bishop), 2
Henry, Jacques-Victor, 178, 179
Henry VIII, 2
Herkimer, Nicholas, 132, 145
Herman, Eleanor, 3
Hermione, 152
Hero, 163, 165
Hispaniola, 2, 24–25, 139
Historic American Buildings Survey (HABS), 54
Hoare, William, 59
Hood, Samuel, 188
Hopkins, Samuel, 19, 37, 73
Hopkins, Stephen, 11, 16–17, 19, 21
Hosier, Harry, 84–85
Housaw, 93
Howard, Martin, 17
Howe, William, 135, 144
Huddy, Joshua, 160
Hugues, Victor, 174
Hutchinson, Thomas, 17–18, 19, 89

Ignatius Sancho (1729–1780, An Early African Composer in England (Wright), 31
Illinois, 149
Indefatigable, 45
India, 41, 122–123
Indian Castle Church, 131–132
Indian Melodies (Thomas Commuck), 48
Indiana, 149, 179, 180
Indigo, 52, 142
Inglis, Charles, 121
Iroquois, 48, 67, 131, 132, 133, 143, 145–147, 179
Irving, Charles, 79
Italy, 25, 41, 47, 169, 178, 187
Ivory Coast, 69

Jackson, Andrew, 13, 90–92, 172
Jackson, Robert, 189–190
Jacome, Manuel Ferreira, 49
Jamaica, 18, 19, 23, 26, 27, 64, 75, 79,
    102, 103, 139–140, 150–152,
    154, 184
Jea, John, 109–110
Jean, Padre, 139
Jefferson, Thomas, 81, 95, 142, 171,
    191
Jersey, 105
Jervis, John, 186
Jesuits, 122, 133
Joaquim, Leandro, 49
Joaquim, Valentim, 49
John VI (Portugal), 43–44
Johnson, Guy, 144
Johnson, Joseph, 85–86
Johnson, Joshua, 54–55
Johnson, Molly Brant. *see* Brant,
    Molly Johnson
Johnson, Samuel, 10–11, 18, 75–77
Johnson, William, 131, 132, 143, 144
Johnson-Sirleaf, Ellen, 39
Johnston, Joshua. *see* Johnson, Joshua
Jones, Absalom, 82–84, 98
Jones, John Paul, 89

Kaufmann, Miranda, 2
Keller, Kate van Winkle, 22
Key, Francis Scott, 108
King, Boston, 99–100
King, Charles Bird, 172
King, Mary, 82
King's College (Columbia University),
    10–11, 143
Knight, James, 18
Knox, Henry, 149
Kofi, Paul, 163–166
Konwatsi'tsiaienni. *see* Brant, Molly
    Johnson
Kweku, Philip, 72–73

La Chlorinde, 153
La Convention Nationale, 152
La Decouverte, 153
La Diane, 167
La Favorite, 152

La Félicité, 173, 175
La Surveillante, 153
La Vertue, 153
Lafayette, James Armistead, 156–158
Lafayette, Marie Joseph Paul Yves
    Roch Gilbert Du Motier,
    Marquis de, 157, 168, 172
Lahoussaye, Pierre, 42
L'Amant Anonyme (Saint-Georges), 32
Land disputes, Shawnee, 179–180
Langdon, John, 155
Latino, Juan, 2
Laurens, John, 6–7
Law, Andrew, 35, 36
Le Cercle de l'Harmonie, 33
Le Cerf, 153
Le Concert des Amateurs, 32
Le Due Gemelle (Nunes-Garcia), 44
Le Duquesne, 153
Le Levrier, 152
Le Marquis de Vaudreuil, 79
Le Redoutable, 189
Le Vengeur, 152
Leclerc, Charles, 161, 167, 181–183
Legge, William, 12
Legge, William, Earl of Dartmouth,
    12, 68
L'Egyptienne, 152
Lenape, 11, 12, 68, 144, 147
L'Eole, 152
Leonard, Joseph, 120–121
Liberia, 38–39, 87, 106, 164, 184
Liberty Hall, 13
Lienas, Juan de, 25
Life Of Johnson (Boswell), 76
Lindsay, Elizabeth, Countess Of
    Mansfield, 100–102
Lindsay, John, 100, 101
Lindsay, William, Earl of Mansfield,
    100–102
Linley, Thomas, 115
Linois, Charles-Alexandre de, 112,
    187
Lisboa, António Francisco, 49–51
Lisle, George, 74–75
Liston, Robert, 148
Lithuania, 176
Livingston, William, 160

Lone Pilgrim, The (Thomas Commuck), 48
Long Island, New York, 61, 66, 67, 68, 145
Loomis, Samuel, 57
Louis X, 18
Louis XVI, 33, 42
Louis XVIII, 178
Louisiana, 52, 54, 90
L'Ouverture. *see* Breda, Francois-Dominique Toussaint
Loyalists, 94, 99, 120–121, 136, 145, 147, 159–161
Luther, Martin, 10, 121
Lutherans, 122, 123, 160
Lyons, Israel, 79

Macaroni, Mungo. *see* Soubise, Julius Othello
Macaulay, Zachary, 137
MacCarthy, Charles, 166
Mackandal, Francois, 139
Madison, James, 121, 165
Malaria, 97, 99, 137
Marengo, 112
Marie Antoinette (ship), 152
Marie-Antoinette (Queen), 32, 33
Marrant, John, 92–94
Marriage, inter-racial, 31, 63, 72, 74, 80, 87, 102, 125, 141, 142, 143, 144, 155, 168, 173, 174, 182
Marsh, Robert, 8–9
Martin, David, 100
Martinique, 52, 59, 60, 152, 173, 174–175, 188
Martyn, Henry, 123
Maryland, 5, 14, 18, 54–55, 58, 84, 89, 97
Masih, Abdul, 122–123
Mason, G. C., 35
Massachusetts, 7, 18–19, 21, 52, 64, 163
Master & Commander: The Far Side of the World (2003), 120, 192
Master-builders, 52–54
McBurney, Alex, xi
McLeod, Cynthia, 63
Meleager, 152

Memoirs, 59, 60, 65, 67, 68, 71, 75, 78, 79–80, 91, 94, 95–96, 99–100, 109, 110, 124, 127
Menshikov, Aleksandr Danilovich, 129
Methodist-Episcopal Church of America, 82, 84, 97, 98
Methodists, 37, 84, 93, 97–98, 99, 103, 120–121
Meude-Monpas, Josse Jean-Olivier, 42
Mexico, 2, 23, 25, 26
Meyers, Terry, 15
Miller, David, 81
Millwrights, 135
Missa Batalla (Rivera, Juan Matias de), 26
Missionaries, 11, 73, 87, 93, 99, 122, 123
Mohawk, 130–134, 143–149
Mohawk-British relations, 147–148
Mohegan, 68, 85
Molly, 20
Moncrieff, William, 118
Monroe, James, 39, 164, 172, 184
Montagu, John, 2nd Duke of Montagu, 26, 29, 30, 59
Montaukett, 67
Moorhead, Scipio, 51–52
Morales, Cristóbal de, 25
Moravian College, 10
Moravians, 10, 13, 37, 56, 121, 126, 127
Morell de Santa Cruz, Pedro Agustin, 64
Morgan, William Sampson, 35
Morro. *see* Sa'id, Omar ibn
Mountain, Jacob, 121
Mozart, Wolfgang Amadeus, 32, 34, 43, 44
Muhlenberg, Henry, 160
Mulattoes
   Boyer, Jean-Pierre, 182–184
   Clairvaux (Clervaux), Auguste, 170
   Delgres, Louis, II, 173–174
   Gines, Micaela, 24–25
   Gines, Teodora, 24–25
   Paquet, Jean-Baptiste, 52
   Petion, Alexandre Sabes, 181–182

Serrant, Joseph, 174–176
MumBet, 21
Murphy, Charles, 8
Murray, Elizabeth, 100, 101
Murray, John, Earl Of Dunmore, 22,
    48, 111, 135, 149, 156, 159
Murray, Joseph, 160
Murray, William, Earl of Mansfield,
    18, 19
Music, polyphonic, 25
*Music of Black Americans: A History,
    The* (Southern), 36
Musical instruments
    bandola, 24
    bassoon, 25
    cello, 24, 45
    fiddle, 115, 117, 119
    flageolet, 115, 117
    flute, 45, 117
    French horn, 92
    treble viol, 24
    vihuela, 24
    viola da gamba, 25
    violin, 24, 32, 33, 36, 41, 42, 45,
        46–47, 92
Muslims, 2, 3, 58–59, 108, 109, 123,
    139, 140

Namur, 113
Napoleon I, Emperor Of The French,
    43, 90, 113, 142, 161, 167,
    169–170, 174, 175, 178, 187–188,
    191
Napoleonic Wars, 112–113, 151–154,
    168–169, 173–176, 178, 186–189
Narragansett, 6, 11, 47–48, 180
Natchez, 74
Native Americans
    Blue Jacket (Weyapiersenwah),
        149–150
    Brant, Molly Johnson, 130–132
    British, relationship with, 143–149
    Commuck, Joseph, 47–48
    conversion to Christianity, 13, 67,
        93, 133
    Cook, Louis-Joseph, 133–134
    Cuffee (Kofi), Paul, 163–166
    education of, 7–17

Johnson, Joseph, 85–86
Lienas, Juan de, 25
memoirs, 68
Occom, Samson, 67–69
Pushmataha, 170–172
Revolutionary War, involvement,
    48, 143–147
Rivera, Juan Matias de, 26
Slender Maker, 57
Tecumseh, 179–181
War of 1812, involvement,
    171–172, 180–181
Native Americans, military and
    political leaders
    Blue Jacket, 149–150
    Brant, Joseph Thayendanegea,
        143–149
    Brant, Molly Johnson, 130–132
    Cook, Louis-Joseph, 133–134
    Pushmataha, 170–172
    Tecumseh, 179–181
Native Americans, portraits, 172
Negroe, The (Williams), 28
Neilson, Peter, 124
Nelson, Horatio, 79, 153, 169, 187,
    189, 191
Netherlands, 18, 23, 62
New Brunswick, 12, 136. *see also*
    Canada
New Hampshire, 21, 86, 87, 124–125,
    154–155
New Jersey, 11, 12, 60, 160
New Orleans, Louisiana, 90, 91, 172
New York, 61, 67, 68, 134, 136, 146
New York City, New York, 12, 55–56,
    107
Newberry Library, 25
Newport, Rhode Island, x, 11, 15–17,
    19–20, 34, 34–37, 73
Nicaragua, 79
Nicholson, Francis, 8, 9
Nigeria, 39, 59, 77, 109, 135
Nkrumah Miereku. *see* Gardner,
    Newport
Nollekens, Joseph, 29
Norfolk, Virginia, 111
North Carolina, 12, 13, 56, 84, 92, 99,
    108, 109, 135

Northcote, James, 76
Nos autem gloriari (Rivera, Juan Matias de), 26
Nova Scotia, viii, 14–15, 22, 35, 74, 75, 78, 81, 92–93, 96, 99, 111–112, 121, 135–136, 159–160, 164. *see also* Canada
Nugent, George, 154
Nunes-Garcia, Jose Mauricio, 43–45, 49

Oaxaca Cathedral, 26
Obechencanough, 7
Occom, Samson, 12, 67–69, 85, 88
Occom, Tabitha, 85
Ocean, The (Wheatley), 89–92
Oglethorpe, James, 10, 59
Ohio, 111, 130, 143, 144, 149–150, 179, 180
Omar (Giddens And Abel), 109
On being brought from Africa to America (Wheatley), 88–89
Oneida, 68–69, 85, 133–134, 144, 145
Onondaga, 146
Ontario, 90, 132, 147, 148, 165, 171. *see also* Canada
Operas, 28, 32, 33–34, 42, 44, 109
Orchestras, 32, 34
Orion, 185, 188, 189
Orléans, Louis Philippe Joseph d', 32, 33
Ouro Preto, Brazil, 49, 51
Owen, Robert, 103, 104

Pachelbel, Carl Theodore, 9, 49
Pacquet, Charles. *see* Paquet, Charles
Pacquet, Claude, 52
Paine, Thomas, 88
Painters, 49, 51–52, 54–55
Pakenham, Edward, 90, 172
Palestrina, Giovanni Pierluigi da, 25
Pamphlet, Gowan (Gavin) Vobe, 74, 80–82
Papillon, Jean-Francois, 140
Paquet, Charles, 52–54
Paquet, Jean-Baptiste, 52, 53
Paramaribo, Suriname, 62, 63

Park Street Congregationalist Church, 37
Parker, Hyde, 152
Parker, Peter, 135
Patriot, 6, 138
Pellew, Edward, 1st Viscount Exmouth, 45, 189
Penelope, 152
Pennsylvania, 20. *see also* Philadelphia, Pennsylvania
Pennsylvania Navy, 105
Pequot, 67
Percy, Hugh Earl, Duke of Northumberland, 145
Perkins, John, 150–154, 161
Perry, Oliver Hazard, 180
Peterloo Massacre, 104
Peters, John, 88
Peters, Phillis Wheatley. *see* Wheatley, Phillis
Peters, Thomas, 135–137
Petion, Alexandre Sabes, 162, 170, 177, 178, 181–182, 183
Petters (Peters), Thomas, 135–137
Philadelphia, Pennsylvania, ix, 11, 13, 14, 19, 22, 56–57, 82, 83, 93, 97, 98, 105–106, 111, 131, 135, 148, 164
Philippon, Armand, 175
Phillis, 88
Phipps, Constantine J., 79
Phoenicians, 2
Pierce, Franklin, 92
Plantations, 53–54, 63, 75, 79, 90, 93, 95, 106, 124, 140–142, 154, 156, 161, 162, 167, 174, 181, 182, 183
Poets, 61–62, 88–89
Poland, 46, 176
Polk, Charles Peale, 55
Polly, will you marry me? (Williams), 115
Polverel, Etienne, 166, 167
Pombal, Antionio, 50
Pontiac's War, 143
Port Royal (Williams), 28
Portraits, Blacks, 41, 49, 59, 71, 76, 100
Portugal, 18, 43–45

Portugal, Marcos, 44
Potter, Richard, 124–125
Potters, 55–56
Powhatan Confederacy, 7
Preachers
    Allen, Richard, 97–98
    Hammon, Jupiter, 61–62
    Haynes, Lemuel, 86–87
    Hosier, Harry, 84–85
    Jea, John, 110
    Johnson, Joseph, 85–86
    Leonard, Joseph, 120–121
    Occom, Samson, 67–69
Presbyterians, 11, 12, 13, 37, 81, 121
Prince, Mary, 125–127
Prince Henry's College, 4, 7
Prince of Wales, 95, 96
Prince Omeroh. *see* Sa'id, Omar ibn
Prince-Regent John (Portugal), 43–44
Princess Amelia, 93
Princeton University, 11, 73
Pringle, Thomas, 126
Prisoners' Opera, The (Ward), 28
Procter, Henry, 180
Promise (Gardner), 37
Protestants, 30
Providence, x–xi
Provoost, Samuel, 121
Punch, 150
Punch, John, 5
Purcell, Henry, 116
Pushkin, Alexander, 130
Pushmataha, 92, 170–172

Quaicoe, Philip, 72–73
Quakers, 36, 37, 57, 60, 78, 79, 97,
    105, 158, 164–165
Quamino, John, 11, 73
Quaque, Philip, 72–73
Quashey. *see* Barber, Francis
Quebec, 10, 52, 121, 133, 143, 146,
    147–148, 165. *see also* Canada
Quebec (ship), 152
Queen Charlotte (ship), 189, 190
Queen Mary, 8
Queen's College (Rutgers University),
    12, 13
Queen's Rangers, 159, 160

Queen's University (Charlotte, North
    Carolina), 13
Queensberry House (Williams), 28
Quien puebla de delicias (Rivera, Juan
    Matias de), 26
Quien sale aqueste dia disfrazado
    (Rivera, Juan Matias de), 26

Race riot, 75
Racehorse, 79
Racial discrimination, 49, 82–83, 101
Racial tolerance, 36
Ranching, 63
Rannie, John, 124–125
Raynal, Guillaume-Thomas, 141
Rego, Do, 122
Remmey, Johannes, 56
Requiem (Nunes-Garica), 44
Reverends
    Allen, Richard, 97–98
    Asbury, Francis, 82, 84
    Bennet, Cornelius, 144
    Berkeley, George, 9, 35
    Bisset, George, 16
    Blackstone, William, 47
    Blair, James, 15
    Bluett, Thomas, 58, 59
    Bradford, William, 87
    Bray, Thomas, viii, 13–14, 35, 96
    Brown, David, 123
    Castro, Matheus de, 122
    Clarkson, Thomas, 33, 136
    Coke, Thomas, 82, 84
    Corrie, Daniel, 123
    Dawson, William, 15
    Duché, Jacob, 82
    Farrand, Daniel, 87
    Frelinghuysen, Theodorus Jacobus,
        60
    Frias, Antonio Joao de, 122
    George, David, 74–75
    Gibson, Edmund, 15
    Haynes, Lemuel, 86–87
    Hopkins, Samuel, 19, 37, 73
    Johnson, Samuel, 10–11, 18, 75–77
    Jones, Absalom, 82–84, 98
    King, Boston, 99–100

(*Reverends continued*)
  Kweku (Quaque, Quaicoe), 72–73
  Leonard, Joseph, 120–121
  Marrant, John, 92–94
  Martyn, Henry, 123
  Masih, Abdul, 122–123
  Moorhead, John, 51
  Muhlenberg, Henry, 160
  Nunes-Garcia, Jose Mauricio,
     43–45, 49
  Occom, Samson, 12, 67–69, 85, 88
  Pamphlet, Gowan (Gavin) Vobe,
     74, 80–82
  Rego, Do, 122
  Stiles, Ezra, 11, 19, 37–38, 73
  Thompson, Thomas, 72
  Wesley, John, 10, 82, 117
  Wheelock, Eleazar, 12, 67, 68, 85,
     143
  Whitefield, George, 10, 82, 88, 92,
     93
  Williams, Solomon, 67
  Witherspoon, John, 11, 73
Revolutionary War, x, 15, 34, 35, 36,
     62, 68, 69, 86, 96, 111, 132, 144–
     147, 150, 156–157, 159–160. *see
     also* American Revolution
Reynolds, Joshua, 76
Rhode Island, X, 4, 5–6, 11, 17, 19–22,
     38, 47–48, 66
Richepance, Antoine, 174
Rigaud, Benoit-Joseph Andre,
     166–167, 181, 183
Rio de Janeiro, Brazil, 43, 49, 50
Rivera, Juan Matias de, 26
Roberts, James, 89–92
Rocha, Jose Joachim da, 49
Rochambeau, Jean-Baptiste Donatien
     de Vimeur Comte de, 153, 161,
     173, 175, 177
Rodney, George Brydges, 151
Roman Catholics, 30, 43, 54, 64, 106,
     107, 122, 133, 141
Rose, x, xi, 120, 191–192
Rough Crossings (BBC), 137
Royal African Company, 3–5, 58, 59,
     69–70, 72, 117
Royal George, 78

Royal Louis, 105
Royal Navy, x–xi, 23, 40, 45, 64, 65,
     76, 77–79, 93, 103, 112–114,
     150–153, 171, 184–192
Royal Savage, 145
Royal Society Of Musicians, 47
Rum trade, x, 11, 17, 66, 189
Rush, Benjamin, 84
Russell, Thomas McNamara, 152
Russia, 128–130, 176
Rutgers, Henry, 12
Rutgers University, 12

Sa'id, Omar ibn, 108–109
Sailmaking, 106
Sailors' Christmas Day, The (Boyce),
     115
Saint Croix, 56–57
Saint-Georges, Joseph Bologne,
     chevalier de, 31–34, 41, 118, 168
Salt, production of, 126
Samson, Elisabeth. *see* Zobre,
     Elisabeth Samson Creutz
Sancho, Charles Ignatius, 18, 29–31,
     41, 101, 118
Santiago de los Caballeros (Domincan
     Republic), 24
Santo Domingo, 177, 178
Saumarez, James, 186, 187
Savannah, Georgia, 22, 74, 75, 93,
     111, 136, 164, 177
Scorpion, 93
Scotland, 18, 76, 103, 125
Sculptors, 49–51
Sea chanteys, x, 25, 45, 115–116. *see
     also* Songs
Seabury, Samuel, 121
Seaflower, 4, 36
Second Congregationalist Church,
     19, 37
Selby, William, 35
Seminoles, 91
Seneca, 48, 146
Senegal, 58, 59, 65, 108, 139, 140
Serrant, Joseph, 174–176
Servants, indentured, 3, 4
Sessarakoo, William Ansah, 69–72
Shannon, Mary L., 120

Sharp, Granville, 79, 95, 136
Shawnee, 8, 9, 48, 147, 149–150, 171,
    179–181
Sheikh Salih. *see* Masih, Abdul
Shepard, Elisha, 159
Shiloh Baptist Church, 16, 38
Shipwrights, 163, 165, 184–186
Siberia, 129
Sierra Leone, 38–39, 55, 74, 75, 77, 80,
    87, 94, 96, 99, 106, 111, 121, 136,
    137, 164–166, 184
Silva, Valentim de Fonseca e, 49
Silversmiths, 56–57
Simcoe, John Graves, 148, 159
Sint Eustatius, 85, 153
Sioberg, Christina Regina, 130
Slave owners, 16
    Armistead, John, 156
    Armistead, William, 156, 158
    Bathurst, Richard, 75
    Berard, Jean, 106–107
    Brant, Joseph Thayendanegea, 147
    Breda, Francois-Dominique
        Toussaint, 141–142
    Campbell, William, 135
    Campbell family, 95
    Chew, Benjamin, 97
    Codrington College, 9
    Corlies, John, 158–159
    Darrell, George, 125, 126
    De Shields, Francis, 89
    Dessalines, Monsieur, 161
    Diallo, Ayuba Suleiman, 58–59
    Doran, James, 78
    Douglas, Alastair, 40
    Douglas, Charles, 3rd Duke Of
        Queensbury, 40
    Galphin, George, 74
    Gardner, Caleb, 34
    Ingham, John, 125
    King, Robert, 78
    Lafayette, James Armistead,
        156–158
    Lloyd family, 61
    Mazange, Leonard, 52, 53
    Monroe, James, 39, 164, 172, 184
    Moorhead, John, 51
    Mumford, Robinson, 65–66

Myners, Charles, 125
Oglethorpe, James, 10, 59
Owen, James, 108, 109
Pailleterie, Alexandre-Antoine
    Davy de la, 168
Pascal, Henry, 77–78
Petrie, Alexander, 57
Shields, Francis De, 89
Smith, Calvin, 89, 92
Smith, Oliver, 66
Stanton, Thomas, 66
Stewart, Charles, 18
Sturgis, Stokeley, 97
Tarrant, Carter, 138
Tolsey, Mr., 58
Triebuen, Angelika, 109
Triebuen, Oliver, 109
Trimmingham, David, 125
Verdelin, Sieur, 18
Vobe, Jane, 80–81
Wainwood's Bakery, 20
Ward, William, 89
Wheatley, John, 88
Wheatley, Susanna, 88
Wheeler, William, 54
Williams, Francis, 26–28
Winslow, John, 64, 65
Winton, Captain, 124
Wood, John Adams, 126
Wynkoop, Abraham, 82
Zobre, Elisabeth Samson Creutz,
    62–64
Slave trade, 69–71
Slave trade, abolishing, 17–23, 29,
    30–31, 33
Slavery, evils of, 86–87, 95–96, 104,
    110
Slavery, history of, 1–7, 71
Slavery laws, 5–6, 18–23, 38–39, 138
Slaves. *see* Blacks, enslaved; Blacks,
    formerly enslaved
Slaves, as indentured servants, 3, 4
Slender Maker Of Silver, 57
Smallpox, 7, 22, 66, 94, 99, 111, 157
Smibert, John, 9
Smith, Venture. *see* Furro, Broteer
Smock, Barnes, 160
Smollet, Tobias, 76

Society for the Promotion of Christian Knowledge (SPCK), 13
Society for the Propagation of the Gospel (SPG), 13
Society of St. John the Evangelist, 2
Solebay, 152
Solomon, Job Ben. *see* Diallo, Ayuba Suleiman
Somersett, James, 18, 101
Son de la Ma Teodora (Cuban folk song), 24–25
Songs, x, 24–25, 45, 68, 91, 114–118. *see also* Sea chanteys
Sons of Africa, 95, 96
Soubise, Julius Othello, 40–41
Sousa, Mathias de, 5, 27
South Carolina, ix, 6–7, 12, 74, 82, 84, 92, 99, 108, 124, 135
Southern, Eileen, 36
Southerne, Thomas, 71
Spain, 2, 23, 25, 53, 64, 65, 90, 101, 113, 129, 140–141, 183, 185–186, 188
Spanish Navy, 64–65
Spanish Town, Jamaica, 27
SPCK (Society for the Promotion of Christian Knowledge), 13
Spence, Thomas, 103
SPG (Society for the Propagation of the Gospel), 13
Spies, 156-158
Spitfire, 152
St. Augustine, Florida, 21, 92, 141
St. Cecilia Mass (Nunes-Garcia), 45
St. John's Church (Calcutta), 123
St. Kitts, 40, 62, 167, 176
St. Lucia, 95, 173, 175, 188
Stag, 76
Starlins, Mark. *see* Startin, Mark
Startin, Mark, 6, 137–139
Sterne, Laurance, 29
Stiles, Ezra, 11, 19, 37–38, 73
Stuart, John, 95–96
Sugarcane farming, 17, 31, 75, 95, 102, 139, 142, 161, 162
Sullivan, John, 146
Suriname, 62, 63
Surprise, x, 192
Switzerland, 175

Tacky Rebellion, 139–140
Tailors, 103
Takyi, Nana Mensah, 139–140
Tarleton, Banastre, 157
Tarrant, Caesar, 138
Tartar, 153–154
Taylor, Charles, 39
Te Deum (Nunes-Garcia), 43
Tecumseh, 171, 179–181
Tenskwataw, 179
Thomas (Apostle), 2, 122–123
Thompson, Thomas, 72
Thornton, John, 88
Tobago, 173
Tota pulchra es Maria (Nunes-Garcia), 43
Toussaint, Pierre, 106–107, 167, 181
Trading, 7, 48, 62, 67, 71, 73, 132, 151, 172
Trail of Tears, 13, 91
Traveller, 163, 163–164
Treatise of Harmony and Counterpoint (Nunes-Garcia), 44
Treaty of Ghent, 181
Trelawney, Edward, 27
Trent, 100
Trinity Church (Newport, Rhode Island), 16, 35, 38
Trip to Kingston, A (Williams), 28
Tryon, William, 12
Turkey, 128
Turks & Caicos Islands, 125–126
Tuscarora, 145
Tye. *see* Cornelius, Titus

Unitarians, 104
University of Havana (Cuba), 23
University of Mexico (Mexico), 23
University of Michoacan (Mexico), 23
University of Pennsylvania, 11, 83
University of St. Thomas Aquinas (Santo Domingo), 23
University of the West Indies (Jamaica), 23

Vanguard, 153
Varnum, James Mitchell, 20
Vassa, Gustavus. *see* Equiano, Olaudah

Verdelin, Sieur, 18
Vermont, 20–21, 86–87
Victory, 186, 189
Viola da gamba, 25
Violin, 24, 32, 33, 36, 41, 42, 45, 46,
    47, 92
Virginia, 4–5, 7–9, 15, 20, 22, 80–81,
    111, 137–138, 156–158, 159, 179
Virginia, Navy, 138
Voltaire, Francois-Marie Arouet de,
    89, 129

Wager, Ann, 14
Walker, James, 153
Wampanoag, 163
War of 1812, 90–91, 165, 171–172,
    178, 180–181
War of the Quadruple Alliance, 129
Ward, Edward, 28
Ward, William, 89
Washington, George, 20, 48, 88, 89,
    142, 146, 148, 149
Waters, William, x, 111–120
Wayne, Anthony, 149
Wedderburn (Wetherburn), Robert,
    102–105
Wedderburn, James, 102
Wedgewood, Josiah, 33
"Welcome, Brother Debtor"
    (Williams), 28
Wellesley, Arthur, Duke Of
    Wellington, 191
Wesley, John, 10, 82, 117
Western Confederacy, 147–148
Weyapiersenwah, 149–150
Whaling, 19, 66, 67, 85, 163
Wheatley, John, 88
Wheatley, Phillis, 52, 61, 73, 88–89
Wheelock, Eleazar, 12, 67, 68, 85, 143
White, Graham, 124
White, William, 83, 98, 121
Whitefield, George, 10, 82, 88, 92, 93
Whitefield College, 10
Wilberforce, William, 33, 103, 136
Wilbraham, Elizabeth, 8, 9, 51
Wilkes, John, 33
*William Waters's Last Will and
    Testament* (Song), 119

Williams, Francis, 26–28
Williams, Solomon, 67
Williamsburg, Virginia, vii–viii, 80
Windsor, Thomas, 4
Winslow, John, 64, 65
Wisconsin, 68, 134
Witherspoon, John, 11, 73
Wren, Christopher, 8
Wright, Josephine R. B., 31
Writers
    Barber, Francis, 75–77
    Davinier, Dido Elizabeth Belle,
        100–102
    Diallo, Ayuba Suleiman, 58–59
    Equiano, Olaudah, 77
    Furro, Broteer, 65–67
    George, David, 74–75
    Gronniosaw, Ukawsaw, 59–61
    Hammon, Briton, 64–65
    Hammon, Jupiter, 61–62
    Haynes, Lemuel, 86–87
    Jea, John, 109–110
    Johnson, Joseph, 85–86
    King, Boston, 99–100
    Marrant, John, 92–94
    Masih, Abdul, 122–123
    Occom, Samson, 67–69
    Prince, Mary, 125–127
    Roberts, James, 89–92
    Sa'id, Omar ibn, 108–109
    Stuart, John, 95
    Wedderburn (Wetherburn),
        Robert, 102–105
    Zembola, Zamba, 123–124

Yale College (Yale University), 9, 19,
    38
Yamma, Bristol Coggeshall, 11, 73
Yellow Fever, 98, 182
Yorktown, Virginia, 9, 81, 157, 160,
    173

Zembola, Zamba, 123–124
Zobre, Elisabeth Samson Creutz,
    62–64
Zoffany, Johann, 100
Zong, 79